Photoshop
Elements 3
Solutions

Photoshop® Elements 3 Solutions

Solutions

The Art of Digital Photography

Mikkel Aaland

SYBEX®   San Francisco • London

Acquisitions Editor: BONNIE BILLS

Developmental Editor: PETE GAUGHAN

Production Editor: LORI NEWMAN

Author's Assistant: ED SCHWARTZ

Technical Editor: GARY COHEN

Copyeditor: SHARON WILKEY

Electronic Publishing Specialist: JAN MARTI, COMMAND Z

Graphic Illustrator: ERIC HOUTS, EPIC

CD Coordinator: DAN MUMMERT

CD Technician: KEVIN LY

Proofreaders: JAMES BROOK, JENNIFER LARSEN, AMY MCCARTHY, NANCY RIDDIOUGH

Indexer: TED LAUX

Book Designer: LORI BARRA, TONBO DESIGN

Cover Designer: JOHN NEDWIDEK, EMDESIGN; LORI BARRA, TONBO DESIGN

Cover Photographs: MIKKEL AALAND, MICHELLE VIGNES

Cover Photo/Illustration: JOHN NEDWIDEK, EMDESIGN

Library of Congress Card Number: 2004109308

ISBN: 0-7821-4363-6

To my daughters

Ana Mikaela and Miranda Kristina

Acknowledgments

Many people have made this book possible. I'll start with Sybex's Bonnie Bills and Dan Brodnitz, with whom I have shared many successful years of creative collaboration and friendship. Studio B's Neil J. Salkind and David Rogelberg stood solidly behind me.

I'd especially like thank my good friend Tom Mogensen, who contributed his wisdom, images, and techniques to the book. Other special friends who were there when I needed them are Rudy Burger, Michael Rogers, Scott Highton, Maggie Hallahan, Monica Suder, Michelle Vignes, Laena Wilder, Paul Persons, Monica Lee, Luis Delgado, Mark Ulriksen, Marcia Briggs, Julie Christensen, Sebastian DeWitt, Jacques Gauchey, and, as always, Sean Parker and Valerie Robbins. I'd also like to thank Michael Angelo, Laura Laverdiere, Maurice Martell, David Miodzik, Tom Morgensen, Brett Newsom, and William Rutledge.

Thank you to Rodney Koeneke, Chuck Snyder, Barbara Smyth, Dennis Fitzgerald, Tara McGoldrick, Richard Koman, Cathryn Domrose, Martha Emmanouilides, Esmeralda Marquez, Craig Sandoski, Anne Compton, Audrey Tomaselli, Diana Howard, Andrew Tarnowka, Tony Barnard, Micha X. Peled, Karen Thomas, Lisa Friedman, Olympus and Joe Runde, Eastman Kodak, Tracy and Chris Cantello, David Robertson, Cindy Adams, Peter Banks, and Jeanne Zimmermann.

It's been an absolute thrill working with several people at Adobe: Mark Dahm, the product manager for Photoshop Elements 3 was always responsive and helpful; Richard Coencas and Chad Rolfs wrote a wonderful Foreword; Kevin Connor, who wrote the Foreword to the first two versions of the book, promised me his full support and proved he is a man good to his word; Susan Doering was helpful; John Peterson, Jeff Chien, Marc Pawliger, Karen Gauthier, Christie Evans, and Gregg Wilensky all gave me valuable advice; and Scott Wellwood was very helpful. Gary Cohen tech-edited the book and patiently answered my many questions.

As you can see by several of the photos in the book, this has been a family affair. Thanks to the Aalands (Kris, Beth, Erik, and Hans), Schneiders (Steve and Francisca), Michael Taggart, Sr., and Michael Taggart, Jr. And to my wife, Rebecca, who kept a seven-year old and a three-year old out of my office while I wrote: I love you.

Thanks to Lori Newman for gently but steadily moving the project forward; Sharon Wilkey for her careful and thoughtful editing; and Hal Leith, a loyal reader, who contacted me and asked revealing questions and gracefully made useful suggestions that I have incorporated in the new edition. Thanks also to Richard Hirschman, another reader who sent e-mails full of helpful corrections and suggestions. And thanks to the many other readers of the earlier versions, many of them loyal viewers of my *Call for Help and Screensavers* appearances, for their support and contributions. I'd also like to acknowledge the input from the community of Photoshop Elements 3 beta testers. The final version of the program, and this book, benefit enormously from such an active and generous support group.

Just about everyone who contributed to the earlier editions of this book helped with this version. I want to thank them all again for their wonderful support and great work. I'd like to thank Lori Barra and Jan Martí for again making a beautiful book, Linda Orlando for editing the second version, and Laura M. Levy for helping me get the earlier versions out on time.

Finally, I want to thank Ed Schwartz, my trusty assistant, who was involved with just about every aspect of the this and earlier versions—from reviewing and writing copy, to grabbing the PC screen shots used in the book, to giving me moral support. Ed, you continue to be such a pleasure to work with!

—Mikkel Aaland, San Francisco, 2004

Foreword

This book rocks! It is not just a revised version; this is a brand new edition. So much has changed in Adobe Photoshop Elements 3 that it is practically a whole new program, and Mikkel Aaland has completed quite an amazing undertaking with *Photoshop Elements 3 Solutions*. What really impresses us about Mikkel is his continued commitment to Photoshop Elements and to his readers. We have worked with Mikkel since version 1.0's inception, and he has had a hand in bringing each of the Elements versions to life, including the latest one. Mikkel has also taken to heart feedback from his readers by refining and improving some of the fabulous techniques in this book, as well as adding at least 20 new ones based on all the new 3.0 goodies.

As we said, Adobe Photoshop Elements 3 has taken a quantum leap from earlier versions, incorporating new powerful organization and editing tools, advanced creations, and more fantastic ways to share your photos. One of the biggest initial changes, which Mikkel gracefully walks you through, is the completely revamped user interface—and we do mean completely! This book introduces you to new and improved version 3 features such as a better Red Eye Removal tool, the Cookie Cutter tool (which scrapbookers will love), and the new dedicated Quick Fix mode that puts the most common tools and fixes into one accessible place. Digital photographers will be extremely happy with the chapters that describe the functionality and tools that have been taken from Photoshop and added into Photoshop Elements—namely the Camera Raw plug-in, the Healing Brush, Photo Filters, the Reduce Noise filter, and 16-bit support. These new features are explained and broken down in step-by-step techniques that tackle real-world problems and issues.

One of the things Adobe has done with Elements 3 is provide the digital photography hobbyist with an integrated end-to-end solution, which Mikkel illustrates throughout the book. With the explosion in digital cameras (last year, digital cameras outsold film cameras for the first time), photographers have more and more images to sort through and organize. Elements 3 to the rescue! Mikkel teaches you how to create tags and categories to group your images easily and visually, allowing you to view by date and create stacks and version sets of related images. Leaving no stone unturned, he explores how to effectively use Elements' powerful Compare function and Photo Review command, which let you, the photographer, quickly sort through your images, marking them for print or correcting rotations on the fly.

Mikkel's approach has always been to teach the hobbyist how to get professional results with digital imaging software. Using Photoshop Elements 3, Mikkel shows how anyone can use the tools in Photoshop Elements to retouch, enhance, and share their photos in ways they never thought possible. You will learn techniques to repair tattered family photographs, bring out detail and color that you thought was lost forever, stitch images into seamless panoramas, and create slide shows and web galleries. What you end up with, thanks to Adobe and Mikkel, are amazing creations that will make your friends, family, and maybe even your boss say, "How did you do that?!?!"

Most importantly, Mikkel makes it fun!

RICHARD COENCAS AND CHAD ROLFS
Adobe Photoshop Elements Quality Engineering

Contents

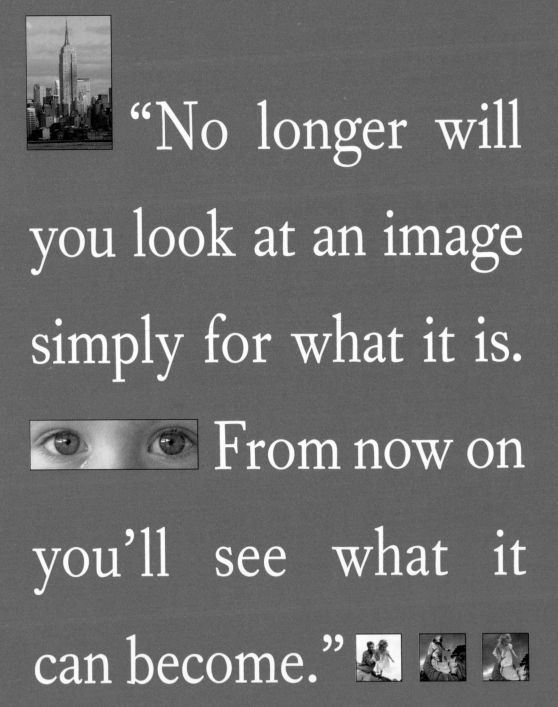

"No longer will you look at an image simply for what it is. From now on you'll see what it can become."

Introduction

The full potential of your digital images will never be fully realized without the help of editing and processing software. Nowadays, there are many such software packages to choose from, but there is only one that combines professional-level quality with consumer ease-of-use and cost—and that's Photoshop Elements.

With Photoshop Elements—and information presented in this book—you'll quickly get up to speed and organize your digital images so they are readily accessible. You'll be able to fix digital images that are over- or underexposed; sharpen images that are out of focus; get rid of annoying red eye; and reduce digital-camera-produced electronic noise. With a little more expertise, you'll be able to remove unwanted objects from outdoor shots, remove and replace distracting backgrounds, add type, create stunning panoramas by stitching together adjacent shots, and much more.

In short, Photoshop Elements and Photoshop Elements 3 Solutions are for anyone familiar with a computer who wants to both organize and create great-looking images. No longer will you look at an image simply for what it is. From now on you'll see what it can become.

What's New in 3?

There is an old saying that the third time is a charm, and that is certainly true for the third version of Photoshop Elements. Once again, Adobe has raised the bar of excellence and value and I'm sure they have yet another hit on their hands.

There are two distinct versions of Photoshop Elements 3: a Windows version and a Macintosh version. Both versions share an upgraded editing application that includes the following new features and improvements:

- Healing Brush and Spot Healing Brush tools that make it easier than ever to seamlessly remove unwanted blemishes and artifacts from an image
- Cookie Cutter tool that crops an image into a shape you can choose
- A radically improved Quick Fix with side-by-side before and after views
- 16-bit support to take advantage of an extended color gamut
- A Camera Raw plug-in that opens and processes most RAW files produced by many digital cameras

- Improved batch processing that includes editing features such as Auto Levels and Sharpen and the ability to add custom labels to batches of images
- An improved File Browser, which makes it easier than ever to organize and work on your digital images
- A completely redesigned workspace with a handy photo and palette bin to streamline workflow as well as new image view controls so you can view and compare open files in multiple ways
- A Divide Scanned Photos command that enables you to scan multiple images together and then automatically split each image into separate files
- New Shadows/Highlights controls to make it easier than ever to balance images with dark backgrounds or light foregrounds
- A new Lens Filter adjustment layer to apply traditional photographic filter effects
- An improved Red Eye brush that really works
- An improved Print Preview so you can choose from several preset paper sizes
- Leading support in the Type tool
- A filter gallery that makes it easier than ever to apply filters and see their effects
- A Reduce Noise filter that automatically diminishes the effect of electronic noise (often caused by shooting a digital camera at a high ISO)
- A new Histogram palette that displays color values along with tonal values

Believe it or not, I've only scratched the surface of Photoshop Elements 3's new and improved editing capabilities. Throughout the book, you'll see references to other useful and well-thought-out features that make working with this program a joy.

On the Windows side, Photoshop Elements 3 is now both a powerful image editor and image organizer. Elements comes bundled with the Organizer, which is really a morphed version of Photoshop Album, previously a stand-alone image management program. What was previously known simply as Photoshop Elements is now referred to as the Editor. Both the Organizer and Editor launch separately, but images can be seamlessly passed back and forth between the two modes.

I won't even try to list all the features offered by the Organizer. Chapters 1 and 12 do that. Let me just briefly say, the Organizer is not only a customizable, professional-level image management system but it also offers a wide range of creative ways to share your images, from interactive slide shows complete with music to custom-made calendars, post cards, greeting cards, and photo album pages. It's a beautiful complement to the Editor and adds tremendous value for Windows users.

What You Need to Know

I've written this book with the assumption that the reader has basic computer skills, such as using the mouse and saving and storing digital files. However, if this is the first time you've worked with a graphics or image-editing program, you may find Photoshop Elements a bit challenging. After all, this is a powerful, feature-rich program. It's unrealistic to think that you can jump right in and get exactly what you want without some trial and error. But the Elements interface is extremely intuitive and will enable you to quickly get up to speed. The Adobe online help is the best I've ever seen. Also, just waving your cursor over a tool brings up the tool's name, and in a separate Hints palette, you'll find a concise explanation of what the tool does.

The CD accompanying this book contains files for almost all of the "before" images shown in this book (the starting images for procedures). Using those files, you can follow along with the procedures to create the "after" images. If you have any specific questions about the material in this book, or the program, feel free to email me at mikkel@cyberbohemia.com.

Platform and OS Differences

As I said earlier, the Windows version includes the Organizer. There is no Organizer for the Macintosh, only the application. As far as this book is concerned, this difference is most noticeable in Chapters 1 and 12, where I've had to devote entire sections to one platform or the other. However, when it comes to actual editing capabilities of the Windows and Mac versions, there is very little difference, and Chapters 2 through 11, which are devoted mostly to these capabilities, should be very straightforward.

The Future Is Now

Twelve years ago I wrote a book titled *Digital Photography* (Random House, 1992). The book was dedicated in part to the great photographer Ansel Adams, who introduced me to digital photography in 1980. In the book I wrote that the future of digital photography is now. I wrote "the new technology would enable people to make photographic expressions for their own amusement, for the enjoyment of others, or for professional gain." Well, I was a little ahead of myself. Adobe had just introduced Photoshop 1, and the first consumer digital cameras and scanners were on the market. I thought it would be just a matter of months or, at the most, a few years, and the digital photography revolution would be in full swing. We all had to grow a little. Photoshop had to evolve and so did digital cameras and scanners. Now, with the introduction of Photoshop Elements 3 and increasingly affordable digital cameras and scanners, that time I anticipated 12 years ago is here. I really enjoyed writing this book and then updating it for version 3, especially since I can truly say: "The future is now."

—MIKKEL AALAND, SAN FRANCISCO, 2004

Importing and Organizing Digital Images

This chapter shows you various options for bringing your digital images directly into Photoshop Elements from a digital camera, card reader, scanner, file, or folder. It also shows you how to organize and manage imported images so you can find the image you want, when you want it. Subsequent chapters focus on the editing and processing capabilities of the program.

1

Importing Digital Images into Photoshop Elements

There are several ways to get your digital images into Photoshop Elements. The way you choose depends on the source of the digital images—folder, digital camera, card reader, scanner, and so forth—and the computer platform you are using—Windows or Macintosh.

Although the editing capabilities of the Mac and Windows versions of Photoshop Elements are virtually the same, significant differences arise when it comes to importing, organizing, and managing digital images.

Windows users benefit from the integration of a popular stand-alone product, Photoshop Album, with Photoshop Elements. The file-management features of Photoshop Album have been collected in an interface called *the Organizer*, and the features that formerly comprised Elements (most of the editing capabilities) have been grouped into an interface called *the Editor*.

The Organizer launches separately from the Editor, but they operate in conjunction. Digital files can be passed relatively easily between the two workspaces. Users can import digital files into the Organizer, where they can be organized, managed, and shared—or transferred to the Editor for extensive editing. Alternately, users can import digital files directly into the Editor and bypass the Organizer entirely.

Mac Photoshop Elements 3 users benefit from a much-improved File Browser, which is totally integrated into the application. (There is no Editor or Organizer "mode" for the Mac version of Photoshop Elements 3; there is simply the "application.") I'll get into all the features of the File Browser later in the chapter, but I think you'll agree that it is a powerful organizing tool as well. (Windows users also have the File Browser integrated into the Editor, but it is slightly more limited than the Mac version.)

Let's start with importing images into the Organizer. (This is relevant only if you are using the Windows platform.) After that I'll show you how to import images directly into the Editor (Windows), or if you are running Photoshop Elements on a Mac, how to import images directly into the application.

Importing Images into the Organizer (Windows Only)

You can bring images into the Organizer from at least three basic sources:
- An existing folder or offline media such as a CD or DVD
- A digital camera or card reader
- A scanner

The easiest and most foolproof method is to bring digital files in from an existing folder, so let's start there.

Importing from an Existing Folder or Offline Media

I'll assume you are starting from the Welcome screen that appears when you first launch the application from your desktop (Figure 1.1).

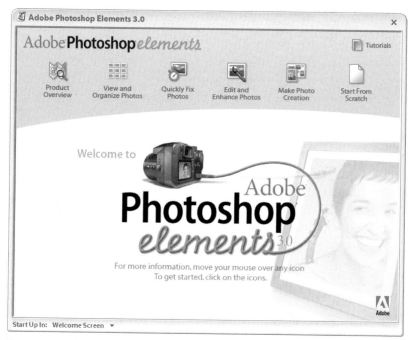

Figure 1.1: *This is what you see when you first launch the Windows version of Photoshop Elements.*

Note: You can bypass the Welcome screen in the future. Simply click Start Up In at the lower-left corner of the Welcome screen, and from the pop-up menu select either Editor or Organizer as your default startup. You can always access the Welcome screen by choosing Window ➢ Welcome from the main menu bar.

1. In the Welcome screen, click View and Organize Photos. This opens the Organizer.

2. Choose File ➢ Get Photos from the main menu bar. Alternatively, you can click the camera icon found in the shortcuts menu bar (Figure 1.2).

Figure 1.2: *Get image files by clicking the Get Photos icon located in the shortcuts menu bar.*

3. Now select From Files and Folders. A window like the one shown in Figure 1.3 should appear.

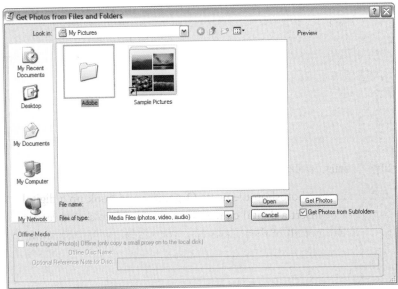

Figure 1.3: When you select From Files and Folders, you'll see a window like this one.

4. Navigate to the files or folders you wish to import.

5. Select the file or folder by clicking the thumbnail; then click the Get Photos button.

 Note: You can also drag and drop files and folders from your desktop directly into the Organizer.

The Organizer is not copying the image file itself. It creates a thumbnail version of the file and a link between your actual image files and the Organizer. Your original image file remains in the original location. (If you move the original file, you'll need to "Reconnect" the link. ᐫ "Reconnecting Photos" later in this chapter.)

If you are importing images from an offline source (for example, from a CD), you have two choices: either copy the entire file or files onto your hard disk, or import only a small proxy (that is, a thumbnail and basic file info) of the file (or files). You can set the size of the proxy thumbnail, from 320×240 pixels to 1280×960 pixels, in the Organizer preferences: Edit ≻ Preferences ≻ Files.

To bring in only a thumbnail version, select the Keep Original Photo(s) Offline check box at the bottom of the Get Photos from Files and Folders window. At first it may seem practical to copy only a small proxy and not the full image. Obviously you'll save space on your hard disk. However, if you try to edit the small proxy, a message appears asking you to insert the offline media (CD or DVD, for example) so a full-resolution version of the image can be accessed. This can take time, especially if you haven't located your offline media quickly. (Personally, I'm shying away from storing images on CD and DVDs. I'm using huge, mega-gigabyte hard disks, which are cheap yet fast and reliable. When I run out of storage space, I just buy another hard disk and daisy-chain it to my computer so all my images are quickly available.)

Importing from a Digital Camera or Card Reader

When you first start using the Photoshop Elements Organizer and hook up a digital camera to your computer or insert a digital camera memory card into a card reader, several scenarios may occur, not all of them desirable. You might get the Microsoft Scanner and Camera Wizard, or you might get the Adobe Photo Downloader, both of which are shown in Figure 1.4.

Figure 1.4: The Microsoft Scanner and Camera Wizard (left) and the Adobe Photo Downloader (right).

It's also possible to get both of these windows or neither. These potential events depend on several factors—namely, the state of your Windows Auto Play settings or the particular software that you have installed on your computer and your Photoshop Elements Organizer preferences.

Before troubleshooting these scenarios, I'll make a suggestion that might make your life a lot simpler: deselect the Adobe Photo Downloader in the Organizer preferences (Edit ➢ Preferences ➢ Camera or Card Reader—see Figure 1.5). You'll still be able to use File ➢ Get Photos ➢ From Camera or Card Reader to load images, but you won't have a pop-up window appearing unexpectedly whenever you put a card into your computer or hook up an external device. If you haven't already done so, you might want to also turn off the Microsoft Scanner and Camera Wizard found in the AutoPlay preferences. (Insert a card in the card reader. Open My Computer. Right-click the card reader icon. Choose Properties and then choose AutoPlay and select Take No Action.)

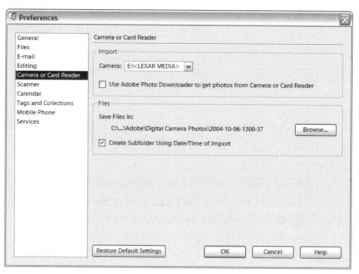

Figure 1.5: Deselect the Adobe Photo Downloader to make life easier.

OK, that's my two bits. Now let's do some troubleshooting.

Case 1: Both wizards open. If you are already familiar with the Microsoft Scanner and Camera Wizard and want to continue to use it, just close the Adobe Photo Downloader when it appears and use the Microsoft wizard. Be aware of two things when using the Microsoft wizard: First, the wizard will rename your pictures. If you select a folder name **Vacation**, for example, the first picture will be renamed **Vacation001.jpg**. Second, the pictures will most likely not be in the order in which you took them. This may or may not be important to you. If you use the Microsoft wizard, you will next have to bring the pictures into the Organizer yourself by opening the program and then using the Get Photo feature.

After the Microsoft Scanner and Camera Wizard finishes, you will be asked whether you want to delete the files from your memory card. You should answer this very carefully; "no" is always the safest answer. After you are sure that the pictures are safely on your hard disk, you can delete the pictures by using the camera.

 Note: Holding down the Shift key while inserting the memory card prevents the Microsoft wizard from starting, but allows the Adobe Downloader to start.

Case 2: Only the Microsoft Scanner and Camera Wizard opens. What you do next depends on what you want. If you want to continue with this wizard, do so in light of the caveats noted in Case 1. If you want to use the Organizer, close the Microsoft wizard and open the Organizer. You can then use the Get Photo feature to import the pictures.

Case 3: Only the Adobe Photo Downloader opens. If this is what you want, simply proceed. If you want the Microsoft wizard instead, turn off the Adobe Downloader in the preferences and enable the Microsoft wizard. (Again, open My Computer, right-click the card reader drive icon, and click AutoPlay. Select Microsoft Scanner and Camera Wizard from the Actions list. After you select OK, eject the memory card and reinsert it. The Microsoft wizard should now work.)

Case 4: Neither wizard opens. If this happens, simply select File ≻ Get Photos from the menu bar (or from the camera icon in the shortcuts bar) and choose from the several choices to import your images. If you want to import them from a card reader, choose From Camera or Card Reader. You can also select From Files and Folders and browse to your card reader drive. With most memory cards, you will have to drill down until you see a folder named **DCIM**. Open this folder, and your images will be there. The former method is the easier of the two.

Where do the images go when you download them? As I said earlier, the Organizer doesn't bring in the actual file but creates a link to the file. When you import from a camera or a card reader, a copy of the file is transferred to your hard disk. You can determine where these files reside in the Organizer preferences (Figure 1.6). By default they go in your **My Documents\My Pictures\Adobe** folder. However, the Organizer still creates a link to those files, and if you move the files from their original location, you will need to reconnect them by choosing the File ≻ Reconnect menu item.

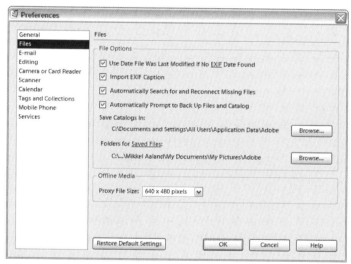

Figure 1.6: You can change where downloaded files reside in the Organizer preferences.

Importing from a Scanner

There are two ways to import from a scanner in the Organizer.

The first way is to select the From Scanner option from the File ≻ Get Photos submenu. The Get Photos from Scanner dialog box is shown in Figure 1.7. You have a choice of saving your files as JPEG, TIFF, or PNG. You can use the Browse button to select the destination for the scans; otherwise, the default location will be used.

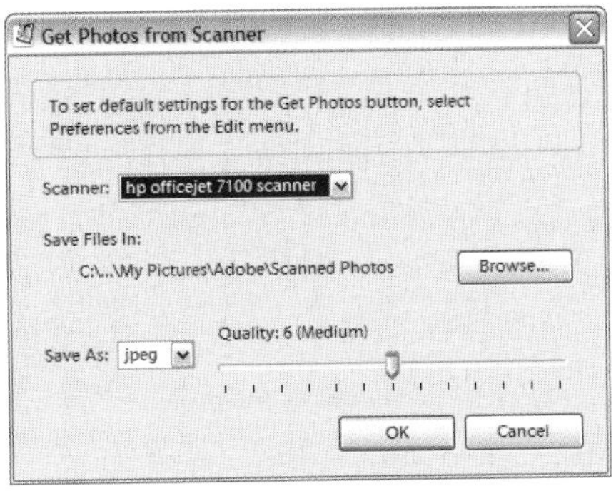

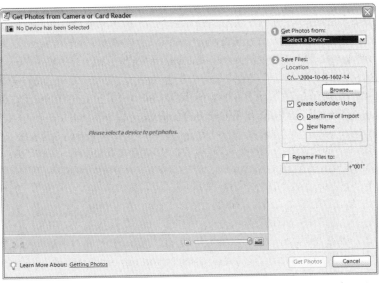

Figure 1.7: The Get Photos from Scanner dialog box.

The second way is to choose File ➢ Get Photos ➢ From Camera or Card Reader (Figure 1.8). Start with step 2, "Save Files," and dictate a file location and naming details. Then move to step 1, "Get Photos From," and select your scanner in the drop-down list box. Do it in this order, because as soon as step 1 is complete, the scanning process begins. If you start with step 1, you can't choose where your files go or the file format; it will always be TIFF.

Figure 1.8: Start with step 2, "Save Files," and pick a convenient location on your hard disk for your files; then move to step 1. Once step 1 is selected, scanning begins.

If you are going to import from your scanner, make sure that the scanner is turned on before you launch the Organizer or the scanner will not be recognized. When you select an option from step 1, make sure that you select a TWAIN version or the scanner may not respond.

Frankly, you may find it better to do all your scanning from within the Editor, not the Organizer (File ➢ Import). If you scan from within the Editor, you have many more choices of file formats for saving files. You also have direct access to a new feature of Photoshop Elements 3 called Divide Scanned Photos (Image ➢ Divide Scanned Photos). With this feature you can scan several images at once, and Photoshop Elements will automatically straighten, crop, and place each image into a separate file.

Opening Images in the Editor (Windows) or Application (Mac)

Here are your choices for opening images from within the Editor (Windows) or application (Mac):

File ➢ Open opens all compatible file formats. This brings up an Open dialog box with controls for locating and previewing files.

File ➢ Open Recently Edited File opens up to 30 of the most recently viewed files. (The default is 10, but you can increase that number in Saving Files preferences.)

File ➢ Import gives you access to any Import plug-in module compatible with Photoshop Elements. You may need to install the specific plug-in yourself. See the documentation for your scanner or digital camera for more instructions. You can also use Import to bring scans or digital camera images directly into Photoshop Elements. Frame from Video is a quick and easy way to bring in individual frames from QuickTime or MPEG movies, or just about any video footage that QuickTime (Mac) or Media Player (Windows) supports.

File ➢ Browse Folders or **Window ➢ File Browser** is one of the most useful ways of opening and managing digital images in Photoshop Elements. I'll get into the specifics of using it later in this chapter.

File ➢ New ➢ Image from Clipboard enables you to create a new file from a selection. Make a selection in an image by using any of the marquee selection tools and then copy that selection (Ctrl+C / ⌘ +C); you can then create a new file containing that selection by choosing File ➢ New from Clipboard.

Clicking the Photo Browser icon in the shortcuts bar (Windows only) opens the Organizer, from which you can also select and import them into the Editor. (Why did Adobe name the icon *Photo Browser* and not *Organizer*? Because clicking it opens the Organizer in Photo Browser mode. I know, it's confusing, but you'll get used to it.)

You can also open files by clicking the Open folder icon (☜) in the shortcuts bar or create a new file by clicking the New icon (▯)in the shortcuts bar. Mac users can open the File Browser from the Browse icon (☜) found in the shortcuts bar.

Finally, Windows users can open files by double-clicking the dark-gray, empty window area, which is called the work area. This brings up the Windows Open dialog box, where you can choose a file or files to open.

Managing Files with the Organizer (Windows Only)

After you have imported your digital files into the Organizer, you can do many things. Not only can you choose the way the images are displayed—single image, multiple images, and so forth—you can also use different criteria to sort and organize the images. With only a little effort you can organize your images according to date, folder location, filename, media type, and more. You can also apply custom or generic *tags* based on the content of the image, and sort and organize the images that way.

Of course, the Organizer is also a gateway to the Editor, where you can use Photoshop Elements' powerful editing and processing capabilities. Furthermore, within the Organizer you can process and print multiple images, labels, and contact sheets, as well as create slide shows, VCDs, photo album pages, greeting cards, postcards, wall calendars, and a web photo gallery. As I mentioned earlier, the editing capabilities of Photoshop Elements are discussed in detail in subsequent chapters. I'll get into the printing and sharing capabilities of the Organizer in Chapter 12.

Let's get up to speed with the organizing and managing capabilities within the Organizer. Again, this information applies only to the Windows version of the program; Mac users should skip ahead to the "Managing Files with the File Browser (Mac and Windows)" section.

Viewing Files with the Organizer

The Organizer is extremely flexible, especially when it comes to the ways it displays your images. You can choose to display images in a variety of ways ranging from tiny thumbnails to large, side-by-side views. Let's look at some of your options.

Viewing Photos in the Photo Well

Look at Figure 1.9. The images are displayed in the Photo Well as small thumbnails and organized by the date they were created, with the oldest displayed first in the upper-left corner. Because most of these shots were created with a digital camera, the Organizer used the date and time information contained in the EXIF data generated by the camera. For other types of digital media, the Organizer uses file-creation information.

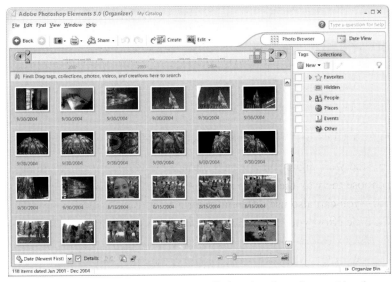

Figure 1.9: Images are displayed as small thumbnails and sorted by date.

Note: You can always change the date and time associated with an image file. Select the thumbnail of the image, right-click, and choose Adjust Date and Time from the pop-up menu. You can also do this by choosing Edit ➤ Adjust Date and Time from the main menu bar or simply by clicking the date at the bottom of the thumbnail.

Now look at Figure 1.10. I didn't do a thing to the images. I changed only two Organizer settings and created a very different view of the same catalog of images.

Timeline Bar

Figure 1.10: Images are now displayed as larger thumbnails and sorted by folder location.

Note: When you import images into the Organizer, it creates a catalog, named My Catalog by default. A catalog can contain an unlimited number of photos, so it is likely you'll need only one catalog. You can create new catalogs if you wish, but only one can be open at a time. To create a new catalog, choose File ➤ Catalog and follow the prompts. To rename your existing catalog, choose File ➤ Catalog ➤ Save As and change the filename in the dialog box.

To create this new view, I selected Folder Location from the pop-up menu that appears at the bottom left of the Organizer (see Figure 1.11). Alternatively, you can use the main menu bar: View ➤ Arrangement ➤ Folder Location. I also increased the size of the thumbnails with the slider found at the bottom right of the Organizer (again, see Figure 1.11). Move the slider to the left and the thumbs are shrunk, to the right and they are enlarged. Obviously, the larger the thumbnails become, the fewer fit into the Photo Well.

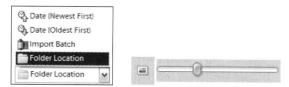

Figure 1.11: View your images with different criteria (left). Change the size of the thumbnails by moving the slider to the left or right (right).

The other arrangement options include Import Batch and Color Similarity (you must select a single image first for comparison) as well as Collection Order, Stack Order, and Version Set Order (you must create a collection, a stack, or version set before these options become available).

Timeline Bar

You can also use the timeline bar to further refine your viewing. The timeline bar is located near the top of the Photo Well (see the indicator back in Figure 1.10). If you chose to view by date, the timeline bar displays the year and 12 marks that represent 12 months. Blocks represent collections of images based on their creation date. The larger the block, the larger the collection. Click and hold and then drag the bottom of the blue frame that hangs on the timeline to the desired month. As you move the frame, thumbnails in the photo well will change accordingly. If you chose to view by folder, you can use the blue frame to scroll between folders. If you select Import Batch, the timeline will change to reflect the relevant criteria.

Note: Remove the timeline bar by choosing View ➤ Timeline from the main menu bar. Bring it back by choosing View ➤ Timeline and reselecting it.

Date View

Figure 1.12 shows yet another viewing option: Date view. Date view doesn't create a calendar (you can do that in the Create menu); it enables you to select a year, month, or day as criteria for viewing your images. You access the Date view by selecting the calendar icon followed by the words *Date View* at the far right of the options bar.

Figure 1.12: Date view is another viewing option.

When you first open this view, you may not see any images, just a calendar with empty boxes. You need to select a viewing range that covers the creation dates of your images. You can do this in two ways. Either click the Year, Month, or Day icons on the bottom of the Date View window and scroll by using the arrows at the top of the window to the correct date(s). Or set a range by clicking the date found in the upper-right of the Date View window. This brings up the Set Date dialog box. Type in the parameters you know will include the dates your images were created.

You can customize Date view in the Organizer preferences to display different holidays or events. Choose Edit ➢ Preferences ➢ Calendar from the main menu bar.

Photo Review and Photo Compare

As if all the preceding options weren't enough, the Organizer also provides yet another way to view your photos: Photo Review and Photo Compare. Figure 1.13 shows the Photo Review and Photo Compare windows.

Figure 1.13: The Photo Review window (left). The Photo Compare window (right).

You access these views via the main menu bar: View ➤ Photo Review, or View ➤ Photo Compare. You can also access Photo Review by right-clicking a thumbnail in the Photo Well and picking it from the pop-up menu or by clicking the Photo Review icon at the bottom of the Photo Well window ( ). (You need to be in the Photo Browser mode for these menu items to be enabled.)

Photo Review and Photo Compare both create an interactive slide show, sequencing one image after another at a pace you determine in the opening Photo Review dialog box shown in Figure 1.14. (Here you can also choose to add music if you like.)

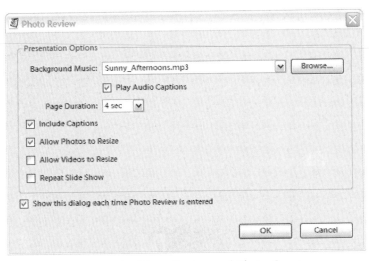

Figure 1.14: Options for Photo Review and Photo Compare.

Don't confuse Photo Review and Photo Compare with the Slide Show Maker found in the Create menu, which is much more versatile and provides a myriad of transition and pacing controls. These are meant to help the editing process. You can stop the slide show at any time, rotate an image, trash it, crop it, Auto Fix it, or attach a tag (more on that later). When you are finished with one image, you can move on to the next image by using familiar VCR-like play and stop controls. When you hit the Play button, the reviewing starts; hit the X button to end the review.

Photo Compare adds the option of selecting a "master" image that remains static, which the other images cycle past. You can use the master image to compare or contrast with the other images. Just hit the X button when you want to stop and compare.

After you are finished reviewing your images in Photo Review or Photo Compare, hit the Esc key to return to the main Organizer window.

Reconnecting Photos

As I said, the Organizer doesn't import image files into the catalog, it creates a link to the image file. If you move a folder or file from your hard disk to another location, you break this link. You know a link is broken when you see a thumbnail like the one in Figure 1.15. To reconnect your image file, choose File ➢ Reconnect from the menu bar. The Organizer will try to find the missing file, or prompt you to browse to the missing file yourself. In the Reconnect Missing Files dialog box (shown in Figure 1.16), navigate to the original file and click Reconnect. When you are finished, click Close.

Figure 1.15: When a link is broken, you get an icon that looks like the one shown here.

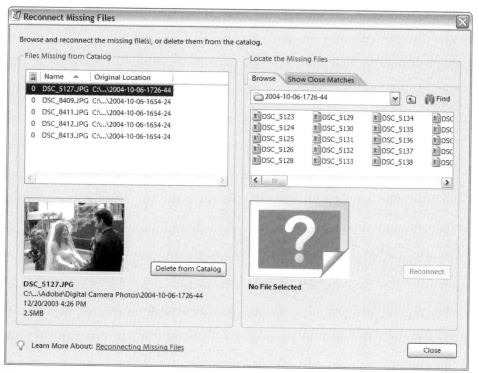

Figure 1.16: Navigate to the missing file and click Reconnect.

Managing Properties

Most image files contain additional information besides the pixels that make up the image. This information includes EXIF data generated by a digital camera, file information created by an application, filenames and file locations, file size, custom tags, and more.

This information is referred to as *properties*, and you can view it by choosing Window ➢ Properties from the Organizer menu bar or by clicking the Properties icon at the bottom of the Organizer window (🖻). Figure 1.17 shows the Properties dialog box, where you can change or add such properties as captions and date and time.

Figure 1.17: The Properties dialog box

Additionally, you can add captions via the menu bar (Edit ➢ Add Caption) or, if the Details button at the bottom of the photo well is selected, by double-clicking a thumbnail in the photo well and typing the caption you want in the caption field at the bottom of the image window. You can also add audio notes to a photo by clicking the Audio icon (🔊) located next to the caption field. (Your computer must be appropriately configured to use the Audio feature.)

Adding and Deleting Tags

The more unique the information that is associated with an image file, the easier it is to find the image later when it is buried in a stack of thousands of other image files. I already mentioned how easy it is to sort and organize a catalog of images by date, filename, or folder location. By adding customized tags, it's even easier.

Figure 1.18 shows the Tags tab found in the organize bin. What you see are the standard preloaded tags that are included by default. You can create your own tags or Tags categories at any time by clicking the New icon at the top of the tab. (You can delete tags or Tags categories by clicking the Trash icon (🗑), or edit tags by clicking the pencil icon (✎).

Figure 1.18: The Tags tab with categories and subcategories. You can create your own as well.

Adding tags to image files is super easy. Simply click and drag the tag from the Organize Bin on top of the image you wish to tag. A tag icon appears and remains associated with the thumbnail. To apply a tag to multiple images, Shift+click to select the images, and then click and drag the tag from the Organize Bin on top of any of them. You can also add a tag by right-clicking a thumbnail and choosing Attach Tag (or Attach Tag to Selected Items if multiple thumbnails are selected).

You can assign as many tags as you wish to a single image. To remove a tag from an image file, select the file in the Photo Well, right-click the thumbnail, and choose Remove Tag from Select Items from the pop-up menu. Do not use the Delete key unless you want to remove the image file from the Catalog or delete the file from your hard disk.

Searching for Tags and Other Properties

You can search for specific images in many ways. In the Find menu you can search by Date, Caption, Filename, History, Media Type, or even color similarity. The easiest way to search is via the Find bar at the top of the Photo Well (Figure 1.19) or, if you have applied tags, via the Tags tab.

Find: Drag tags, collections, photos, videos, and creations here to search

Figure 1.19: Search criteria can be dragged and dropped into the Find bar.

To use the Find bar, simply drag a thumbnail of an image containing the criteria you are looking for (for example, date or color) to the find bar. You can also drag tags from the Tags tab into the Find bar and search that way. To search by tags, simply double-click the tag you want to search or click the check box next to the tag. A binocular icon appears, signifying your selection (Figure 1.20). You can also search for multiple tags by selecting more than one check box. Matching items will appear in the Photo Well.

Figure 1.20: When you select the check box next to a tag, a binocular icon appears signifying your selection. You can select multiple tags.

Using Collections and Stacks

Collections and stacks provide another way to customize your image collection.

To stack a series of related images, first select more than one image by Shift+clicking the image icon. Choose Edit ➤ Stack ➤ Stack Selected Photos from the menu bar. All your selected images are combined into one icon, designated by the icon you see in Figure 1.21. To reveal the contents of the stack, right-click the image icon and choose Stack ➤ Reveal Photos in Stack from the pop-up menu. If you select Unstack Photos, all the images in the stack will revert to individual thumbnails that appear in the Photo Well. If you select Flatten Stack, all the photos except the top photo in the stack will be deleted from the catalog.

Figure 1.21: The icon in the upper right of the thumbnail designates this a stack of grouped images.

To create an image collection, click the Collections tab in the Organize Bin (Figure 1.22) and select New. Collections are especially handy when you use the Organizer's Create options. For example, if you want to create a slide show, place all the appropriate images into a collection. When you choose Create Slide Show from the Create menu, simply select Add Photos and navigate to the relevant collection.

Figure 1.22: Creating a collection is another way to customize your images.

Working on and Fixing Photos

The Organizer provides some rudimentary editing tools accessible from the Edit menu. For example, you can rotate images or apply an Auto Smart Fix command. You can also open an Auto Fix window and crop and apply some basic image processing to your images (Figure 1.23).

Figure 1.23: The Organizer's Auto Fix window. Here you'll have only basic editing capabilities.

As you will see in Chapter 2, I suggest you do most of your editing in the Editor, not the Organizer. To bring an image into the Editor, simply select it and choose either Edit ➤ Go to Quick Fix or Edit ➤ Go to Standard Edit. Either command takes you out of the Organizer and into the Editor. (You can also use the Edit button in the shortcuts bar.)

Using Version Sets

When you crop, rotate, or otherwise edit an image in the Organizer, Photoshop Elements creates a new version of your original image. You can tell that an image has been edited by the presence of a small icon in the upper-right corner (🖼). This signifies a version set. If you right-click the image and choose Version Set ➤ Reveal Photos in Version Set from the pop-up menu (Figure 1.24), you can view all the versions of a particular image (Figure 1.25). The original image is left untouched unless you right-click the image and choose Version Set ➤ Flatten Version Set. From this pop-up menu, you can also revert to the original and delete all the subsequent versions.

Copy	Ctrl+C	
Delete from Catalog...	Del	
Rotate 90° Left	Ctrl+Left	
Rotate 90° Right	Ctrl+Right	
Auto Smart Fix	Ctrl+Shift+I	
Auto Fix Window...		
Go to Quick Fix...		
Go to Standard Edit...	Ctrl+I	
Adjust Date and Time...	Ctrl+J	
Add Caption...	Ctrl+Shift+T	
Update Thumbnail	Ctrl+Shift+U	
Set as Desktop Wallpaper	Ctrl+Shift+W	
Photo Review	F11	
Play Video or Audio		
Edit 3GPP Movie...		
Stack	▶	
Version Set	▶	Reveal Photos in Version Set
		Flatten Version Set...
Attach Tag	▶	Revert to Original...
Remove Tag	▶	Set as Top Photo
Add to Collection	▶	
Remove from Collection	▶	
Show Properties	Alt+Enter	

Figure 1.24: When you right-click an edited image, you get this pop-up menu and choices.

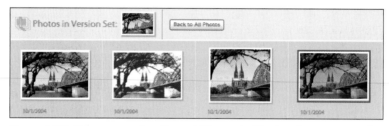

Figure 1.25: When you select Reveal Photos in Version Set, you can view all the versions of a particular image.

When you bring an image from the Organizer into the Editor and work on it there, versions work slightly differently. As soon as an image is brought in and worked on in the Editor, a padlock appears on the icon of the image in the Organizer (Figure 1.26), signifying an edit in progress. When you are finished editing an image in the Editor, save it (File ➤ Save from the Editor menu bar). This brings up the dialog box. Notice under Save Options the option to Save in Version Set with Original. If you select this check box, Photoshop Elements will automatically save both the original and the edited version. Now when you look at the thumbnail of your image in the Organizer, you'll see the familiar version icon.

Figure 1.26: When you work on an image in the Editor, this icon appears on the thumbnail of the image in the Organizer.

By the way, the Organizer saves copies of your work in predetermined locations. You can change the location in the Preferences (Edit ➤ Preferences ➤ Files).

Backing Up and Archiving

You can use the Organizer to create backups of your image files either offline on a CD or DVD or onto another hard disk. Choose File ➤ Burn or File ➤ Backup from the Organizer menu bar. Either command brings up the dialog box.

Managing Files with the File Browser (Mac and Windows)

Both Mac and Windows users can use the File Browser—a totally integrated feature—to organize and manage digital images. Figure 1.27 shows a Mac screen shot of the File Browser, but the Windows version is basically the same—albeit missing the Automate and flagging features.

Figure 1.27: The Mac File Browser. The Windows version is basically the same, without the Automate and flagging features.

To open the File Browser from the application (or from the "Editor" in Windows parlance), do *one* of the following:

- Select File ➢ Browse Folders from the main menu bar. (A reminder for Windows users: I am talking about the Editor main menu bar. You cannot get to the File Browser from within the Organizer.)
- In the shortcuts bar, click the Browse icon (). (The Windows version doesn't have this icon in the shortcuts bar. You can access the File Browser only from the main menu bar in the Editor.)

After the File Browser is open, you need to navigate to a folder containing the images you wish to view. The upper-left pane of the File Browser dialog box displays the folders on your computer. When you click a folder, any images contained in it appear as thumbnails on the right.

To open an image from the File Browser into the Editor, either double-click its thumbnail or select Open from File in the File Browser menu bar. To open multiple images, hold down the Ctrl/Shift key while clicking to select them, and then double-click any one of them or select Open from the pop-up menu. You can also right-click / Control+click a thumbnail to display a pop-up menu with several options including Open, Delete, and Rename.

Note: You can add files or folders from your computer's desktop to the File Browser at any time by dragging and dropping them onto the File Browser window.

Viewing Files with the File Browser

The File Browser window is totally customizable. Not only can you change the size of the thumbnail displays via View in the File Browser menu bar, but you can change the size of the entire window by placing your cursor in the lower-right corner of the window and clicking and dragging the window to the desired size. To change the size of the tab items on the left side of the window (Folders, Preview, and Metadata), click the top, right, or bottom border and drag to the desired size. (I often increase the size of the Preview tab to get a larger view of my selected image.)

You can change the order in which images are displayed via Sort in the File Browser menu bar. Your choices are shown in the pop-up menu shown in Figure 1.28.

Figure 1.28: Change the order in which your images are displayed via Sort in the File Browser menu bar.

Deleting, Moving, and Copying Files with the File Browser

To delete files from the File Browser (and completely from your system) select the file or files you want to delete, and do *one* of the following:

- Click the Trash button at the top of the File Browser window.
- Drag the files to the Trash button.
- Press the Delete key.
- Choose File ➤ Delete from the File Browser menu bar.

To move a file from within the File Browser window, select the file, and then drag it to a different folder or even the desktop.

To copy a file from within the File Browser window, select the file, and then Alt+drag / Option+drag it to a different folder.

You can also create new folders by choosing New Folder from File in the File Browser menu bar. To rename a folder, select it in the folder tree (left pane), right-click / Control+click to open the pop-up menu, and then choose Rename. To rename the files, click the filename type a new one. Press the Tab key to go automatically to the next one. Or select the files you want to rename and choose File ➤ Rename Multiple Files from the File Browser menu bar.

> **Note:** ☞ "Setting Proper Orientation" in Chapter 2 to learn about rotating files from within the File Browser window.

Adding Flags (Mac Only)

You can add flags to some of your image files to differentiate one from another. This is an option only if you are using a Mac. To apply a flag, select one or more of the files you wish to flag and click the flag icon at the top of the File Browser ( ). You can choose to view only flagged files or only unflagged files by selecting from the Show menu at the top right of the File Browser window. To remove a flag, select the file or files you wish to remove the flag(s) from and select the flag icon at the top of the File Browser.

Searching for Files with the File Browser

To search for specific files, choose File ➤ Search from the File Browser menu bar or click the binocular icon at the top of the File Browser window (👀). When you do this, a dialog box much like the one shown in Figure 1.29 appears. Choose a source folder from Look In by clicking Browse. Set your Criteria and then click the Search button. The results of the search will be displayed in the File Browser window.

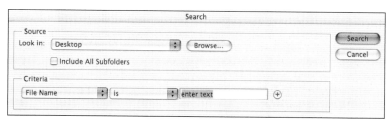

Figure 1.29: Search by different criteria including Date Created and EXIF Metadata. The results of your search are shown in the File Browser window.

Running Automated Tasks from the File Browser

On a Mac you can run automated commands directly from the File Browser via the Automate menu. Figure 1.30 shows the various tasks available from within the File Browser that can be applied to selected image files. On Windows the Automate menu is missing, but you can still apply Process Multiple Files and the Multi-Page PDF to PSD Automation tool to selected files via the Editor File menu. Throughout the book I've shown when it is appropriate and useful to run Automate commands directly from the File Browser.

Figure 1.30: On a Mac you can run several Automate tasks directly from within the File Browser.

Where Do You Go for Help?

Within Photoshop Elements, there are several ways to get help on specific subjects without ever taking your eyes off the screen. Adobe has provided some of the best screen help I've encountered, and because Photoshop Elements is such a powerful program with so many features, I encourage you to use the help whenever you have a question about a particular tool or feature.

The How To palette, located in the Editor's palette bin, is full of useful step-by-step instructions, including "how tos" that help you enhance text, correct color and brightness, design web graphics, and retouch photos.

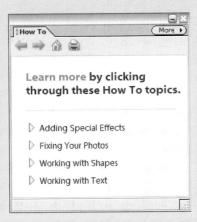

On the Help menu, you'll find Help and Photoshop Elements Tutorials, both of which are useful HTML-based systems. Help is a hyperlinked version of the printed manual, with a powerful index and search engine so you can quickly get the answer to just about any Photoshop Elements question. The tutorials walk you step-by-step through various tasks by using images that come on the program disk.

If you position your mouse over a tool or palette and hold it there, a tiny pop-up box will appear telling you the name of the tool and what keyboard shortcut (if any) to use.

There are many useful keyboard shortcuts in addition to those mentioned in this book and the Adobe resource material. A good source for this information is a list compiled by Don Fukushima and found on Jay Arraich's site. The main part of Jay's site is also a good source for a whole range of other Photoshop Elements tips and techniques:

http://www.arraich.com/elements/keyboardshortcuts.htm
http://www.arraich.com/elements/psE_intro.htm

Your Images: Global Solutions

It doesn't matter whether an image is taken with a low-resolution camera phone or a high-end digital camera. Truth is, most digital images benefit from software tweaking. This chapter focuses on using Photoshop Elements' Quick Fix and Standard Edit to make improvements that affect your entire image, including cropping; optimizing color and tonal range; removing unwanted dust, scratches, and camera noise; sharpening; and resizing. (Other, subsequent chapters concentrate on more localized problems that require you to work on a specific area or part of an image.)

2

Chapter Contents

Choosing an Editing Workspace

Photoshop Elements 3 offers two primary modes, or workspaces, in which to fix your image: Quick Fix and Standard Edit. You *can* do some photo enhancing in the Organizer (Windows only), but the editing is inherently limited. Standard Edit is the default workspace that appears when you first open the Editor. (Mac users have only the application; there is no separate Editor or Organizer as there is in Windows.)

You can tell you are in Standard Edit when you see the extensive toolbar on the left of the screen and the palette bin on the right. You can access Quick Fix by clicking the Quick Fix icon found to the far right of the shortcuts bar, in the grayed out area that looks like a folder tab. The icon is located next to the Standard Edit icon, which takes you back to that mode from Quick Fix. (In Windows, you can also access the two choices directly from the Organizer. The Edit icon is located in the middle of the shortcuts bar, and the pop-up menu gives you a choice of edit workspaces.)

Figure 2.1 shows the Quick Fix workspace. Figure 2.2 shows the Standard Edit workspace.

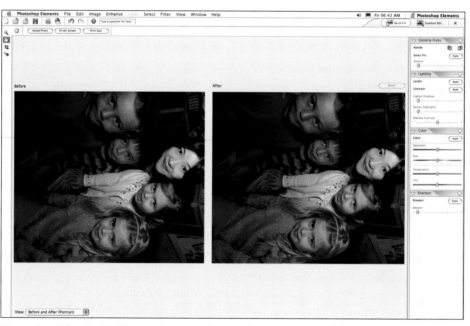

Figure 2.1: The Quick Fix workspace. The Windows version will look slightly different.

Figure 2.2: The Standard Edit workspace. The Mac version will look slightly different.

As you can see, Quick Fix is a streamlined version of the Standard Edit, with an abbreviated toolbar and a Control Center on the right instead of the palette bin. Once you are in Quick Fix, many of the menu commands such as Image Size, Rotate, Adjust Lighting, and most of the filters are still available. Shortcuts are also available. I really like Quick Fix, and especially like the ability to view before and after versions of your work side by side. What you don't see—and what you don't have access to—are many of the toolbar tools, including the selection tools, brush tools, shape tools, and eraser tools.

Quick Fix is ideal for many of the image enhancement tasks outlined in this chapter. However, just about anything you can do in Quick Fix can also be done in Standard Edit—albeit without the side-by-side reference. As I go through the steps of improving an image, I'll be sure to note both the Quick Fix and Standard Edit equivalents and let you know when a particular task is best done in one or the other.

I'll also note when a particular editing task can be done in the Organizer (Window users only); however, keep in mind that when you edit in that workspace you won't have nearly as many options or the flexibility offered in the Editor. The Organizer editing tools are for those wanting to make some quick changes or adjustments without leaving that workspace. (The Organizer was originally Photoshop Album, a stand-alone program, and many of the image-editing capabilities were left in when it was combined with Photoshop Elements.)

Deciding What Comes When

Quick Fix streamlines your workflow, and like Standard Edit, it doesn't force you into any one way of doing things. When it comes to fixing a typical digital image, however, some tasks are best done before others.

Here is an order I suggest you follow when working on images:

1. Rotate the image if it is in the wrong orientation.
2. Use the Smart Fix command. If that doesn't work satisfactorily, use Auto Levels. For even more tonal control, use Levels. (I'll get into the specifics of how to do this shortly.)
3. Use the Reduce Noise filter to reduce digital-camera-specific noise.

(If you are working in Quick Fix, from this point on I suggest you leave and go to Standard Edit.)

4. Use the Clone Stamp tool (⚓) or Spot Healing Brush (🖊) to remove unwanted dust and scratches and other kinds of flaws.
5. Save a copy of your work in the Photoshop file format (File ➢ Save As). Do this now, before cropping, resizing, and sharpening. Cropping throws away data you may want later, and resizing and sharpening always degrade an image to some degree.
6. Use the Crop tool (🔲) to crop an image to its essential elements.
7. Resize the image to meet the specific needs of its final destination, be it the Web, a high-resolution ink-jet print, a printed document, or an e-mail attachment.
8. Use the Unsharp Mask filter to sharpen images that were shot out of focus or that look particularly soft for some reason and to optimize the image for printing.
9. Use File ➢ Save As to save your image. Be sure to rename your file to differentiate it from the copy you saved before resizing and then select an appropriate file format (JPEG, PSD, TIFF, and so on).

At this point, if you follow my suggestions, you'll have three versions of your image—the original, an "optimized" image, and, finally, an optimized, cropped, resized, and sharpened image. If memory storage is an issue, consider saving only the original and final image.

You can vary the order of these tasks slightly. For example, there is no logical reason why you'd need to optimize colors and tonal values before removing unwanted dust, scratches, and electronic noise. However, whatever order you follow, always keep resizing and sharpening for last. Throughout this chapter, I'll give you exact details about how to perform these tasks.

Setting Proper Orientation

It's difficult and unnecessary to work on an image that is not properly oriented. Look at the image in Figure 2.1. I shot the photo on assignment for a labor magazine and held the camera in the portrait, or vertical, orientation to capture kids huddled around their day care provider. This is how the image appears when I first bring it into Photoshop Elements. Obviously, the image needs rotating before I can move on to other tasks. To do this, click the Rotate Photo 90 Degrees Counterclockwise icon located in the upper-right side of the Quick Fix Control Center. Both the "before" and "after" views will rotate.

Note: If your image contains multiple layers, only the selected layer will be affected by Quick Fix commands. The exception is the Quick Fix rotate command, which rotates all layers. Also, if you have an active selection, only the selected areas will be affected by Quick Fix commands.

You can also rotate an image from the main menu bar regardless of whether you are in Standard Edit or Quick Fix (Image ➤ Rotate).

If you are in File Browser (File ➤ Browse Folders), you can rotate one or more selected images via the rotate icons located in the File Browser menu bar. To select more than one image for rotation at a time, hold the Ctrl/⌘ key while selecting, and then apply the rotate command. Keep in mind that when you do this you are rotating only the thumbnail version of the image. To apply the rotation to the actual image file, you'll need to either choose Edit ➤ Apply Rotation from the File Browser menu, or open the file and do a File ➤ Save or File ➤ Save As from the main menu bar. If you are working with JPEG images, I suggest you avoid the Apply Rotation command from within the File Browser menu. If you use this command, your file is automatically saved back in the JPEG file format with a very slight loss of quality. (See the note at the end of this section.)

What Do You Do When You Mess Up?

It's comforting to know that when you are working within Photoshop Elements, it's difficult to permanently damage a digital image. There is hardly a mistake you can make that can't be fixed by using the Undo History palette or the Undo command. Even if you accidentally save your work, as long as you haven't closed the file you can revert to a previous version. Here are your choices if—and when—you mess up:

The simplest way to undo an action you've just made is to click the Undo button (↺) in the shortcuts bar or use the keyboard shortcut Ctrl+Z / ⌘ +Z. This button is connected to the Undo History palette, and each time you click it you move backward through the various recorded states in the Undo History palette. You can continue stepping backward this way until you reach the end of the recorded states in the Undo History palette. To redo the operation, click the Redo button (↻) in the shortcuts bar or use the keyboard shortcut Ctrl+Y / ⌘ +Y. (You can customize the keyboard command by choosing Edit ➢ Preferences ➢ General.)

You can also go directly to the Undo History palette to correct mistakes. By default, the Undo History palette records 50 states, or changes, to your image. You can increase this number in the Preferences (↻ "Setting Preferences" in the appendix). States are added to the palette from the top down, with the most recent state at the bottom. The name of the tool or command you used is included. To undo a mistake, simply select a state above the one you want to redo, and the Undo History palette will revert your image to that state.

You can also choose Edit ➢ Undo from the menu bar. Or you can use the keyboard command Ctrl+Alt+Z / ⌘ +Option+Z. To redo, choose Edit ➢ Redo or use Ctrl+Alt+Y / ⌘ +Option+Y. When using almost any tool, it's important to use small steps (release the mouse frequently); that way, you will need to undo only a small amount of work.

As a last recourse, you can always revert to the last saved version. To do this, choose Edit ➢ Revert to Saved. If you decide this isn't what you want, you can always undo Revert in the Undo History palette.

Fixing a mistake is easy, but most people will find a way to mess up so badly that the methods just described won't help. For example, say you resize an image and save and close the file. Oops, you really didn't mean to save the resized version. What do you do now? Unless you have a backup, you are out of luck. That's why throughout this book you'll see that I strongly advocate creating a copy of your digital image and working on that file. It won't matter as much if you mess up because you'll always have an original to go back to.

If you are using the Windows platform, you can also rotate images while in the Organizer. Simply select the Rotate Left or Rotate Right icons at the bottom left of the screen. (You can also use the keyboard commands Ctrl+Left arrow or Ctrl+Right arrow. You can also use the rotate controls at the bottom of the Auto Fix window (Edit ➢ Auto Fix Window), but if you are working on a JPEG image, your edited image will be slightly degraded because it will be recompressed and saved as a JPEG when you exit. (See the following note.)

Regardless of how you do it, don't worry if you rotate your image the wrong way. Most of the time you can undo your mistake by rotating your image until you get it right or by using one of the various Undo controls and trying again (☞ "What Do You Do When You Mess Up?" earlier in this section).

> **Note:** If you start with a JPEG file, rotate the image as I have described, and then save the final version in the JPEG file format, the saved image can become slightly degraded. This is because every time you decompress, change, and then compress a JPEG file, there is a slight loss of quality. Although the effect is minimal, it is cumulative—the more times you open, change, and close a JPEG, the more you'll degrade the image (another reason to leave your original image intact and always do a File ➢ Save As of your edited work). This is not an issue if you rotate and then save your file as a PSD or TIFF or other lossless file format.

Making Dull Images Shine

Look at the image in Figure 2.3. It's a nicely composed scene, but something is wrong. It looks "flat" and suffers from a poor distribution of tonal values and poor color saturation. The hang glider blends into the sky without strong distinction. In the case of this photo—taken with a digital camera—it's a matter of a wrong exposure. My auto-exposure exposed for the sky and not for the hang glider. Sometimes the quality of light will make a digital image look flat. Think fog or haze.

Figure 2.3: Before applying Smart Fix.

I use one of three methods to improve images that suffer from this "dull" syndrome: Smart Fix, Auto Levels, or Levels. All three methods are available in Quick Fix or Standard Edit.

If you prefer to remain in the Organizer (Windows only), you can try using Edit ➢ Auto Fix Photo from the Organizer menu bar, or Ctrl+Shift+I. You can also try the Auto Fix controls (Edit ➢ Auto Fix Window from the Organizer menu bar). If you don't get satisfying results with these methods, switch to either Standard Edit or Quick Fix and try one of the methods outlined later in this section. (In Chapter 11, I'll explain a more powerful, yet complex way of using adjustment layers and masking to fix more problematic images.)

Calibrate Your Display

To get the most out of your digital images, you'll need to calibrate your monitor and make sure that when it comes to color and brightness, you are at least in the ballpark. How else will you know how much contrast or brightness to add to your carefully optimized image, or how will you know when your colors are right? If the monitor is off, there is no way to predict what the image will look like when it is printed.

If you are really into precision, it pays to spend a few hundred dollars and get a sophisticated calibration device that attaches to your monitor and physically measures the colors and brightness. These products produce a color profile that can be applied to compatible desktop printers for even more consistent results.

The following are two popular products that include a colorimeter and profiling software:

MonacoOPTIX (http://www.monacosys.com/products/monacooptix/ monacooptix_xr.html) creates monitor profiles for both the Mac and Windows operating systems, LCD or CRTs, for about $300.

Eye-One Display (http://www.i1color.com/products/i1_display.asp) can be used for both Mac and Windows, LCD or CRTs, and costs about $249.

A less expensive way that requires just software and your own eyes is to use the Adobe Gamma utility found in Photoshop Elements' **Goodies** folder (Windows only). If you are using a Mac, use the OS X Display Calibrator Assistant found in the **Utilities** folder. Both utilities walk you step-by-step through the process of calibrating your monitor. They also produce a color profile that can be applied to desktop printers.

Before you proceed with either Adobe Gamma or the Mac OS X Display Calibrator Assistant, keep the following in mind:

- Set your operating system display preferences to the maximum number of colors, usually millions.
- If you are using a CRT monitor, let it warm up for at least 30 minutes before performing the calibration.
- Avoid calibrating in a brightly lit room.
- Set your desktop background to a neutral/non-distracting color, preferably mid-tone gray.
- When adjusting the monitor to the target, it helps to blur your vision by squinting your eyes and leaning back at a distance from the screen.
- Calibrate your monitor regularly, two or three times a month. Settings inadvertently change, and monitors dim with time.

For a useful on-line calibration tutorial, go to **http://epaperpress.com/monitorcal/**.

Other third-party calibration software includes the following:

PowerStrip ($29.95): http://entechtaiwan.net/util/ps.shtm

QuickGamma (free): http://quickgamma.de/indexen.html

Smart Fix

Figure 2.4 (left) shows what happens when I apply Smart Fix and its default settings to the hang glider shot. Smart Fix adjusts for lighting, color, and contrast all at once and can be quite effective for some images but not at all for others.

Figure 2.4: Smart Fix applied at default settings (left). Smart Fix boosted about 75 percent (right).

To apply Smart Fix, use one of these methods:

- In Quick Fix mode, click the Smart Fix button located in the upper right of the Control Center, below the rotate commands. A status bar at the bottom of the Quick Fix window informs you of the progress. If you aren't satisfied with the results, click the Reset button located near the After version of your image. You can also use the keyboard command Ctrl+Z / ⌘+Z.
- In Standard Edit mode, choose Smart Fix from the Enhance menu (Enhance ➢ Auto Smart Fix).

In this example, there is improvement. But I can do better with Smart Fix by increasing the amount of correction:

- In Quick Fix mode, boost the strength of Smart Fix via the slider located below the Smart Fix command.
- In Standard Edit mode, use the Enhance menu (Enhance ➢ Adjust Smart Fix). In the dialog box, just move the slider over until you get the results you want, or type in a percentage from 0–200 percent. If you select Auto, the fix amount will automatically adjust to 100 percent.

Figure 2.4 (right) shows what happens when I slide the Smart Fix setting in Quick Fix by about 130 percent. Much better. (Each hash mark on the slider is equivalent to 50 percent.) After you determine the proper amount of correction by using the slider, click the Commit button (✔) located at the top of the Smart Fix box, next to the words *General Fixes*. If you can't find an adjustment that works, click the Cancel button (⊘). The Commit and Cancel icons appear only after you adjust the slider amount. They are not available when you use the Auto option. You can also select any of the other options in the Control Center, and your Smart Fix adjustment will automatically be committed. Note that the Reset button found above the After view is dimmed until you either Commit or Cancel the Smart Fix adjustment.

Auto Levels

Sometimes, regardless of how much you increase the strength, Smart Fix doesn't do the job. Look at Figure 2.5. I tried using Smart Fix, but it was way off. Instead I'll try another method, Auto Levels.

Figure 2.5: Smart Fix didn't work on this image.

Auto Levels finds the darkest and lightest pixels of an image and then remaps the intermediate pixels proportionally. Color casts may be removed or introduced because Auto Levels adjusts the red, green, and blue channels individually.

In Standard Edit, you apply Auto Levels via the menu bar (Enhance ➤ Auto Levels) or via the keyboard (Shift+Ctrl+L / Shift+⌘+L.) In Quick Fix, in the Lighting group in the Control Center, click Auto next to Levels.

That's what I did to the shot, and you can see in Figure 2.6 that it worked. Figure 2.7 shows the image's histogram before and after Auto Levels. Notice that the fixed shot has a much better distribution of tonal values.

Figure 2.6: After Auto Levels.

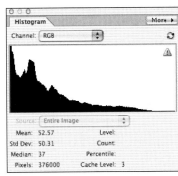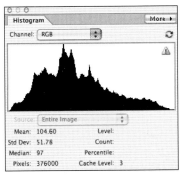

Figure 2.7: The image's histogram before Auto Levels (left): a narrow distribution of tonal values. After Auto Levels (right): a wider distribution of tonal values.

Auto Contrast, by the way—found just under Auto Levels in the Enhance menu and in Quick Fix under Lighting—isn't nearly as useful for color images. It adjusts the overall contrast and mixture of colors but it does not adjust each color channel (red, green, and blue) individually. I rarely use Auto Contrast, and when I do it's mostly for grayscale images.

The Lighten Shadows, Darken Highlights, and Midtone Contrast commands found in the Quick Fix Control Center are basically the same commands you get when you choose Enhance ➤ Adjust Lighting ➤ Shadows/Highlights from the main menu bar. These controls are very useful when you want to correct images with a strong backlight and a dark foreground, or vice versa. I'll use these commands later, in Chapters 3, 4, and 7. (When you adjust the Lighten Shadows, Darken Highlights, and Midtone Contrast sliders, Commit and Cancel icons appear next the word *Lighting*. Select Commit when you are satisfied with the image. Select Cancel if you are not. Until you select either the Commit or Cancel icon, the Reset button located above the After version of your image is dimmed and inoperable.)

More Control: Levels

The Auto Levels command also doesn't always work satisfactorily. The bag in Figure 2.8, shot with a digital camera for a commercial website, lacks color intensity and contrast. But applying Auto Levels makes it look worse. At times like this, I turn to the Levels controls found in the menu bar under Enhance ➤ Adjust Lighting ➤ Levels. (You also have access to Levels from Quick Fix.) The truth is, I probably use Levels more than any other single Photoshop Elements control. It enables me to manually adjust the intensity of my shadow, midtone, or highlight areas. Not only does it give me sophisticated control over the look of my digital images, it is intuitive and relatively easy to use.

Figure 2.8: The original image (left) lacks color intensity and contrast. Auto Levels didn't help (right).

Here is how I used Levels to make the bag look more attractive and saleable:

1. I chose Enhance ➢ Adjust Lighting ➢ Levels. This opened the dialog box shown in Figure 2.9.

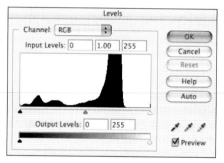

Figure 2.9: Levels graphically show the distribution of tonal values and provide a means to individually adjust shadows, midtones, or highlights.

2. Looking at the Levels histogram, I saw the problem. Most of the values were to the left, toward the shadow areas. I needed to spread the values across the spectrum and increase the contrast. To do this, I dragged the Input Levels white triangle (at the lower-right corner of the histogram) to the left, toward the edge of the tall black mound. As I did this, I saw the whites, or highlights, in my actual image lighten and the overall contrast increase. (Be sure you have selected the Preview check box in the Levels dialog box. With this option selected, any changes you make in the Levels dialog box will be shown in the actual image.)

3. Next I adjusted the midtones by dragging the Input Levels gray triangle (found in the middle of the bottom edge of the histogram) to the right. This darkened and intensified the midtones. The numbers in the three boxes above the histogram represent numerically, in order, shadows, midtones, and highlight areas. As you move the triangle sliders, you'll see these values change to reflect the new values. You can also enter numeric values into these boxes, but it's a lot easier to manually slide the sliders.

4. At various points in the process, I found it useful to carefully examine the effects of my changes on detailed parts of the image. For example, when I adjusted the midtones, I wanted to make sure I didn't lose any details in the gold embroidery. Even though the Levels dialog box was open, I could still use my navigation keyboard commands to magnify and scroll around the image. (This works only in Standard Edit, not in Quick Fix.)

5. The shadow areas (again, represented in the left side of the histogram) looked fine, but I went ahead and moved the black triangle anyway. In Figure 2.10, you can see how I adjusted the Levels so that the shadow areas became too dark. At this point I could have slid the black triangle back to its original position, but I decided to start over completely and reset the image to its original state. To do this, I held down the Alt/Option key and clicked the Reset button in the Levels dialog box.

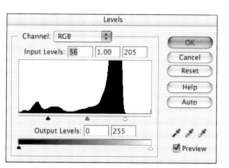

Figure 2.10: Changes made in the Levels dialog box (left) are reflected in the image window (right). In this case, sliding the shadow triangle to the right made the dark areas too dark.

6. I went back and adjusted my highlights and midtones and left the shadows alone. When I was finished, I clicked OK (see Figure 2.11).

Figure 2.11: Corrected image using Levels.

More Levels

If you click Auto in the Levels dialog box, you'll get the same results as you would using the Auto Levels command. This dialog box also enables you to change the brightness and contrast of the image by dragging the gray slider at the bottom. This affects all the pixels equally and does not affect the color values. You can also choose to work specifically on a red, green, or blue channel by selecting from the Channel drop-down menu at the top of the dialog box. Unless I know one specific color is off, I work in the default composite RGB mode. The eyedroppers found under the Auto button can also be used to adjust Levels according to a tonal priority. Select the eyedropper on the left and click directly on the area you want to be the darkest area of your image. Observe the changes as Levels forces those areas to black and adjusts the corresponding tonal values accordingly. Select the middle eyedropper and click midtone or gray areas (areas without any color) and watch the effect. Select the eyedropper on the right and click on an area you want to be the white area of your image and watch the effect. You can also customize the black, gray, and white targets by double-clicking the corresponding eyedropper tool. This opens the Color Picker, where you can select colors to adjust the three tonal values. This can be useful if you want to adjust the tonal parameters of your image to match the capabilities of your printer. If you hold the Alt/Option key, the Cancel button becomes Reset. This enables you to start over without closing the Levels window.

Correcting Color

A digital image can contain an unwanted color cast, perhaps because of an improper white balance setting, or a mismatch between film and ambient light, or a poor scan. You can rid a digital image of unwanted colors or make colors truer in several ways by using Photoshop Elements. The easiest way is using the Auto Color Correction command (Enhance ➢ Auto Color Correction, or Color: Auto in Quick Fix). If this doesn't work satisfactorily, and you want more control, try the Color Cast command (Enhance ➢ Adjust Color ➢ Remove Color Cast) or Color Variations (Enhance ➢ Adjust Color ➢ Color Variations), both of which I'll describe in this section. (You can also adjust colors individually with Levels, as described earlier.)

Auto Color Command

Auto Color Correction does both independent and composite adjustments of the red, green, and blue channels. Auto Color Correction often does a better job of fixing color cast problems than Auto Levels, which does only an independent adjustment for each color channel.

Here's how to access Auto Color Correction:

- In Quick Fix, Auto Color is found in the Color group in the Control Center.
- In Standard Edit, the command is found in the Enhance menu (Enhance ➢ Auto Color Correction).

Try it, and if it doesn't work, move on to one of the following methods.

Removing an Unwanted Cast with One Click

Figure 2.12 shows a photograph I took of a new MRI scanner at the University of California Medical Center in San Francisco. The balance between daylight film and ambient light was off, and the result was a greenish tint.

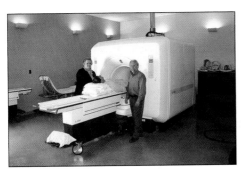

Figure 2.12: A mismatch between film sensitivity and ambient light caused the greenish tint.

It was easy to fix the image by using Photoshop Elements' Color Cast command, which analyzes color samples taken from selective parts of the image and attempts to shift the color cast to a neutral color.

Here's what I did:

1. I chose Enhance ➤ Adjust Color ➤ Remove Color Cast to open the dialog box (shown on the left in Figure 2.13). You can do this from within either Standard Edit or Quick Fix.

2. Using the Eyedropper tool (✐), I clicked different areas in the image. I was specifically looking for areas that I knew should be gray, white, or black but weren't because of the unwanted color cast. The image changed according to the color I selected. When I didn't like a result, I simply clicked on another area of my image or clicked on the Reset button, and the image reverted to its original state. The Color Cast eyedropper samples only one pixel at a time. To be precise about where you are sampling, you need to magnify your image.

3. I poked around until I got what I was looking for and then I clicked OK. The resulting image is shown in Figure 2.13.

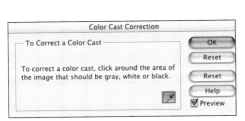
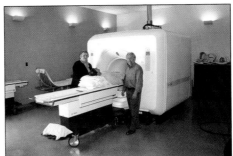

Figure 2.13: The Color Cast Correction command (left) helps remove unwanted color casts. The image with the color cast removed (right).

Note: Usually I find the notes that Adobe includes in their dialog boxes to be excellent. However, I must confess that reading the note in the Color Cast Correction dialog box confused me at first. It reads: "To correct a color cast, click around the area of the image that should be gray, white, or black." The first time I read this, I didn't pay particular attention to the word *should*. Instead I tried to find an area in my image that was gray, white, or black. I didn't have good results until I realized that I needed to look for areas that *should* be a neutral color such as gray, white, or black. The tool works by taking a sample from any one these areas you choose and then assuming that you want the sampled area to be neutral—in other words, to consist of equal amounts of red, green, and blue. It then shifts all the colors to create this neutral state.

Shooting Digital: Use the Right Side of Your Brain

When shooting with a digital camera—or, for that matter, any camera—keep in mind that photography is a visual language dependent on light and form. It works best when it speaks to the nonverbal, intuitive side of the brain, complementing words but not necessarily competing with them. A billboard framed against a brilliant blue sky is interesting not only because of the words on the billboard but because of its shape and the way that light strikes it, and the inherent tension between something man-made and something natural. I always tell my students that the best way to learn this language is to take classes and examine images in books and see what works and what doesn't. I tell them to go to exhibitions and art galleries, and by all means, just pay attention to the way the summer light strikes a gnarled old oak tree or glances off a sleeping child's face.

Using Color Variations to Get the Color Right

While on assignment for *Wired* magazine, I used daylight film to shoot the portrait of Cold War warrior and futurist Andrew Marshall in the fluorescent-lit halls of the Pentagon. (Yeah, believe it or not, I still shoot film occasionally.) The mismatch between outdoor film and the indoor lighting caused Marshall to be bathed in an interesting combination of magenta and green light, as shown in Figure 2.14.

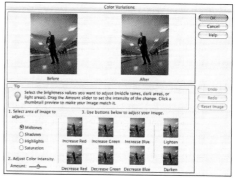

Figure 2.14: The colors in this photo (left) needed to be adjusted. The Color Variations command (right) is a good way to visually adjust color, contrast, and saturation.

To tone down the strong casts, I used Photoshop Elements' Color Variations command. The Color Variations command lets you adjust the color balance, contrast, and saturation of an image by showing you thumbnails of alternatives. Like the Color Cast command, Color Variations is most useful for images that don't require precise color adjustments.

I followed these steps:

1. I chose Enhance ➤ Adjust Color ➤ Color Variations to create the adjustment thumbnails (see Figure 2.14). Color Variations is also available while working in Quick Fix. The thumbnail in the top left corner of the dialog box shows the original image (Before). As I made adjustments, the After thumbnail on the right changed to reflect my choices. When I went too far and wanted to revert to my original, I simply clicked the Before thumbnail or the Reset Image button. You can also click Undo to step backward through your changes. In the lower-left corner of the Color Variations dialog box, dragging the Amount slider determines the amount of each adjustment. Also, by selecting one of the Shadows, Midtones, or Highlights radio buttons before making adjustments, you can emphasize adjustment of the dark, middle, or light areas. (Midtones is the default setting.) To change the degree of hue in the image, select Saturation.

2. I didn't need to adjust the brightness of this particular image, but I could have by clicking the Lighten or Darken thumbnails on the right side of the dialog box. Instead, I adjusted the color by clicking the Decrease Green thumbnail. That took care of some of the green cast. Next I clicked the Increase Blue thumbnail, and that took care of some of the magenta cast. Neither adjustment removed all the magenta or green cast, but I still liked the result

3. When I was finished, I clicked OK. Figure 2.15 shows the adjusted image.

Figure 2.15: The adjusted image.

Scanning Digital: Scanning Old Black-and-White Photos

When scanning old black-and-white photos, keep your scanning software set at RGB. Don't scan in grayscale even though that might seem like the logical way to go. Most old photos contain subtle colors or tints, caused by the aging process or the characteristics of the photographic paper. It's these colors that make the image look authentic.

Tinting Images

I like grayscale images. I really do. But sometimes they benefit from a color tint. The tint need not be overwhelming. In fact, sometimes a subtle shade of yellow or red is all it takes to give a grayscale image an added pop so it jumps from a page.

Take, for example, the 1761 engraving from a Russian bath shown in Figure 2.16. The image was published in black-and-white in a book I wrote on bathing. It looked fine. However, when I went to place the image on my website, it was lacking. It needed to stand out more.

Figure 2.16: The original grayscale image.

This is what I did:

1. I opened the Hue/Saturation dialog box (Enhance ➢ Adjust Color ➢ Adjust Hue/Saturation), shown in Figure 2.17.

Note: This will not work if you are in Grayscale or Bitmap mode—it works only if you are in RGB or Indexed Color mode. If you need to, choose Image ➢ Mode ➢ RGB or Image ➢ Mode ➢ Indexed Color to convert the image.

2. I selected Colorize. The image was converted to the hue of the current foreground color—in this case, red.
3. I then slid the Hue and Saturation sliders to select variations of color.
4. When I got the tint I wanted, I clicked OK. The tinted image is shown in Figure 2.17.

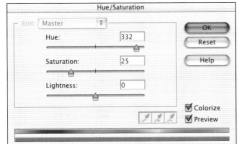

Figure 2.17: To tint, make sure the Colorize option is selected in the Hue/Saturation dialog box (left). The tinted image (right).

You can tint an image using the Hue/Saturation dialog box (Enhance ➢ Adjust Color ➢ Adjust Hue/Saturation) from within Quick Fix as well. You can also use the Quick Fix Color group. Start by sliding the Saturation slider completely to the left. Then adjust the Tint slider to introduce a tint. You can then use the Hue slider to introduce new tints. (When you adjust the Saturation, Hue, Temperature, and Tint sliders, Commit and Cancel icons appear next to the word *Color.* Select Commit when you are satisfied with the image. Select Cancel if you are not. Until you select either the Commit or Cancel icon, the Reset button located above the After version of your image is dimmed and inoperable.)

Eliminating or Diminishing Dust, Scratches, and Electronic Noise

Most digital images suffer from dust, scratches or other marks, or electronic "noise." Even high JPEG compression can cause unwanted artifacts, which show up as "blocks" and are especially obvious in areas of continuous tone such as a vast blue sky or skin, and can appear as chunky blocks of pixels. Any of these flaws can detract from the look of a digital image. With smaller prints, or when viewed on a monitor, these artifacts are not as noticeable, but as prints get larger—or if an image is magnified over 100 percent—these artifacts can be quite visible. Fortunately, Photoshop Elements offers several tools for getting rid of them.

N o t e : Low-cost, third-party solutions to reducing noise are available. Check out Dfine, a Photoshop plug-in from nik multimedia that offers more options than Photoshop's new Reduce Noise filter. (A trial version of Dfine is included on the CD.)

Reduce Noise Filter

The newest and most useful tool in the Photoshop Elements arsenal is the Reduce Noise filter. The filter can be applied from either Quick Fix or Standard Edit. Look at Figure 2.18 (left) and you'll see a shot I took in extremely low light. I managed to get the shot without using a flash by boosting my digital camera's ISO setting to 1600. I got the shot, but increasing the ISO introduced a lot of "noise" or "grain" into the image. Figure 2.18 (right) shows a magnified view and reveals the noise more clearly.

 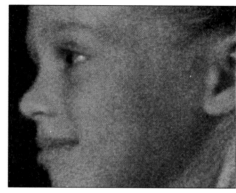

Figure 2.18: I shot this in low light without a flash by boosting my digital camera's ISO to 1600 (left). The magnified view shows the noise clearly (right).

To reduce the noise, I used the Reduce Noise filter (Filters ➤ Noise ➤ Reduce Noise). The filter is available in both Standard Edit and Quick Fix. Figure 2.19 shows my settings and the results.

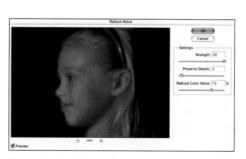 

Figure 2.19: My Reduce Noise filter settings and the results.

How did I come up with my settings? I just used trial and error until I got something that looked less "noisy" but still maintained edge detail as well.

Spot Healing

Sometimes flaws are not global but specific. The flaws you see in Figure 2.20, for example, were caused by dust accumulating on the electronic sensor of my Nikon D100. Similar artifacts can be caused by a smudge or speck of dust on the lens. A dirty scanner glass will also produce similar results.

Figure 2.20: The flaws on this image were caused by dust on the electronic sensor.

The Spot Healing Brush is especially effective in removing these kinds of image flaws. To use this new Photoshop Elements brush, you'll need to be in Standard Edit.

The Spot Healing Brush tool is found in the same spot on the toolbar as the Healing Brush tool (use the keyboard command J and repeatedly press J to cycle between tools). Why use it rather than the Healing Brush tool? The Spot Healing Brush tool is easy to use. You don't need to establish a sample area by holding the Alt/Option key and clicking, as you need to do with the Healing Brush and Clone Stamp tools. You only need to select a brush, position your cursor, and click over an area you wish to heal. You can also click and hold the mouse and drag to "paint" over a complex shape. After you stop painting and release the mouse, the Spot Healing Brush tool goes to work. Like the Healing Brush tool, it automatically samples the areas outside the selection and blends the results with the area within the selection.

In the example shown in Figure 2.20, the Spot Healing Brush worked great. This what I did:

1. I selected the Spot Healing Brush tool from the toolbar.
2. I chose a Hard Round 30 pixels from the options bar. I chose this size because it was about 20 percent larger than the area I wished to remove. Using a brush 10–30 percent larger than the area you wish to remove is a good rule of thumb to follow. (You can play around with a soft or hard-edged brush. In most cases, hard is the way to go, but sometimes a soft brush produces a smoother edge transition.)
3. I set the Type to Proximity Match. (Pattern generates an obvious pattern, which isn't appropriate if you are trying to seamlessly remove a flaw.)

4. I placed my cursor over the large flaw in the middle and clicked. I then selected a smaller, Hard Round 20 pixels brush and clicked the smaller flaws sprinkled throughout the image. Done.

The result is shown in Figure 2.21.

Figure 2.21: Flaw fixed with the Spot Healing Brush.

If you try the Spot Healing Brush on large flaws, say over 300 pixels, you'll quickly see why it is called a "spot" healing brush. The tool seems to get confused, and produces unpredictable and often unsatisfactory results. You'll also find it works best when the area around the objects you are trying to remove is surrounded by uniform color or texture.

Combining Tools and Techniques

Sometimes you'll want to use a combination of tools to fix a particularly challenging job. For this example, I used a combination of the Dust & Scratches filter, a selection tool, and the Clone Stamp tool to fix the 50-year-old photo shown in Figure 2.22.

Figure 2.22: This 50-year-old photo is full of scratches and other artifacts of age.

In Standard Edit, here's what I did:

1. I cropped the edges of the scan by using the Crop command (↩ "Cropping to the Essential Parts" later in this chapter).

2. I applied Auto Levels to optimize the colors and tone (↩ "Making Dull Images Shine" earlier in this chapter).

3. At a magnification level of 300 percent, I noticed the sky was filled with dust and scratches and other artifacts of age (see Figure 2.23). As I scrolled around, I saw there were also moiré patterns caused by the scanning process. Glass against glass often causes a swirling pattern, called a *moiré*, to form. The old transparency was sandwiched between two pieces of glass. I was tempted to use the Dust & Scratches filter to clean up the entire image but I knew this wasn't a good idea because it would blur the image. Instead I selected the sky by using the Lasso selection tool (◯) and applied the filter only to this selected area. I set the Radius at 4 and the Threshold at 0 (see Figure 2.23). In general, higher Radius values effectively remove more dust and scratches but blur other pixels in the image as well. Depending on the image, you can still remove dust and scratches but diminish the blur caused by higher Radius values by selecting higher Threshold values.

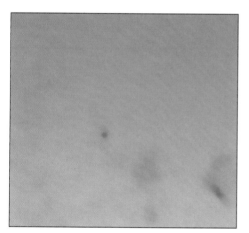
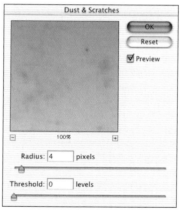

Figure 2.23: A magnification of 300 percent reveals the details of the problem (left). Applying the Dust & Scratches filter (right) to the selected background removed many of the artifacts and left the foreground area sharp.

4. Although the filter got rid of most of the smaller artifacts, the larger ones remained. To get rid of these, I selected the Clone Stamp tool (♨) from the toolbox. In the options bar, I selected the following options for the Clone Stamp tool:

    Brush: Soft Round 100 pixels
    Mode: Normal
    Opacity: 100 percent
    Aligned: selected
    Use All Layers: selected

I positioned the cursor slightly to the side of a scratch or smudge, in an area of the sky devoid of spots. While holding the Alt/Option key, I clicked and sampled. Then I clicked and "stamped" over a flawed area, careful not to drag and smear the pixels and cause an unnatural-looking blur.

5. After deselecting the sky, I turned to the foreground and to the woman on the road (see the left side of Figure 2.24). This area wasn't as bad as the sky but it still needed some cleaning up. Again, I used the Clone Stamp tool to selectively rid the woman's arm and face of spots, this time using a smaller brush setting for the smaller areas.

This was a particularly difficult image, and, frankly, I had to draw the line at how much time I was going to put into it. I could have continued to use the Clone Stamp tool to make each and every detail perfect. However, I was satisfied with cleaning up the sky and most of the woman. After all, it is a historical photo and I wanted to keep some of its authenticity. The final image is shown on the right in Figure 2.24.

Figure 2.24: I used the Clone Stamp tool to selectively clean up the woman on the road (left). The final image (right), after applying the Dust & Scratches filter and using the Clone Stamp tool for extensive cloning.

Converting Color Images to Black-and-White

There are several reasons why you might convert a color image to black-and-white: black-and-white images stand out in a world saturated with color images, they are often more economical to print, and, if you save an image in Photoshop Elements' Grayscale mode, they take up less file space.

The image in Figure 2.25 was shot by San Francisco, California, resident Julie Christensen for a local newspaper. The newspaper prints only black-and-white photos, and Julie gave me a color print to scan and convert.

I scanned the print in color and converted it to black-and-white simply by choosing Enhance ➤ Adjust Color ➤ Remove Color (see Figure 2.25). This command converted the colors in the image to gray values, assigning equal red, green, and blue values to each pixel in the RGB image. The lightness value of each pixel did not change and, because the image remained in RGB mode, the file size didn't change either.

Figure 2.25: The original image (left). Quickly convert to black-and-white (right) by choosing Enhance ➤ Adjust Color ➤ Remove Color. (Photo by Julie Christensen)

If you want to keep your file size down, I suggest you convert an image to black-and-white by simply changing modes from RGB to Grayscale (Image ➤ Mode ➤ Grayscale). If you use this method, you won't have access to many Photoshop Elements filters and effects, which work only in RGB mode. But because grayscale images are only 8 bits per pixel, versus 24 bits per pixel, your file size will be about 75 percent smaller.

Cropping to the Essential Parts

Cropping is one of the most important ways to improve your digital image. Not only does cropping strengthen the composition of an image, it also reduces the overall size with no degradation in quality. In Photoshop Elements, using the Crop tool or Crop command is one of the easiest things you can do. This is a good time to emphasize the value of working on a copy of your original digital image. I can't tell you how many times I've cropped an image to what I thought was an optimal composition but then later decided I needed more sky or more foreground. I would have been in trouble if I didn't have the original to go back to.

In Figure 2.26 you'll see how with a little cropping I emphasized the child and her day care provider, and made a more compellling image.

Figure 2.26: Before cropping, the image is unnecessarily large and not as effective. The shaded area outside the bounding box denotes the area that will be cropped.

This is what I did:

1. I selected the Crop tool (⊐). In Quick Fix—shown here—it's located to the far left of the window. In Standard Edit, it's in the toolbox.

2. I clicked and dragged over the part of the image I wanted to keep—in this case, the child and day care provider. When I released the mouse button, the crop marquee appeared as a bounding box with handles at the corners and sides.

3. The area to be cropped appears gray by default, which makes it easier to visualize how my image will look after it is cropped.

Note: The Crop tool's default shield color, gray—or more precisely, black at 75 percent opacity—is fine for most images. However, if you are working with images that contain large dark expanses, the gray shield may not be visible, In such cases, you can choose a lighter color and opacity by using the color selection box and the opacity pop-up slider in the options bar. This option appears only after you select the Crop tool and click and drag on your image.

4. I then adjusted the size of the crop marquee by dragging the corner handle. You can move the marquee to another position by clicking inside the bounding box and dragging. To rotate the marquee, just position the pointer outside the bounding box—the pointer turns into a curved arrow—and drag. You can constrain the proportions by holding down Shift as you drag a corner handle. If you hold the Ctrl key while dragging the bounding box near the edge of an image, you can avoid the "snap to edge" effect. Now when you drag, the transi-

tion will go smoothly. Holding the Alt/Option key while dragging any handle causes the crop window to grow from the middle. If you use the Shift and Alt/Option keys together, you can draw a symmetrical crop window from the center. The center is where you first clicked.

5. After I finished, I clicked the Commit button (☑) in the options bar. I could have double-clicked inside the crop marquee, selected a different tool, or pressed Enter/Return. If I had decided not to crop, I could have clicked the Cancel button (⊘) in the options bar or pressed the Esc key.

In Standard Edit, I also could have cropped this image by using the Crop command on the Image menu. In that case, I would have had to do the following:

1. Select the part of the image I wanted to keep by using any of the marquee selection tools (✍ "Selection Tools" in the appendix). Keep in mind that regardless of the shape of your selection, the final cropped shape will always be rectangular, based on the outermost parameter of the selection.

2. Choose Image ➢ Crop from the menu bar.

In the Organizer (Windows only), you can also crop in the Auto Fix window. (To open the Auto Fix window, choose Edit ➢ Auto Fix Window from the Organizer menu bar, or right-click on the image and choose Auto Fix Window from the pop-up list.) The Crop tool is located at the top right of the Auto Fix window and is fairly intuitive to use. It even has fixed aspect ratios to choose from with a variety of commonly used sizes such as 4 × 6 inches and 8 × 10 inches. When you are finished with your crop, simply click the Apply button.

At times you'll want to crop to a specific resolution and size. Figure 2.27 (top) shows a series of thumbnail shots that I created for **Newsweek.com**. I started with literally hundreds of screen-sized images, all of which required a smaller, thumbnail version to be used as a navigation device. The job was so big that any extra steps added unwanted time to the process. Instead of cropping and then resizing each cropped image, I simply put the required size and resolution values of the thumbnail version into the Width, Height, or Resolution text boxes in the options bar. (Clicking the Clear button in the options bar resets the values to their defaults.) The options bar is shown in Figure 2.27 (bottom). I then followed the preceding steps, used in the day care example. After I finished making my cropping selection, I clicked Commit (☑) and ended up with exactly the size and resolution I needed—in this case, 30 × 30 pixels at 72 dots per inch (dpi).

Figure 2.27: The Crop tool can be set to crop to a specific size and resolution (top). (Photos by Peter Turnley, with permission from Newsweek, Inc.) The Crop tool options bar (bottom).

Although this procedure saved time, there was a trade-off in quality. By resizing so radically in one jump, I degraded the final image more than I would have if I had taken it down slowly in increments (☞ "Resizing," next).

Knowing Your File Size

Just as you wouldn't lift something without knowing its weight for fear of injuring your back, you shouldn't begin working on a digital image without knowing its pixel size. Why? The larger the image, the more the pixels, and the more "processing" power it takes to do even the simplest tasks.

How do you determine file size?

Choose Window ➤ Info from the menu bar. Look at the bottom of the Info window. Click the triangle and choose Document Sizes from the pop-up menu. The number to the left is the approximate size of the saved, flattened file in the Photoshop format. The number next to it is the file's approximate size, including layers. If an image contains only one layer, the numbers will be the same. (On a Mac you can also look at the bottom of the document window and look at the middle section. Click the triangle in the status bar and choose Document Sizes to get information on the amount of data in the selected image.) These numbers are useful to know when working on an image within Photoshop Elements. However, the numbers aren't representative of the file size of the image if it is saved in other file formats such as JPEG or GIF. For that, you'll have to either leave the program and check the file size where it's stored, or open Photoshop Elements' Save for Web plug-in and check the file size in the lower-left corner. In Windows, just click File ➤ Open from the menu bar and click on the icon on the left of the "Open" dialog. Here you will get a choice of views, including "Details." This reveals more info about your files, including their size and date modified. This is handy for determining JPEG file sizes without leaving Photoshop Elements.

Resizing

One of the secrets of success in digital imaging is matching the size of your digital image to the requirements of your output. This means that if your digital image is destined for print, you'll need more resolution than you would if it were destined for a monitor (☞ Chapter 12). Most likely, the original image that you are working with is larger or smaller than needed, and you'll have to resize. Keep in mind that resizing, up or down, always involves some loss of image quality. It is also the next-to-last step that you want to perform, just before sharpening.

Figure 2.28 shows a 720 × 480 at 72dpi video frame grab from filmmaker/producer Micha X. Peled's acclaimed PBS film, *Store Wars: When Wal-Mart Comes to Town*. Micha wanted to use the frame for a publicity shot, but it didn't have enough resolution for the higher demands of print.

Figure 2.28: A low-resolution frame from a video grab contains obvious scan lines.

Here is what I had him do to boost the resolution and make the image more acceptable:

1. I had him apply the De-Interlace filter (Filter ➤ Video ➤ De-Interlace), keeping the default settings: Odd Fields and Interpolation. This removed the odd interlaced lines and, by interpolation, replaced the lines with adjacent pixels, which made the video grab appear smoother. Just from this simple move, the picture quality greatly improved. See Figure 2.29.

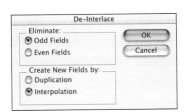

Figure 2.29: The De-Interlace filter dialog box. With its scan lines removed and its resolution increased, the video grab is now a perfectly acceptable still image.

2. I had him choose Image ➤ Resize ➤ Image Size to open the Image Size dialog box (see Figure 2.30). I made sure that the Constrain Proportions and Resample Image options were selected. I had him change the resample image interpolation method from Bicubic—the default setting—to Bicubic Smoother. (Bicubic Smoother is the preferred interpolation method when enlarging images—Bicubic Sharper is often preferred when reducing images, but more on that shortly.)

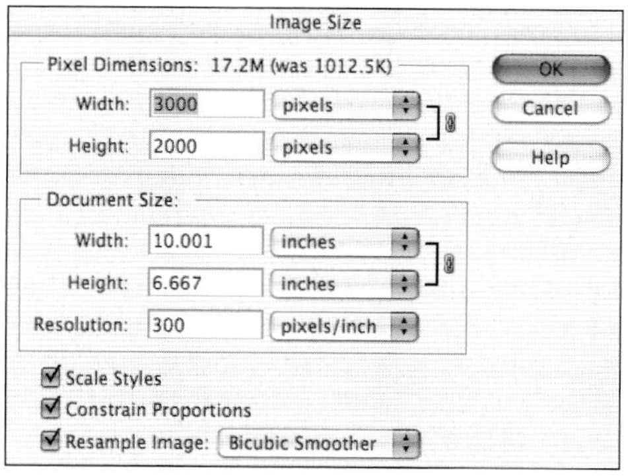

Image Size

Pixel Dimensions: 17.2M (was 1012.5K)

Width: 3000 pixels

Height: 2000 pixels

OK

Cancel

Help

Document Size:

Width: 10.001 inches

Height: 6.667 inches

Resolution: 300 pixels/inch

☑ Scale Styles
☑ Constrain Proportions
☑ Resample Image: Bicubic Smoother

Figure 2.30: The Image Size dialog box.

3. I had Micha enter 300 pixels/inch in the Resolution box, and voila! He had a digital image that would look great in a magazine as long as it wasn't published much larger than 4 × 6 inches.

What about going the other way—making a large image small? This is a common task when you are resizing digital images for the Web or for e-mail transmission to many people. You'd think all you'd have to do is enter the values into the Image Size dialog box and leave it at that. That's fine if you are reducing the image to, say, only 50 percent and you use the Bicubic Sharper resample image interpolation method—but it's a big mistake if you need to shrink it more than that.

Take the image shown in Figure 2.31. It is 2700 × 1932 pixels at 288 pixels/inch. Now look at the image on the left in Figure 2.32. I've reduced it to 675 × 624 pixels at 72 pixels/inch in one swoop. The image looks mushy and soft. It's best to reduce your file size in increments of no more than 50 percent at a time and to apply the Unsharp Mask after each step. It takes a little longer to resize this way, but the results make it worthwhile, as you can see on the right in Figure 2.32.

Figure 2.31: The original image started at 2700 × 1932 pixels. (Photo by Monica Lee)

Figure 2.32: Resizing in one step to 675 × 624 pixels at 72 pixels/inch creates this mushy looking image (left). Resizing incrementally, with an Unsharp Mask filter applied between each step, results in a sharper-looking resized image (right).

Sharpening

If you have a digital image that appears soft or blurry, Photoshop Elements gives you several options for sharpening it. The Sharpen filter globally increases the contrast of adjacent pixels, whereas the Sharpen Edges filter sharpens only the areas of a major brightness change and leaves smooth areas untouched. The toolbox also has a Sharpen tool, which sharpens specific areas of an image. Quick Fix's Sharpen command has an auto-sharpen feature plus amount controls.

But the tool I consistently use is the Unsharp Mask filter, which can be accessed from either Standard Edit or Quick Fix. This filter is based on a traditional film compositing technique that creates a blurred negative version of the image. It then averages this copy with the original, and through three controls—Amount (percentage), Threshold, and Radius—gives you precise control over the amount of sharpening and the way the sharpening is applied. (Quick Fix's Sharpen command utilizes the Unsharp Mask filter, albeit without Threshold and Radius controls. When you adjust the Sharpen Amount slider, Commit and Cancel icons appear next to the word *Sharpen*. Select Commit when you are satisfied with the amount of sharpening. Select Cancel if you are not. Until you select either the Commit or Cancel icon, the Reset button located above the After version of your image is dimmed and inoperable.)

Here is how I used the Unsharp Mask filter to improve the photo (1700 × 1680 pixels, 72 pixels/inch) shown on the left in Figure 2.33.

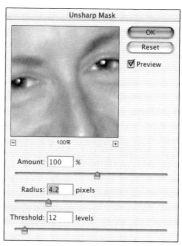

Figure 2.33: The original image (left) is lacking sharpness. The Unsharp Mask dialog box (right). Your settings will vary depending on the size and content of the image.

1. I chose Filter ➤ Sharpen ➤ Unsharp Mask and made sure the Preview check box was selected.

2. I then dragged the Amount slider until it reached 100 percent.

3. I set the Threshold at 12. (Setting the Threshold slider at a higher value forces the Unsharp Mask filter to leave the flesh tones, or other areas containing contiguous pixels of similar tonal values, relatively alone. Leaving the Threshold set at 0 forces the filter to sharpen all the pixels in the image equally and may introduce unwanted artifacts in flat-colored areas such as the skin.)

4. I then slid the Radius slider until I was visually happy with the amount of sharpening. In the case of this image, a value of 4.2 was just about right.

Note: If the Preview check box is selected, you can see the effects of the Unsharp Mask on the image in the document window. Selecting and deselecting the Preview option gives you a way to toggle back and forth between a sharpened and unsharpened version of your image. You can also view the effect of the Unsharp Mask in the dialog box's small preview window. If you click the image in the preview window, you'll see how the image looks without the effect of the Unsharp Mask. In the preview window, you can also drag to see different parts of the image and click the plus sign (+) or the minus sign (-) to zoom in or out. To see a particular spot in your image in the preview, just click on it in the image window. You may have to move the Unsharp Mask window out of the way to do this.

5. I then clicked OK. Figure 2.34 shows the resulting image.

Figure 2.34: Image sharpened with the Unsharp Mask filter.

The values that you use for your image will vary depending on such factors as the image's content, size, and final destination. For an average-sized image that contains a lot of detail—say an architectural shot at 1600 × 1800 pixels—try setting your percentage at 150 percent and your Radius at 2. For these kinds of images, I generally leave the Threshold setting at 0, which forces the Unsharp Mask filter to sharpen all the pixels equally.

For an image of the same size that contains expanses of color and tone, such as a face, I recommend setting your Amount at 100 percent, your Radius between 0.5 and 1, and your Threshold between 2 and 15. Playing with your Threshold setting will help you avoid introducing noise in the flat areas of color. Increase these numbers if you are working with larger images. Decrease them for smaller images.

Note: On the enclosed CD is a trial version of nik Sharpener Pro, a Photoshop Elements plug-in. Using the plug-in takes the guesswork out of using the Unsharp Mask filter. It also automatically optimizes sharpening for different display outputs.

Grabbing Digital: Which File Format Should You Choose?

Many popular video frame grabbers give you the option of saving your image in various file formats, such as JPEG, TIFF, PICT, or PSD. Which one should you select? For the best quality, choose TIFF or PSD, which is Photoshop Elements' native file format. If you do this, your file won't be as small as it would be if you saved it as a JPEG, but the TIFF and PSD file formats are lossless, which means no data is thrown away during the conversion. PICT is a Mac-only file format and is therefore inherently limited.

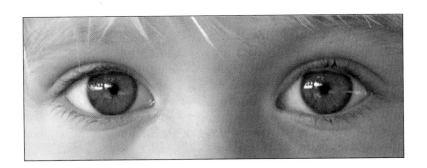

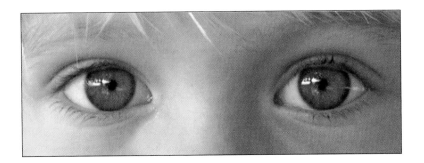

Better Faces

How many times have you seen someone look at a picture and heard them say, "That doesn't look like me!" You may even have said it as you stared at a picture of yourself. Sometimes the criticism is based entirely on vanity. But often the fault lies with the photograph. Blame it on the camera, the lens, the lighting—or even more likely, the photographer. With the help of Photoshop Elements—and especially with the new Healing Brush tool—there are no more excuses. You can make better faces. This chapter shows you simple tips and techniques for using Photoshop Elements to intensify eyes, eliminate red eye, reduce wrinkles, and otherwise help improve digital images of the human face.

3

Chapter Contents

What Comes First

Before starting to work on a face or faces, I usually begin by cropping the image to its essential parts and optimizing the tonal values (↪ "Cropping to the Essential Parts" in Chapter 2). What I do next depends on the image, the person depicted in the image, and where it is ultimately going to be shown or published.

Many times a face needs only a little tweaking to get it just right. Sometimes this means removing red eye with the Red Eye Removal tool, whitening the white part of the eyes and teeth, slightly increasing the color saturation of the eyes and lips, or selectively diminishing wrinkles with Photoshop Elements 3's amazing Healing Brush tool. Other relatively easy tasks include selective burning and dodging, and applying a digital fill flash.

Some faces are more challenging than others. For example, when a face is distorted because of natural or unnatural causes, I use various Transform commands or the Liquify filter to get it right. Although it is relatively easy to change the color of hair, or to lighten or darken hair, removing or adding hair requires a little more work, and for this I almost exclusively use the Clone Stamp tool. Blurring a distracting background can also improve a portrait, and for this I use a combination of selection tools and the Gaussian Blur filter.

The last thing you'll ever do to a digital image is resize and sharpen it to the needs of your final destination (↪ "Resizing" and "Sharpening" sections in Chapter 2). Be sure to keep an original, full-sized version of your image for future purposes.

Note: How far do you want to go? The possibilities for improving or changing a face by using Photoshop Elements are almost unlimited. That's why I suggest you ask yourself how far you want to go and how much time you want to spend. There are no easy answers, and no hard rules to follow. The answers to these questions invariably depend on the wishes of your subject and the final destination of the image. If the picture is just for fun and the person in the picture has a good sense of humor, well, anything goes. If you are preparing an image for a corporate brochure or other serious purpose, tread lightly and make subtle changes.

Whatever you do, please keep in mind that it's a special day when the subject of your work actually likes their own portrait. Unless you've really messed up their face, you can chalk up any complaints to vanity and human nature!

Working the Eyes

The first thing we usually notice about someone is their eyes. Are they bright, dull, or shiny? Red? Bloodshot? Yellow? Sick? The eyes are the gateway to the soul, and that is where I usually start.

Eliminating Red Eye

Red eye occurs when light from an on-camera flash reflects off the blood vessels in the back of the eye, giving someone a demonic look (see Figure 3.1). Red eye is such a common problem in color images that Photoshop Elements 3 includes an easy-to-use tool devoted to fixing the problem: the Red Eye Removal tool. This is not the red-eye brush of previous versions of Photoshop Elements. (The earlier Red Eye Brush has morphed into another useful Photoshop Elements tool, the Color Replacement tool, which I'll describe in more detail later in this chapter and in the appendix at the end of the book.)

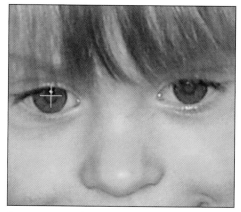

Figure 3.1: Before using the Red Eye Removal tool. Note the position of the cursor in the middle of the pupil.

Here is what I did to get rid of the red eye shown in Figure 3.1:

1. I selected the Red Eye Removal tool (✐) from the toolbar.
2. I placed my cursor—which turned into a plus sign—on the center of the pupil and clicked. Depending on the image, you need not be precise where you click. Sometimes you can even get away with clicking anywhere in the vicinity of the eye, and the tool automatically differentiates between the eye and other parts of the face and applies the appropriate red eye removal. In one instance I accidentally clicked a nose, and the red eye was removed!
3. When the red eye was removed from one eye, I turned to the other eye and repeated step 2. (The tool is smart, but not smart enough to do both eyes at once!)

Done. That's all I did to get the results for both eyes shown in Figure 3.2.

Figure 3.2: After using the Red Eye Removal tool and the one-click-per-eye method.

It's remarkable how well the one-click method worked on this image. Sometimes, however, the one-click method doesn't do the trick. There is no hard-and-fast rule to follow, but I've noticed problems with the one-click method when the edge of the red is less defined and the color spills randomly across the iris. In any case, if it doesn't work, you can use another method. You use the same tool, just a different method.

This is what I did to get rid of the red eye shown in Figure 3.3:

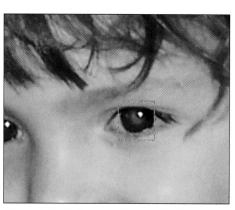

Figure 3.3: If the one-click method doesn't work satisfactorily, try defining a parameter for the Red Eye Removal tool by clicking and holding the mouse and dragging a selection around the iris.

1. I selected the Red Eye Removal tool ( ) from the toolbar.

2. I clicked and held the mouse *and dragged* a rectangular selection with my cursor just outside the parameter of the iris, as you can see in Figure 3.3. When I released the cursor, the tool went to work and nearly instantly gave me the results you see in Figure 3.4. Varying the size and position of the selection will affect the outcome, and once again, you may need to experiment to get it right.

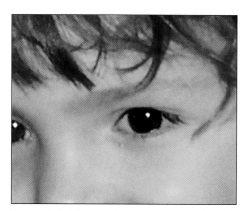

Figure 3.4: The results of clicking and holding while dragging a selection.

Although I used the Red Eye Removal tool for both the one-click and click/hold/drag methods, these two methods employ fundamentally different mathematical algorithms to do the job. You can tell they are different just by comparing the amount of time the methods take to remove red eye. The one-click method takes longer because it first identifies the eye and *then* removes the red. The click/hold/drag method is much faster because *you* define the work area with a selection. (There are other, more technical reasons why the methods are different, but I'll spare you the details.) I suggest you try the one-click method and if that doesn't work to your satisfaction, try the click/hold/drag method. Experiment and figure out which is best for a particular image.

Regardless of which method you use, you can fine-tune the results with two options available in the Red Eye Removal tool options bar, shown in Figure 3.5(a). Note the default setting for Pupil Size is 50 percent, and the default setting for Darken Amount is also 50 percent. Using these settings, I got the results shown in Figure 3.5(b). Figure 3.5(c) shows what happened when I increased the Pupil Size to 100 percent and increased the Darken Amount to 100 percent: the pupil is larger, and the density of the black is increased. Figure 3.5(d) shows what happened when I set the Pupil Size to 1 percent and the Darken Amount to 1 percent. I think you get the idea. Again, you'll have to experiment to find the right settings for your particular image.

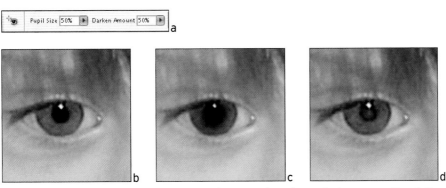

Figure 3.5: (a) The Red Eye Removal tool options bar (b) Default settings: Pupil Size 50 percent and Darken Amount 50 percent. (c) Increasing Pupil Size and Darken Amount to 100 percent. (d) Setting both Pupil Size and Darken Amount to 1 percent.

Eliminating Dog Eye

Dog eye occurs when you use a flash to take a picture of a dog. Dog eye is similar to red eye in people, but much worse. For better night vision, dogs, like cats and many other animals, have extra cells behind the retina that act like a mirror. This mirror reflects light back, giving the rods and cones a second chance to pick up the small amount of light available at night. This is what makes cats' and dogs' eyes seem to glow in the dark. It's also what gives their eyes a hellish glow when photographed with a flash.

Recently I received an e-mail from reader John Howell who attached a picture of his dog Reuben displaying a classic case of dog eye (see Figure 3.6). He wanted to know how to fix the shot.

Figure 3.6: Dog eye can't be fixed with the Red Eye Removal tool.

Photoshop Elements' Red Eye Removal tool isn't much use for this kind of problem. No matter which method you use—one-click or click/hold/drag—the tool looks only for variations of the color red. If the variations aren't there the tool doesn't do anything.

I suggested John try two other methods, which I'll share here.

Method 1 is the simplest way I can imagine to make Reuben appear less threatening:

1. Magnify and zoom in on one of the eyes by using the Zoom tool found in the toolbar.
2. Select the Paint Bucket tool (⬧) from the toolbar.
3. Make sure the foreground color in the color swatch at the bottom of the toolbar is set to black.
4. Position the Paint Bucket tool over the blown-out highlights of one eye and click.
5. Repeat steps 1–4 for the other eye.

This fills the white area with black. It's certainly not a perfect solution, but if you zoom out or print the shot small, it doesn't look too bad (see Figure 3.7).

Figure 3.7: Using the Paint Bucket tool is the simplest solution.

Method 2 results in a more realistic-looking image, shown in Figure 3.8.

Figure 3.8: Adding a "Glass" eye is more realistic.

1. Magnify and zoom in on the dog's eye by using the Zoom tool.
2. With the Magic Wand tool (✎)—or selection tool of your choice—make a selection of the blown-out areas of the eye. Slightly feather the selection 2–3 pixels (Select ➢ Feather).
3. In the Layers palette, make a new layer (Layer ➢ New ➢ Layer).
4. With the new layer active, fill your two selections with black or another color (Edit ➢ Fill or use the Paint Bucket tool as described in method 1).
5. In the Styles and Effects palette located in the palette bin, select Layer Styles and Glass Buttons from the pop-up menus.
6. Choose a "glass" color. (I chose Black Glass.) If you're satisfied with black, you can stop here; the remaining few steps show you how to change the color to anything you want.
7. Flatten the layers (Layer ➢ Flatten Image).
8. Select the Color Replacement tool from the toolbar. (It shares the same spot on the toolbar with the Brush tool, which uses keyboard shortcut B; repeatedly hitting the B key cycles through the brushes.) In the options bar, choose the following options:

    Mode: Color

    Sampling: Continuous. For some images, Once also works fine. Background Swatch is not appropriate for this example.

    Limits: Contiguous. Discontiguous can work too if you paint carefully.

    Tolerance: 30 percent. A higher percentage replaces adjacent pixels with a broader range of color values. A lower percentage replaces only a few adjacent pixels with similar color values.

9. Select a color from the foreground color swatch at the bottom of the toolbar. (Click the foreground color swatch, and the Color Picker will open.) I chose blue.
10. Click the area you want to change and then "paint" the replacement color over it.

Figure 3.9 shows the results.

Figure 3.9: Change to any color by using the Color Replacement tool.

And you thought this chapter was only about people!

Whitening the Whites

Both of the methods I use to whiten the whites of the eyes use the Dodge tool. One method is slightly quicker than the other but less precise.

Here's method 1:

1. Select the Dodge tool (●) from the toolbox; it shares the same place on the toolbar as the Sponge and Burn tools. Press the letter O on your keyboard and repeatedly hit the O key to cycle through the three tools.

2. In the options bar, select Midtones from the Range menu, and 50 percent from the Exposure menu. (Remember that no one has perfectly white whites, and at 100 percent exposure it's easy to overdo the amount of whitening. I chose 50 percent exposure because it gives me more control over the amount of dodging.)

3. Select an appropriate brush size. (To alter the image shown on the left in Figure 3.10, I chose a Soft Round 35 pixels brush, which fit nicely in the space between the eyelids and the pupils.) The brush size that works in your image will depend on the size of your image and the white space itself.

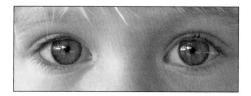 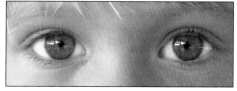

Figure 3.10: Before dodging (left). After dodging (right).

4. Start by clicking and dragging carefully over the parts of the eye that you want to whiten. If you need a better view of the area you are working on, magnify the image by using one of the View tools. Dodge incrementally, dragging over a small area and then releasing the mouse button. By doing this, you can undo incrementally as well. If you do all your dodging in one click, the Undo command will undo all your work to the point of that first click.

5. When you achieve the look you want, stop. Remember, it's tempting to go too far and make the white perfectly white. Don't. It won't look natural. My final shot is shown on the right in Figure 3.10.

The second method I use is similar to the first one, but this time I create a selection that protects the nonwhite areas from the effects of the dodging. This way, the size of my brush isn't so important and I don't need to be nearly as precise when I dodge. Here's method 2:

1. Select the Lasso selection tool ( ) from the toolbox. In the options bar, make sure that the Anti-aliasing check box is selected. I also set the Feather option to 3 pixels. Anti-aliasing softens the color transition between edge pixels and background pixels and smoothens the jagged edges of a selection. Feathering causes some loss of detail at the edge of the selection, but when you apply the Dodge tool, feathering also creates a smooth transition between the white and adjacent areas.

2. Carefully select one white area, as shown in Figure 3.11. Then, while holding down the Shift key, select the white area on the other side of the pupil. A plus sign appears next to the pointer. While holding down the Shift key again, select the whites in the other eye.

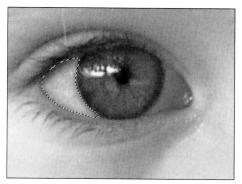

Figure 3.11: A selection protects the nonwhite areas from the effects of the Dodge tool.

Note: You can also add selections by clicking the Add to Selection icon ( ) in the options bar.

3. Select the Dodge tool from the toolbar. This time you can choose a fairly large brush because the selection will protect the rest of the image. Then dodge incrementally, just as in the first example, until you get the effect you want.

4. To deselect the selection, use the keyboard command Ctrl+D / ⌘+D. You can also deselect a selection by choosing Select ➤ Deselect from the menu bar or by clicking anywhere in the image outside the selected area.

Note: You can control the size of the brush by pressing the left or right bracket keys.

Enhancing the Color

It's easy to enhance the color of the eyes. I use a method similar to the one I just described, but instead of using the Dodge tool on the white areas of the eye, I use the Sponge tool to saturate the colors of the iris (see Figure 3.12).

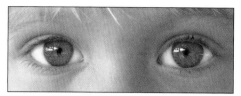

Figure 3.12: Use the Sponge tool to saturate the colors.

To create this effect, I did the following:

1. I selected the Sponge tool (🔘) from the toolbox. It shares a place in the toolbar with the Burn and Dodge tools.
2. In the options bar, I selected Saturate from the Mode menu, and 50 percent from the Pressure menu.
3. I then selected an appropriate brush size. For this image, I chose a Soft Round 65 pixels brush.
4. I started by clicking and dragging carefully over the parts of the eye that I wanted to enhance. I saturated incrementally, dragging over a small area and then releasing the mouse button.
5. When I got the saturation I wanted, I stopped. It's easy to go too far and make the eyes look unnatural.

If you want to be more precise, you can also make a selection as described in the preceding section, and then saturate only the selection.

Changing the Color

It's easy to change the color of the eyes from, say, green to blue. Although there are other ways of doing this, I recommend a simple yet effective method using the Color Replacement tool. I outlined a similar method earlier in the chapter to change the color of a dog's eye from black to blue. Take a look at Figure 3.13.

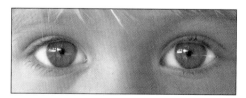

Figure 3.13: Change color by using the Color Replacement tool.

This is what I did to change the color of the eyes:

1. I selected the Color Replacement tool ( ) from the toolbar.

2. I chose a brush size from the pop-up palette in the options bar. I chose a Soft Round 75 pixels brush, but the brush you choose will depend on the specifics of your particular image.

3. I set my options in the Color replacement tool options bar to the following:

    Mode: Color

    Sampling: Continuous

    Limits: Contiguous. Discontiguous can work too if you paint carefully.

    Tolerance: 30 percent. A higher percentage replaces adjacent pixels with a broader range of color values. A lower percentage replaces only a few adjacent pixels with similar color values.

4. I specified a replacement color by selecting a light blue from the Color Picker. (Click the foreground color swatch found at the bottom of the toolbar; then, when the Color Picker opens, select the color of your choice.)

5. I clicked the iris. This set a "target" color. Then I dragged over the irises. The parts of the eye that matched the target color were colorized with the light blue. To sample new target colors, I simply released the mouse and clicked again on another part of the iris. If you find the color spilling over to other areas of the eye, reduce the Tolerance setting; if the color isn't flowing evenly, you may need to increase Tolerance. For some images, you may find that no matter what Tolerance setting you choose, the color still spills onto unwanted areas of the eye, for example, the eyelashes. If this happens I suggest that you make a selection around the iris and then apply the Color Replacement tool.

Enlarging the Eyes

Portrait painters learned long ago that they could make their wealthy patrons happy by slightly enlarging the eyes of their female subjects. Enlarged eyes evoke youth, innocence, and receptiveness. When it's appropriate, you can easily do something similar by using the Liquify filter. The Liquify filter enables you to warp, twirl, expand, contract, shift, and reflect areas of your image. It's as if your image were turned into easily manipulated molten pixels ("Liquify Filter" in the appendix). I used the Liquify filter to enlarge the eyes shown in Figure 3.14.

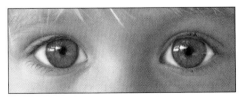

Figure 3.14: Use the Liquify filter to enlarge the eyes.

Here's what I did:

1. I chose the Liquify filter (Filter ➤ Distort ➤ Liquify). This opened the dialog box shown in Figure 3.15. Keep in mind that the Liquify filter works on the selected layer of an image. In my case, the image had only one layer, so selecting a layer wasn't an option.

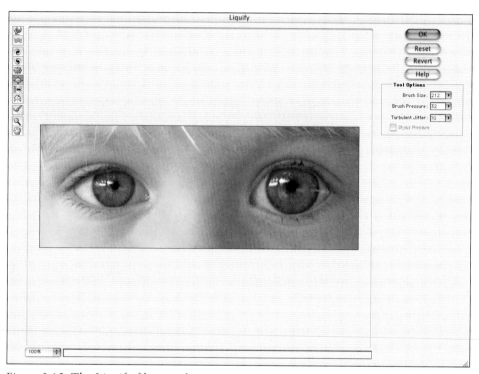

Figure 3.15: The Liquify filter work area.

2. I selected the Bloat tool (⬦) and then adjusted the brush size so the brush would fit over the entire eye. I then adjusted the brush pressure. I chose a low brush pressure so that changes occurred more slowly and it was easier to stop when I got what I wanted.

3. I placed the brush over one of the eyes, and then clicked and held the mouse without moving the cursor. The Bloat tool moved pixels away from the center of the brush, effectively making the eye bigger.

Note: If you go too far, you have a few choices: You can revert to the original version by clicking Revert. You can also Alt+click (Windows) or Option+click (Mac), and the Cancel button turns into Reset. Or you can use the Reconstruct tool (✏) and hold down the mouse button and drag over the distorted areas.

4. When the first eye looked the way that I wanted it to, I did the same to the other eye, making sure to apply the same amount of enlarging. Then I clicked OK.

Sometimes it's enough to slightly enlarge the pupil, or the dark part of the eye. To do this, simply choose a smaller brush size and apply the Bloat tool to just that area.

Working on Lips

After the eyes, the next area I work on is the lips. Again, a lot of what I do is very subtle and yet very effective. Mostly, I slightly enhance the color of the lips by using the Saturate tool. Sometimes it's fun to change the color of the lips as well. To perform either of these tasks, I suggest you follow the step-by-step instructions used earlier in the chapter to enhance eyes (☞ "Enhancing the Color" and "Changing the Color"). Just focus on the lips instead of the eyes. If you want to imitate a Julia Roberts look, use the Liquify filter to add fullness. Here is how to produce the results shown in Figure 3.16:

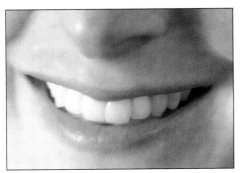 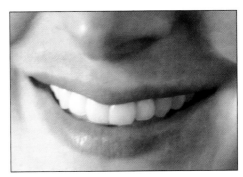

Figure 3.16: Before the Liquify filter (left). After the Liquify filter (right).

1. Select the mouth by using any of the selection tools.
2. Choose Filter ➢ Distort ➢ Liquify.
3. Select the Bloat tool (◇) and choose an appropriately sized brush and a relatively low brush pressure.
4. Place the brush over the lips. Click and selectively add fullness. If you don't overdo it, the effect can look realistic. Go too far, and it's pretty outrageous!

Whitening and Fixing Teeth

People spend a lot of money making their teeth look good. After the eyes and the lips, teeth are probably the most noticed part of the face. You can do someone a big favor by removing years of coffee or tobacco stains with a few selective brush strokes. Whatever you do, don't go too far. Teeth that are perfectly white look unnatural.

To use the Dodge tool to whiten teeth:

1. Select the Dodge tool (●) from the toolbox.
2. In the options bar, select Midtones from the Range menu, and 50 percent from the Exposure menu.
3. Select an appropriate brush size.
4. Click and drag carefully over the parts of the teeth that you want to whiten. Magnify your image if needed. Dodge incrementally, dragging over a small area and then releasing the mouse button.
5. Stop when you get the look you want. You've gone too far if the teeth look unnatural or if you lose the texture of the teeth. Figure 3.17 shows before and after shots.

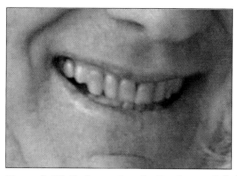
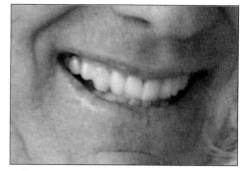

Figure 3.17: Before using the Dodge tool (left). After using the Dodge tool (right).

To use the Brush to whiten teeth:

1. Choose a color to paint with by selecting the Eyedropper tool (✐) from the toolbar. Click the lightest section of a tooth. Now click the foreground color swatch (▪) in the toolbar, which now contains your sampled color. This opens the Color Picker. Select a color that is brighter than the sampled color. On the left in Figure 3.18, you can see the sampled color shown in a small circle. The larger circle shown above and to the left of the sampled color is the mouse cursor, which you can move around to select a lighter color. When you click the cursor on a color, that color appears in the upper half of the color rectangle to the right of the color slider, with the sampled color appearing in the lower half of the rectangle.

2. Select the Brush tool (✐) from the toolbar.

3. Select an appropriately sized soft-edged brush from the options bar. Set the Mode to Lighten and the Opacity to 15–20 percent.

4. Paint carefully over the teeth until you get the effect you want.

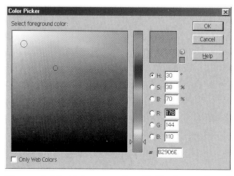
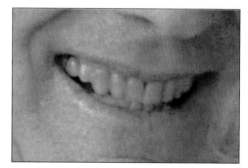

Figure 3.18: Select a color (left) that is brighter than the tooth (right).

To fix a tooth with the Liquify filter:

1. Make a selection around the area you want to fix.

2. Choose Liquify from the Filter menu (Filter ➢ Distort ➢ Liquify).

3. Select the Bloat tool (⟡) if you want to enlarge a tooth, the Pucker tool (⟡) if you want to shrink one, or the Warp tool (⟡) if you want to straighten one. Choose an appropriate brush size and a relatively low brush pressure.

4. Place the brush over the area you want to fix. It will take some experimentation, but you can shrink the gaps between teeth, fill in a missing piece of enamel, or straighten a crooked tooth.

In Figure 3.19 you can see how I've fixed two teeth by using the Liquify filter and the Bloat tool.

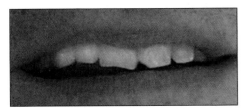 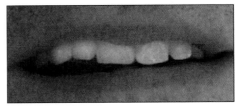

Figure 3.19: Before applying the Liquify filter (left) and after (right).

Selectively Removing Wrinkles and Blemishes with the Healing Brush

Personally, I like wrinkles; they show character and maturity. However, I know that not all wrinkles are caused by age and character. Many times they are unwanted artifacts of a high-speed contrasty film or harsh lighting.

Getting rid of wrinkles and removing blemishes and other unwanted artifacts from the face is especially easy with Photoshop Elements' Healing Brush tool, which is similar in practice to the Clone Stamp tool. You start by clicking and defining a source. Then you "paint" over the area you wish to replace or "heal." But the Healing Brush tool does much more than simply duplicate and replace pixels. It matches the texture, lighting, transparency, and shading of the sampled pixels to the source pixels. The result is often a seamless blend that leaves little or no trace of the original underlying flaw.

To use the Healing Brush tool to eliminate wrinkles or other small skin blemishes:

1. Select the Healing Brush tool (⟡) from the toolbar.

2. In the options bar, select a brush size. The brush size will vary depending on the target. In general, it's a good idea to pick a size 30 percent or so larger than the crease of the wrinkle or circumference of the blemish. Hard-edged brushes are usually more effective than soft-edged ones. The Healing Brush tool applies a complex blending algorithm to the edges of the brush, and a soft-edged brush adds a variable to the equation that makes the results unpredictable.

3. From the Healing Brush tool's options bar, set the remaining options as follows:

Mode: Normal. Choosing "Replace" basically turns the Healing Brush tool into a Clone Stamp tool, which isn't what you want for this exercise.

Source: Sampled. The Pattern choice blends a chosen pattern over the target area, which isn't useful for this kind of cosmetic healing.

Aligned. You can go either way with this setting depending on the size and location of the flaw you are healing. Selecting Aligned means pixels are sampled continuously, always at a relative distance from the target. Deselecting Aligned means that after you click to define a source, Photoshop Elements will use that initial source point as a reference when you click and paint with the Healing Brush—no matter where you move on the image. It will continue to use the original defined source even if you release the mouse button and click another target area.

Use All Layers. Select this if you want to sample data from all visible layers. Select All Layers is particularly useful if you want to keep your original image untouched. In this case, simply create a new layer (Layer ➢ New ➢ Layer), make it active, and follow the subsequent steps for using the Healing Brush tool. The healing will occur on the new layer, leaving the underlying layer untouched. When you are completely satisfied with your results, you can choose Layer ➢ Merge Down or Layer ➢ Flatten Image. Or you can save the layered PSD file.

4. Pick an area adjacent to the wrinkle or blemish and sample it by holding down the Alt/Option key and clicking. Now click and hold the mouse, and paint over the wrinkle or blemish. When you release the mouse, the Healing Brush goes to work. If the area you painted over is large, it may take time to complete the healing process. If the healing is acceptable, you are finished. If not, use the Undo command (Ctrl+Z / ⌘ + Z, or Edit ➢ Undo) and start over. Often it is just a matter of changing the brush size to get it right. Sometimes, if the area you want to heal is adjacent to a detail with strong contrast—for example an eyelid or a lip—you'll need to isolate the target area with a selection and then apply the Healing Brush tool.

I used this method to remove the wrinkles shown in Figure 3.20 and to remove the blemishes shown in Figure 3.21.

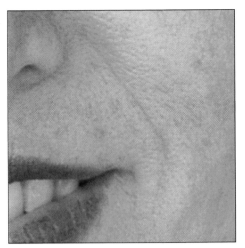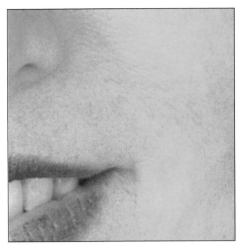

Figure 3.20: Before (left) and after (right) using the Healing Brush tool.

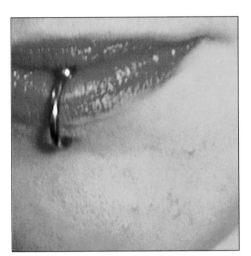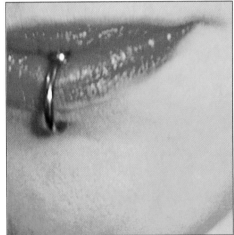

Figure 3.21: Before (left) and after (right) using the Healing Brush tool.

Keep in mind that wrinkles are technically shadows on a digital image. If you want to diminish their appearance—and not get rid of them completely—you can just lighten them up.

To use the Dodge tool to reduce wrinkles:

1. Select the Dodge tool ( ) from the toolbar. Set it to Midtones and use an appropriately sized, soft-edged brush. If needed, magnify your image so the wrinkles fill the screen.

2. With a very low exposure—say 10–20 percent—gently stroke the wrinkle away with the brush. Don't go too far. Before you make a final judgment, you should zoom back to normal magnification. That way, you'll have a more objective view of your work.

Diminishing and Straightening the Nose

Wide-angle lenses or oblique camera angles can make a nose seem much larger than it is. Again, the Liquify filter is a good way to diminish an unnaturally large nose—or to straighten a crooked one.

To use the Liquify filter to diminish or straighten a nose:

1. Select the nose by using any of the selection tools.

2. Choose Liquify from the Filter menu (Filter ➤ Distort ➤ Liquify).

3. To diminish a nose, select the Pucker tool (🔅). Pick a brush size that fits over the entire nose. Select a brush pressure less than 50. Hold the cursor over the nose and click incrementally until you get the effect you want.

4. To straighten a nose, select the Warp tool (👋). Click and drag to shift the nose into a straighter position.

I used a combination of these techniques to achieve the effects shown in Figures 3.22 and 3.23.

Figure 3.22: Before applying the Liquify filter (left). After applying the Liquify filter (right).

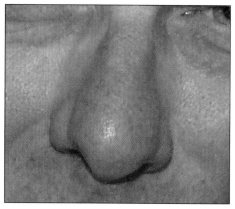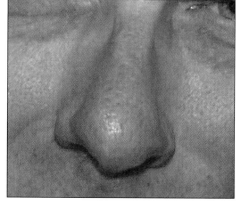

Figure 3.23: Before applying the Liquify filter (left). After applying the Liquify filter (right).

Making People Glow

In the "old days" I used to stretch a nylon stocking over my darkroom enlarger lens to give a portrait a glamorous, dreamy glow. It's easy to simulate this look with Photoshop Elements.

Look at the difference between the images in Figure 3.24.

Figure 3.24: The original photo (left). It's easy to create a softer look (right).

Here's what I did to create the softer effect:

1. I selected and made a copy of the background layer and named it **Blur**.
   You can copy a selected layer by choosing the Duplicate Layer command either from the Layer menu on the main menu bar or from the Layers palette menu. You can also duplicate a layer by selecting it and dragging it to the New Layer button (▣) at the top of the Layers palette. Windows users can right-click the selected layer—but not the thumbnail—and choose Duplicate Layer from the pop-up menu. Mac users can do the same by Ctrl+clicking the layer bar.

2. With the **Blur** layer selected, I applied a strong Gaussian blur (Filter➤ Blur ➤ Gaussian Blur). The exact amount of blurring will depend on the size of your image. In the case of this image, I chose a Radius of 30 pixels from the Gaussian Blur filter dialog box.

3. In the Layers palette, I selected Overlay from the Blending Mode drop-down list (see Figure 3.25). (You can also experiment with the Soft Light, Hard Light, and Screen blending options.) I diminished the Opacity setting in the Layers palette to 90 percent, which gave me the effect I wanted. Again, the exact opacity that looks the best will depend on your image.

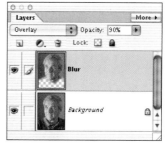

Figure 3.25: The soft look is created with a combination of blurring and different Layers settings (left). The blur effect is selectively removed from the neck and chest area with the Eraser tool (right).

4. I liked the effect of the blurring on the face. However, I wasn't pleased with the way the effect blurred the clothes. To selectively remove the effect from that area, I chose the Eraser tool ( ) from the toolbox and selected an appropriately sized, soft-edged brush. With the **Blur** layer selected, I used the eraser to remove the blur effect from the tie and shirt (see Figure 3.25).

As you can see in Figure 3.26, the effect also works well in grayscale. To soften this image, I followed the same steps; however, before I began, I desaturated the image by choosing Enhance ➤ Adjust Color ➤ Remove Color from the main menu bar. I also chose Screen, instead of Soft Light, from the Blending Mode pop-up menu and dropped the Opacity setting to 25 percent. I also could have turned the color image into black-and-white by changing the mode from RGB to Grayscale (Image ➤ Mode ➤ Grayscale from the main menu).

Figure 3.26: The soft-focus effects work with a black-and-white image as well.

Creating a Grainy 35mm Black-and-White Look

What do you think of when you see an old, grainy, black-and-white print? To me it evokes the '60s and '70s and movies like *Blow-Up*. Whatever. The fact is, it's easy to simulate this grainy, gritty look with Photoshop Elements.

That's what I did to a contemporary color photo I took of TechTV guest host and Apple Computer cofounder Steve Wozniak (see Figure 3.27).

Figure 3.27: *The original color image (left). The image after applying desaturation and the Noise filter (right).*

Here's how I created the effect I wanted:

1. I desaturated the color image (Enhance ➤ Adjust Color ➤ Remove Color).
2. I increased the contrast by a factor of +12 (Enhance ➤ Adjust Lighting ➤ Brightness/Contrast).
3. I applied the Add Noise filter (Filter ➤ Noise ➤ Add Noise). In the Add Noise filter dialog box, I chose Gaussian rather than Uniform to authentically duplicate the erratic size and shape of the film's silver halide crystals. To prevent the introduction of color, I selected the Monochromatic check box (see Figure 3.28). I played with the Amount setting until I got the look I wanted. In this case, 30 percent was about right.

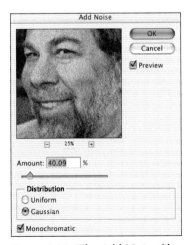

Figure 3.28: *The Add Noise filter dialog box and settings.*

To duplicate a similar effect, you can also try the Mezzotint filter (Filter ➤ Pixelate ➤ Mezzotint). I prefer the Add Noise filter because I have more control over the way the image looks, but some people may prefer the Mezzotint look.

Creating a Digital Fill Flash

It's common to take a picture of a person against a bright background. However, if you don't use a fill flash or specifically expose for the skin tones, a face will turn into a silhouette (see Figure 3.29). Photoshop Elements includes a useful Shadows/Highlights command that does a good job of creating a digital fill flash, balancing the foreground with the background. (In earlier versions of Photoshop Elements, a less sophisticated version of Shadows/Highlights was called Fill Flash.)

Figure 3.29: Before applying Shadows/Highlights, the face is too dark (left). After applying Shadows/Highlights (right), both the face and the background are fine.

Here is what I did to fix this picture of San Francisco Giants slugger Barry Bonds:

1. I selected Shadows/Highlights from the Enhance menu (Enhance ➤ Adjust Lighting ➤ Shadows/Highlights).
2. I left the Lighten Shadows slider settings at 50 percent, which made the face look right. I also left the other settings alone.
3. I clicked OK. That's all. It was that easy.

Note: One of the most effective ways of emphasizing the features of someone is to isolate their face from the background. If you shoot a portrait with a longer than normal focal length and a wide f-stop, the background will naturally fade out of focus. However, when this shooting this way isn't possible, or if you inherit a photo with a distracting background, you can use Photoshop Elements to save the day. Later in the book I'll show you how to use the Gaussian blur filter to isolate an object from its background, ↝ Chapter 4, "Adding Selective Focus."

Making Distorted Faces Normal

Facial distortion is often caused by inferior optics or by the inherent effect of wide-angle lenses. It can also be caused by illness or certain prescription drugs. I've noticed that some faces are more puffy in the morning than later in the day, or at certain times of the month. Whatever the cause, if the distortion is unwanted, you can use Photoshop Elements' Transform tools to compress and reshape a face.

Figure 3.30 shows an example of distortion caused by poor optics. In this case, artist Tom Mogensen used a digital video camera at a San Francisco Giants baseball game to capture a still image frame of the legendary Bobby Thomson and Debby Magowan, the wife of one of the owners of the Giants. Instead of selectively fixing just one face, as I did in the preceding example, Tom applied a global fix to the entire image.

Figure 3.30: This distortion is global (left) and affects the entire image. After applying the Transform ➢ Distort command, the image looks normal (right).

Here is what he did:

1. He selected the entire image (Select ➢ All or Ctrl+A / ⌘ +A).
2. He chose Image ➢ Transform ➢ Distort.
3. He dragged the right side handle slightly toward the center, then dragged the left side handle toward the center. He went back and forth until the faces looked just right. When he was finished, he clicked the Commit button (✔) at the top of the options bar. The results are shown on the right in Figure 3.30.

Fixing Hair

You can do a lot to hair with the help of Photoshop Elements. You can tint it, you can change the color entirely, you can shape it, and you can even add or delete it. As usual, a subtle approach is the most realistic.

Adding Hair

Hair, or the lack of it, can be a sensitive subject. I want to thank another friend, Jonathan, for agreeing to let me use a before and after shot of him and his family to illustrate what Photoshop Elements can do to … well, to add hair. Check out Figure 3.31.

Figure 3.31: Jonathan and his family before (left). Jonathan and his family after (right).

Here is what I did to go from the before shot to the after shot:

1. I made a new layer and named this layer **Hair** (Layer ➢ New ➢ Layer).
2. I selected the Clone Stamp tool (⚓) and chose an appropriately sized, soft-edged brush from the options bar. I set the Mode to Normal and the Opacity to 80 percent. I made sure that All Layers was selected in the options bar.
3. With the **Hair** layer selected, I sampled Jonathan's son's hair with the Clone Stamp tool. (To take a sample, click the desired area while holding the Alt/Option key.) I then brushed Jonathan's head, filling it with the hair from his son. This new set of hair was painted on its own layer, keeping the real Jonathan intact for future reference (see Figure 3.32).

Figure 3.32: The new hair is on its own layer.

4. When I was finished, I selected the background layer containing Jonathan and his family and, using the Burn tool (), burned in his beard.

Note: If you are getting serious about retouching and restoring photographs, I highly recommend Katrin Eismann's *Photoshop Restoration & Retouching* (New Riders, second edition 2003). It's written with Photoshop in mind rather than Photoshop Elements, but it is a very practical book that will give you easy-to-follow techniques for resurrecting old photos, improving portraits, and touching up glamour shots.

Shooting Digital: Making a Better Portrait

Getting a person to relax is essential to taking a good portrait. And before they can relax, you must relax too. If you are nervous or unsure of yourself, your subject will respond accordingly. Make an effort to smile, be confident, and at least act like you know what you're doing. It helps also to know ahead of time where you will be shooting the picture. Scout out a quiet spot with good light (natural light outside or by a window works well) and a simple, uncluttered background. Many digital cameras enable you to instantly view a picture on an electronic display. Show your subject a few shots and engage them in the process. Before you know it, that fake smile will disappear and be replaced by a real one.

Changing Color, Tinting, and Trimming Hair

My hairdresser, Robert, tells me that most of the colorizing he does is really lightening and darkening certain parts of the hair to model or mold it. The secret, he says, is to lighten the front part so it creates a glow around the face while darkening the back to bring out the highlights in the front. He also adds streaks of light and dark to give the hair a sense of depth. All of this is easy to do in Photoshop Elements. Look at the difference between the images in Figure 3.33.

Figure 3.33: Before (left) and after (right) adding highlights.

Here is what I did to add the highlights:

1. I chose New layer from the Layer menu (Layer ≻ New ≻ Layer). This opened the dialog box shown in Figure 3.34. Here I chose Color Dodge from the Mode pop-up menu and selected Fill with Color-Dodge-Neutral Color (Black). I named this layer **Highlights**. Then I clicked OK.

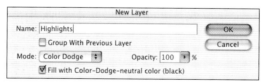

Figure 3.34: By selecting a new layer with these settings, you can literally paint highlights onto an image.

2. I selected the Brush tool ( ) from the toolbar and then selected the Airbrush icon in the toolbar ( ). I selected an appropriately sized, soft-edged brush from the options bar and set the Mode to Normal and the Opacity to 4 percent. In the Color Picker at the bottom of the toolbox, I selected white for the foreground. On the layer called **Highlights**, I applied the Airbrush to the hair in the front, airbrushing lightly until I got the right amount of "modeling."

3. To enhance the shadows, I created another new layer (Layer ≻ New ≻ Layer). This time in the dialog box, I chose Color Burn from the Mode pop-up menu and selected Fill with Color-Dodge-Neutral Color (White). I named this layer Shadow. I applied the Airbrush tool to this layer, but this time I painted the back of the hair with a black foreground color instead of white. Figure 3.35 shows all my layers after painting with the Airbrush.

Figure 3.35: Highlights and shadows are painted onto their own layers.

It's also easy to add color to hair by using the Color Replacement tool. Compare the two images in Figure 3.36.

Figure 3.36: Hair before using the Color Replacement tool (left) and after using Color Replacement (right).

Here's what I did to go from the first image to the second:

1. I chose the Color Replacement tool (✎) from the toolbar. In the options bar, I chose the following:

   Mode: Color
   Sampling: Continuous
   Limits: Contiguous. Discontiguous will work too.
   Tolerance: 30 percent. A higher percentage replaces adjacent pixels with a broader range of color values. A lower percentage replaces only a few adjacent pixels with similar color values.

2. I clicked the foreground color swatch in the toolbar to access the Color Picker. I used the Eyedropper (✐) to sample a color from the bird. (The cursor changes to the Eyedropper when moved outside the Color Picker. You can also choose a color directly from the Color Picker.) After selecting my color I clicked OK.

3. Then I simply used the Color Replacement tool and broad strokes with my brush to apply the color to the hair.

My friend Tracy took the photo on the left in Figure 3.37 of her husband, Chris, in their backyard in Chico, California. Tracy told me that she wanted to see her husband without the gray. "And, oh, by the way," she asked, "could you trim his beard as well?"

Figure 3.37: Chris in real life (left). Chris with his beard trimmed and all of the gray removed (right).

This is what I did:

1. I selected the Burn tool (✎) from the toolbar.

2. I selected an appropriately sized, soft-edged brush and set the Range to Midtones and the Opacity to 50 percent.

3. I burned until the beard was the right shade.

4. I selected the Clone Stamp tool (♨) and carefully trimmed the edges.

The results are shown on the right in Figure 3.37.

Getting Rid of Glasses Glare

Glare from glasses is always distracting. Look at the image on the left in Figure 3.38. The glare on the left is noticeable but slight, and it is easy to fix. The glare on the right fills the lens and blocks part of the eye. Although it takes a bit more work, it's also relatively easy to fix. The image on the right shows the results.

Figure 3.38: The glare on the left lens is easy to fix; the glare on the right lens takes a little more work (left). Glare gone (right).

To fix the glare on the left:

1. I selected the Clone Stamp tool (⚒). In the options bar, I chose an appropriately sized, soft-edged brush and set the Mode to Normal and the Opacity to 75 percent.

2. I sampled an area outside the glare and then "cloned" this area to the glare.

To fix the glare on the right:

1. I used the Lasso tool (⌾) to make a selection of the left eye. I then made a copy of this and pasted it onto its own layer (Ctrl+C / ⌘+C and then Ctrl+V / ⌘+V). I named this layer **Right Eye**.

2. I selected the eye in the layer called **Right Eye**. (An easy way to do this is to put the pointer on the layer bar—but not the thumbnail—and then click while holding the Ctrl/⌘ key.)

3. I chose Image ➤ Rotate ➤ Flip Selection Horizontal from the main menu bar. This effectively made the left eye a right eye.

4. I moved the eye by using the Move tool (▸⊹) in the toolbox. I positioned it over the glare on the right side.

5. I used the Clone Stamp tool to touch up the edges and make the fit perfect.

Better Outside Shots

4

Outside shots depend a lot on the undependable. The weather may not cooperate. Power lines, telephone poles, or even people can get in the way. It may be the wrong time of year or the wrong time of day. It may even be day when you really want night. You lose a lot of control when a picture is taken outside, but with the help of Photoshop Elements you can get some of that control back.

Chapter Contents

Intensifying the Sky

Many outside shots benefit from a dramatic sky filled with intense colors or interesting cloud patterns. Techniques I described earlier will help many skies reach their full potential (☞ "Making Dull Images Shine" in Chapter 2). However, if your digital image inherently suffers from a boring sky, you can use some other simple Photoshop Elements' techniques to "clone" a dramatic sky from one digital image and place it instead on another.

Cloning Clouds

On the left in Figure 4.1 is a photograph I took on the Spanish island of Menorca. It's not a bad photograph, but a dramatic sky would make it a lot better. By using Photoshop Elements, and working in the Standard Edit mode, I was able to create the new image shown on the right. You can apply these techniques to make your own dramatic sky.

Figure 4.1: By cloning a sky from another image, this photo (left) will become a lot more interesting. The same photo with a new sky (right).

This is what I did to create the new image:

1. I opened the image shown in Figure 4.1 and another image containing a dramatic sky, shown in Figure 4.2. Both of these images came from a Kodak Photo CD and were opened at 1536 × 1024 pixels at 144 pixels/inch. (If your images have resolutions that are different from each other, you should resample the image containing the dramatic sky to match the resolution of your target image. To resample, choose Image ➤ Resize ➤ Image Size and type in the matching pixel values.)

Figure 4.2: These clouds will liven up almost any sky.

2. In the image containing the man and the horse, I created a new layer and called it **Clouds** (Layer ➤ New ➤ Layer). I did this because I wanted to clone the new sky to its own layer and keep the old sky intact.

3. I selected the Clone Stamp tool (⚒) from the toolbar and selected the image containing the dramatic sky. In the options bar, I selected the following: Brush: Soft Round 300 pixels; Mode: Normal; Opacity: 100 percent; Aligned: selected; Use All Layers: selected. (The brush size you choose will depend on your image.)

4. I positioned the cursor at the top far left of the dramatic sky and, while holding the Alt/Option key, I clicked and sampled.

5. I placed the cursor on the top far left of the image of the man and the horse and "painted" the new sky. I started with a horizontal stroke, going from left to right, filling in the top 33 percent of the sky. Then, *and this is very important*, I changed the opacity of the Clone Stamp tool in the options bar to 65 percent. I painted another horizontal layer of sky, this one just under the one that was painted at 100 percent opacity. I painted about 40 percent of the sky this way and stopped just above the top of the horse and the top of the rock talus. At this point, I wasn't very precise and some of the clone spilled over the horse and the rock talus. However, it didn't matter because the new sky was actually going on its own layer, the layer I called **Clouds**, and I would go back later and fix the overlapping areas (see Figure 4.3).

*Figure 4.3: By keeping **Clouds** as its own layer, I can go back and edit or enhance it at any time.*

6. When I was finished cloning the new sky onto the old, I selected the Move tool
    (⊹) from the toolbar. With the layer called **Clouds** still selected, I put my cursor
    on the image window, and clicked and dragged the sky around until it was posi-
    tioned exactly as I wanted.

7. I chose the Eraser tool (⌀) from the toolbar. I selected the following options
    from the options bar: Brush: Soft Round 100 pixels; Mode: Brush; Opacity: 100
    percent. On the layer called **Clouds**, I carefully erased the clouds and sky away
    from the horse, the man, and the rock. (For the detailed areas, I used a Soft
    Round 35 pixels and a Soft Round 17 pixels brush.)

8. I enhanced the clouds by applying Levels to the **Clouds** layer only (Enhance ➢
    Adjust Lighting ➢ Levels). Finally, I used the Crop tool (⊐) to crop off a small
    part of the right side of the image, where the cloned sky didn't fit quite to the
    edge.

9. At this point, I could have flattened my image (Layer ➢ Flatten Image, or
    Flatten Image from the Layers palette menu), or just saved my image with the
    two layers intact. Keeping the two layers increases the file size, but I kept them
    because I wanted the option of going back and tweaking my image, or even
    restoring the original sky if I wanted.

In some cases, when you are transferring an entire sky from one image to another, it's not a bad idea to use a copy-and-paste technique rather than using the Clone
Stamp tool. For this particular image, however, I needed to gradually blend the two
skies. The Clone Stamp tool enabled me to do this by giving me the ability to change
the opacity as I painted.

Changing the Time of Day

Photographers and artists love morning and evening light. It's when the sun is angled
to the horizon and the shadows are long and dramatic. Sunset light is especially pleas-
ing when the light passes through a thick layer of particulates, such as smog, moisture,
or dust. Midday light, on the other hand, is much more difficult to work with.
Depending on the time of year and the place, the light is harsh, and shadows are short
and intense.

With Photoshop Elements, you can imitate the golden light of a sunset or even
change day to night. Here are some specific examples with techniques you can use on
your own digital images.

Midday to Sunset

Figure 4.4 shows a beautiful scene taken in San Francisco around 3 P.M. by professional photographer Monica Lee and a shot of the Manhattan skyline by me.

Figure 4.4: These photos are beautiful but they could benefit from warm sunset light. (Photo by Monica Lee (left) and the author (right).)

I thought both photos might benefit from warmer, more golden sunset light. Here are two ways to do this with Photoshop Elements. The first method requires a few more steps but gives you more control. (It also prepares you for using a similar method in the example following this one, "Morning to Sunset.") The second method uses one of Photoshop Elements 3's photo filters. Both methods require working in the Standard Edit mode.

Method 1:

1. I opened the image and made a new layer called **Sunset Light** (Layer ➢ New ➢ Layer). I set my layer Opacity to 56 percent and the Mode to Color Burn.

2. I selected an appropriate color for my warm tint. I did this by clicking the foreground color selection box in the toolbox. This brought up the Color Picker, where I chose a color with the following RGB values: Red = 255, Green = 204, and Blue = 102 (see Figure 4.5).

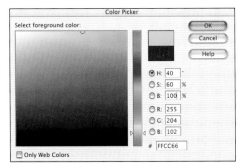

Figure 4.5: Choose a warm tint like this one from the Color Picker.

3. I selected the Gradient tool (■) from the toolbox. I chose the following settings from the options bar: Gradient Picker: Foreground to Transparent; Type of Gradient: Linear Gradient; Mode: Normal; Opacity: 100 percent (see Figure 4.6). Then, with the empty **Sunset Light** layer selected, I applied the Linear Gradient tool (■) to the image I did this by holding the Shift key and dragging the cursor from the bottom of the image window halfway up, just past the top of the row of houses. Holding the Shift key while I did this constrains the angle

to multiples of 45 degrees. (I used the Linear Gradient tool to apply the warm tint, but you can instead apply the tint selectively by using the Brush tool (✐). Just be sure to apply the color to a layer of its own, using the color values from step 2 and the **Sunset Light** layer specifications from step 1.)

Figure 4.6: Set the Gradient tool options as shown.

4. After I applied the warm tint, I noticed that the sky looked too light for the late hour I was trying to imitate. To darken the sky, I created a Levels adjustment layer and adjusted the entire image so the background darkened appropriately. I then selected the Gradient tool and kept the same settings as described in step 3. However, I clicked the Default Colors icon (▣) (you can also use the shortcut key D) to set the colors in the color selection box to their default colors in the toolbox, and reset my foreground and background colors to black-and-white. I then used the Gradient tool on the adjustment layer to create a mask that prevented the levels adjustment from affecting the foreground (see Figure 4.7). More information on this technique is provided later in this book (☞ "Layer Adjustments with Masks" in Chapter 11). The result is shown on the right in Figure 4.7.

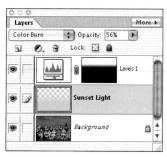 

Figure 4.7: Note the Layer options for **Sunset Light** *and the adjustment layer mask (left). The new image is now bathed in sunset light (right).*

Method 2:

1. I opened the image and made a copy of the background layer (Layer ➢ Duplicate Layer).

2. On the duplicate layer I applied a photo filter (Filters ➢ Adjustments ➢ Photo Filter). I chose Warming Filter (85) from the Filter pop-up menu; I set Density to 76 and kept Preserve Luminosity selected. (You can also apply the photo filter as an adjustment layer and forgo step 1. However, you'll see shortly why I chose to apply it as a normal filter to a copy of the background layer.)

3. At this point, for some images, all you need to do is select OK and you are done. The filter does the job. However, for this image the filter made the sky look strange, as you can see in Figure 4.8. To correct this, I selected the Magic

Eraser tool ( ) from the toolbar and after a little experimentation set the Tolerance to 40 in the options bar. I left Contiguous selected. (Tolerance settings depend on how wide a range of similar colors you want to erase and will vary depending on the image. Selecting Contiguous assures that only pixels sharing a boundary or touching each other will be erased.)

Figure 4.8: The photo filter gave the buildings the glow I was looking for, but didn't do a good job on the sky.

4. On the duplicate layer, I clicked the sky. The Magic Eraser erased most of the sky on the duplicate layer. (The Layers palette and final image are shown in Figure 4.9.) Now the original sky—which was OK without the filter—shows through from the layer below. (If I had applied the photo filter as an adjustment layer, I couldn't have conveniently used the Magic Eraser selectively on the sky area.)

Figure 4.9: Note how the Magic Eraser selectively deleted the sky in the top, duplicate layer (left). This enables the sky from the background layer to show through (right).

Morning to Sunset

The image on the left in Figure 4.10 is a shot I took of the ancient Mayan ruins in Tikal, Guatemala. Even though it was early morning and the jungle mist hadn't cleared, the light had a bluish tint.

Figure 4.10: This jungle scene (left) lacked warmth. I used the layer blending and Opacity settings (right) to make it more tropical.

I wanted the image to feel warmer, more tropical, so I did the following:

1. With the Tikal image open, I made two copies of my background layer and named these layers **Sharpen** and **Blur**. I created a new layer and called it **Tint**. My Layers palette is shown on the right in Figure 4.10. The layer order is important.

Note: The easiest way to duplicate a layer is to select the layer in the Layers palette and drag it to the New Layer button (🔲) at the top of the Layers palette. The easiest way to create a new layer is to click that button. Remember, the Layer palette is located by default in the palette bin. However, by clicking/holding/dragging on the top tab of the palette you can move the palette anywhere you want on the screen.

2. To the layer called **Blur**, I applied a strong Gaussian blur (Filter ➢ Blur ➢ Gaussian Blur) and set the Radius setting to 5.7. I left the **Blur** layer blending Mode to Normal and set the layer Opacity to 58 percent.

3. To the layer called **Sharpen**, I applied an Unsharp Mask (Filter ➢ Sharpen ➢ Unsharp Mask). I used the following settings: Amount: 100 percent; Radius: 1.9 pixels; Threshold: 0 Levels. I then set the **Sharpen** layer Opacity to 61 percent and left the blending Mode at Normal.

4. I filled the **Tint** layer with a light orange tint. To do this, I clicked on the foreground color selection box in the toolbox to open the Color Picker, and then I selected a color with the following RGB values: Red = 255, Green = 204, and Blue = 102. I selected fill layer from the Edit menu and chose the settings from the dialog box shown on the left in Figure 4.11. You can also use the Paint Bucket tool (🖌) to fill the **Tint** layer. Just be sure your Fill option in the option

bar is set to Foreground and not Pattern. (I want to acknowledge Photoshop master Brad Johnson for concocting this particular tint, which I use often.)

5.	I set the Mode of the **Tint** layer to Color Burn, and the Opacity to 44 percent, and I was done. The final image is shown on the right in Figure 4.11.

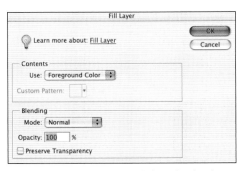

Figure 4.11: Fill settings (left). The final image (right).

It may seem counterintuitive to apply both a Sharpen and Blur effect to the same image, but rather than canceling each other, the combination of the two effects gave my image a soft, dreamy look and yet kept much of the sharpness in some of the detailed areas. I also could have modified the effects of these two layers by using the Eraser tool ( ) and selectively erasing each effect from certain areas.

Shooting Digital: The Rules of Good Composition

Regardless of whether you are shooting a digital camera or a film camera, the rules of good composition remain the same. Somewhere in your picture there should be a focal point. This can mean arranging your shot to include a blooming branch in the foreground, or a large rock in the middle ground, or a dramatic sky in the background. Don't make the common mistake of assuming that, simply because a scene looks breathtaking to the eye, it will work as a photograph. Without a strong focal point, the camera translates the scene into a mush of small objects that are visually boring. Because most digital cameras don't capture very high resolution, shots without careful composition are especially uninteresting.

Day to Night

Figure 4.12 is a still frame grabbed from a Lexus TV ad. The shot was taken during the day, but the director, Melinda Wolf, decided afterward that it should have been shot during the night. Special-effects wizard Michael Angelo was called. Before working on the actual footage, Michael used digital editing to show the director what the scene might look like at night. Michael used Photoshop to create this image originally, but he kindly modified his procedure to show how it could be done using Photoshop Elements.

Figure 4.12: This is how the shot looked during the day (left). This is how it would have looked at night (right).

This is what Michael did to get the results shown on the right in Figure 4.12:

1. He made a duplicate layer and called it **Night**. To duplicate a layer, select the layer and drag it to the New Layer button (▣) at the top of the Layers palette.

2. With the **Night** layer selected, Michael removed the color by choosing Enhance ➤ Adjust Color ➤ Remove Color. Then he selected Enhance ➤ Adjust Color ➤ Adjust Hue/Saturation and selected the Colorize option in the dialog box. He tinted the image blue by sliding the Hue slider to the right. He left the Saturation in the middle, set at 50. Then he darkened the overall image by sliding the Lightness slider to the left. Because he selected Preview in the dialog box, all his changes were visible on the actual image and he could easily modify his settings to get exactly what he wanted (see Figure 4.13).

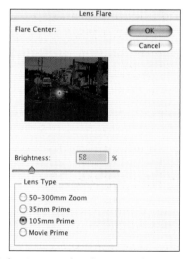

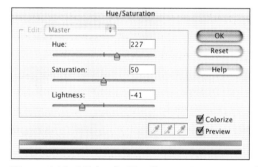

Figure 4.13: Michael's Hue/Saturation settings (left). Settings for the Lens Flare filter (right).

3. He created a duplicate layer of **Night** and called it **Lens Flare**.

4. To the **Lens Flare** layer, he applied the Lens Flare filter (Filter ➤ Render ➤ Lens Flare). See Figure 4.13 for the settings he used. He dragged the flare over one of the headlights and selected OK. He repeated these steps, selecting the Lens Flare filter again to apply another "headlight."

5. He duplicated the **Lens Flare** layer and called this layer **Final**. On this layer, he used the Dodge tool (✦) from the toolbox to paint the reflection of the head-lights in the pavement.

The conversion of a single frame from day to night was a piece of cake for Michael compared to what he had to do to convert the entire film footage into night. That was a task for another program and a subject for another book!

Making Weather

If you don't like the weather, use a Photoshop Elements effect and make some of your own. That's what I did to turn the relatively calm day shown on the left in Figure 4.14 into the blizzard shown on the right.

Figure 4.14: All it takes is a Blizzard effect to add drama to the image on the left.

To do this, simply select Effect and Image Effects from the pop-up menus in the Styles and Effects palette, located by default in the palette bin. Then select and apply the Image Effect called Blizzard. (To apply the effect, double-click its icon, or click and drag the icon on top of the image window.)

Remember, all effects can be easily removed and sometimes altered. To remove an effect, you can either choose Edit ➤ Undo Blizzard (Ctrl+Z / ⌘ +Z), or select the effect layer in the Layers palette and click the trash can at the top of the palette. For the Blizzard effect, try varying the blending and Opacity settings found at the top of the Layers palette. Color Dodge and Soft Light blending choices work well.

Working with the Midday Sun

The image on the left in Figure 4.15 shows a field of wheat shot in the middle of the day by field biologist Laura Laverdiere of the Syngenta Crop Protection company. She used a digital camera to document the effects of different fertilizers and insecticides. The midday sun washed out much of the color, making it more difficult to see the difference between the healthy and unhealthy plants. The right side of Figure 4.15 shows the same field after Laura used Photoshop Elements to fix the shot.

Figure 4.15: The midday sun washes out color (left). With a little help from Photoshop Elements, this is now a useful image (right). (Photos by Laura Laverdiere)

Making this right was a simple matter: Laura applied Auto Levels to her image (Enhance ➢ Auto Levels). Then she slightly increased the saturation (Enhance ➢ Adjust Color ➢ Adjust Hue/Saturation).

Adding Lighting Effects

Look at the image on the left in Figure 4.16. The light is flat and monotonous. If we could just part the gray veil and bring out the sun, it might help. Well, with Photoshop Elements and its Lighting Effects filter, we can do just that.

Figure 4.16: This photo (left) is waiting for a little divine intervention. The sun (right), thanks to the Lighting Effects filter. (Photos by Monica Lee)

Here is what I did to create the final image shown on the right in the figure:

1. I made a copy of the background layer.
2. I selected the Lighting Effects filter (Filter ➢ Render ➢ Lighting Effects, or select Filters and Render from the pop-up menus in the Styles and Effects palette, located by default in the palette bin). This brought up the dialog box shown in Figure 4.17.

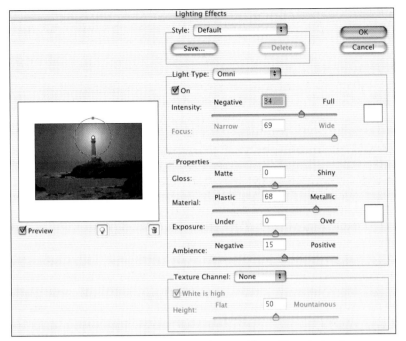

Figure 4.17: Photoshop Elements' Lighting Effects filter dialog box.

3. For Style, I chose Default.

4. For Light Type, I chose Omni, which created a light that shined in all directions. I selected the On check box (below the Light Type) and an Intensity of 34. Still in the Light Type section of the dialog box, I clicked in the color box and then chose white from the Color Picker.

5. I adjusted the Omni light by dragging the center circle in the preview window just over the top of the lighthouse. I played with the size of the light by dragging one of the handles defining the edges of the light until I got what I wanted.

6. To set the light properties, I dragged the corresponding sliders and chose the following:

- For Gloss (which determines how much a surface area reflects), I left the slider at a neutral 0. (Matte creates a dull reflection, whereas Shiny creates a high reflectance.)
- For Material, I slid the slider more toward Metallic.
- I kept my Exposure at 0.
- For Ambience, I moved the slider toward the positive, which increased the overall brightness of my image.
- I left the color of the Ambience light white. (To change the ambient color, click the color box to the right of the Ambience slider and use the Color Picker that appears.)

How did I come up with these choices? To be honest, it was a lot of trial and error. Any time I made a choice, the image in the preview window changed, reflecting that choice. I played around until I got the quality of light that looked appropriate.

7. After I was finished, I clicked OK.

As you can see, the Lighting Effects filter offers many options for changing the quality and direction of light in your digital image. It takes some time and experimentation to fully master its potential, but the extra effort is worth it.

Removing Unwanted Objects

Many times a picture is perfect except for a power line or an unwanted sign or, for that matter, an unwanted person who wanders into your shot. Sometimes all it takes to get the picture right is a little Photoshop Elements blur here, or a burn there. Other times you'll need to remove the object entirely, and that's when other techniques come in handy. In Chapter 7 I'll show you how to use the Clone Stamp and Healing Brush tools to remove annoying power lines that often appear in outdoor shots. In this section, I'll show you a couple of ways to remove other kinds of unwanted objects.

Removing a Tarp from the Golden Gate Bridge

Photographer Monica Lee needed a shot of the Golden Gate Bridge, but on the day she picked to shoot it, the Highway and Transportation District wasn't cooperating. As you can see in Figure 4.18, they placed a yellow tarp right in the middle of the bridge. Monica got the shot, and I helped her remove the unwanted blemish.

Figure 4.18: Who put that yellow tarp in the middle of my picture? (Photo by Monica Lee)

This is what I did:

1. I made a selection from a nearby part of the bridge by using the Rectangular Marquee tool (⬚), as shown in Figure 4.19. I copied this selection and pasted it on a layer that I called **Fix**.

Figure 4.19: I made a selection from a clean part of the bridge.

2. I used the Move tool (⊹) from the toolbox to slide the fix into place over the yellow tarp. It didn't match up perfectly, so I selected the Free Transform command (Image ➢ Transform ➢ Free Transform) and turned the fix slightly so it did fit (see Figure 4.20).

Figure 4.20: I used the Free Transform command to position the pasted fix (left), then used the Clone Stamp tool to clean it up. The fixed image (right).

3. I then used the Clone Stamp tool (⬚) to remove the last bits of yellow on the bottom.

The results are shown on the right in Figure 4.20.

Removing a Person

My wife, Rebecca, writes and photographs for a monthly column in *Parents' Press*. Mostly she takes pictures of our daughters and the daughter of her coauthor, or photos of other known kids. If an unknown child slips into a photograph, Rebecca is required by the magazine to get a model release before the magazine can use the picture. Occasionally she gets a shot that she wants to submit but that doesn't have a model release.

That's what happened on the left in Figure 4.21. The person sliding down the slide is our daughter, so no problem using her image for the magazine, but who is the person behind her? Using Photoshop Elements, I made the image publishable, as shown on the right.

Figure 4.21: The child in the background is recognizable (left). After using the Burn tool, the background child is no longer recognizable (right).

Here's what I did to remove the unknown person: I first made a duplicate layer of the background. Then I selected the Burn tool (✎) from the toolbox and selectively darkened the boy's face until it was unrecognizable.

For other pictures that contained unwanted or unusable faces, I've used the Blur tool (◊) to achieve a similar goal. You can also use the Mosaic filter (Filter ➤ Pixelate ➤ Mosaic) to achieve the blurred-face look used on real-life television shows to protect someone's privacy.

Adding Selective Focus

Field biologist Laura Laverdiere is hindered not only by the difficulties of shooting under a midday sun. The digital camera she uses doesn't give her much creative control. For example, the camera is fully automatic, and it's impossible for her to choose a lens aperture and thereby increase or decrease the depth of focus. She gets around this limitation by using Photoshop Elements' Gaussian Blur filter selectively to create a sense of depth. By doing this, she calls attention visually to the critical parts of her image.

In the photo shown on the left in Figure 4.22, Laura wanted the chemically damaged leaf to stand out.

Figure 4.22: A narrower depth of focus would be helpful (left). Now the damaged leaf jumps out (right). (Photos by Laura Laverdiere)

To emphasize the leaf, she did the following:

1. She created a duplicate layer and called this layer **Blur**.
2. With the Lasso tool (⌇), she made an outline around the chemically damaged leaf and feathered this selection by 3 pixels (Select ➤ Feather). Then she chose Select ➤ Inverse from the menu bar.
3. She applied a strong Gaussian blur with a 4.4 pixel setting to the selection (Filter ➤ Blur ➤ Gaussian Blur). She then deselected her selection (Select ➤ Deselect or Ctrl+D / ⌘ +D). The results are shown on the right in Figure 4.22.

This is a perfect example of a time when the Selection Brush might be used instead of the Lasso tool for making a selection. Simply click the Selection Brush in the toolbar (⫸) and "paint" your selection over the plant. After you do this, follow the rest of the steps in this procedure to feather and inverse the selection and then move on to step 3. To make the Selection Brush tool feel even more like painting, choose Mode: Mask from the menu bar, and the selected area will appear "masked" in the overlay color of your choice. If you use the Mask mode, however, keep in mind that you do not need to inverse your selection. Mask mode works the opposite way from Selection mode. What you paint over is "protected" or "masked" as if you used masking tape, and not "selected." In other words, by painting over the damaged leaf in Mask mode, you've automatically protected it from the effect of the Gaussian blur—so you don't need to inverse your selection as you would otherwise. (For more on the Selection Brush, see "Selection Tools" in the appendix.)

By working on a duplicate layer, Laura kept her original image intact. Also, if she wanted to selectively remove the Gaussian blur effect, all she had to do was use the Eraser tool (✎) selectively on the Blur layer, and the unblurred areas in the background layer would be revealed.

Creating a Large-Scale Digital Fill Flash

I used Photoshop Elements' Shadows/Highlights command elsewhere in the book to illuminate a person and a room (☞ "Creating a Digital Fill Flash Effect" in Chapter 3, and "Balancing the Light" in Chapter 7). Shadows/Highlights also works well as a large-scale digital fill flash on outdoor objects, as shown in Figure 4.23.

Figure 4.23: Before Shadows/Highlights is applied (left). After Shadows/Highlights is applied (right).

To get this kind of effect without software help would have required a powerful off-camera strobe or large reflector to fill in the shadows—neither of which I usually carry in my camera bag. Also, if you try to correct this image with Levels or other Enhance controls, you can't control either the shadow or highlights independently and get satisfactory results.

To fix the photo (taken at California's Morro Bay State Park), I opened it, selected Enhance ➤ Adjust Lighting ➤ Shadows/Highlights, and adjusted the sliders using the settings shown in Figure 4.24.

As you can see, I adjusted the Shadows slider to "open" up the shadows and I also darkened the highlights slightly with the Highlights slider. Often, with images like this, I get away with adjusting only the Shadows. Just experiment. As long as you have the Preview check box selected, you'll get instant feedback.

Figure 4.24: My Shadows/Highlights settings.

Scanning Digital: Digitizing without Owning a Scanner

You don't have to own an expensive slide scanner to digitize your 35mm or APS film. A variety of retail outlets will take your film and in return give you a floppy disk or a CD containing a digitized version of your work. Just keep in mind that although these services are economical and convenient, they may not provide the image resolution you need.

The Kodak Picture CD, which is widely available at most photo-finishing outlets, provides a 1536 × 1024 pixel file in the JPEG file format. This file has less resolution than that produced by many digital cameras, although the resolution is adequate for monitor viewing or for making small prints.

For higher-resolution scans, I recommend stepping up to the Kodak Photo CD process. Kodak Photo CDs are more expensive than Picture CDs, and services that offer them are less widespread. (For a listing of businesses in your area that provide Photo CD service, go to **www.kodak.com/US/en/digital/products/photoCD.shtml.**) However, the Kodak Photo CD process scans and stores your negative or slide in a proprietary format, which allows for a single image to be stored in up to six different resolutions, ranging from 192 × 192 pixels all the way up to 2048 × 3072 pixels.

Photoshop Elements is especially good at opening these files via the File ➤ Open menu commands. Just go to the Photo CD file folder named **Photo_CD** and open the images from a folder titled **Images**. (Mac users: Do not open your images from a folder titled **Photos**, which contains images saved in the PICT format and intended for screen display, not hard-copy output.) A Kodak PCD Format dialog box appears after you select an image, offering you choices of resolution and color profiles and thereby making it possible to open an image that meets your exact requirements.

Better Product Shots

It doesn't matter if you are selling a camera on eBay or a vintage sports car through a community bulletin board. A professional-looking image will help sell your stuff. Sure, it helps to have a fancy photo studio or a high-end advertisement budget. But you can make a product shot taken with a consumer digital camera in your living room look significantly better just by using various Photoshop Elements tricks and techniques. In this chapter, you'll learn how.

Chapter Contents

Separating a Product from Its Background

Just about anything you do to enhance or fix a product shot begins by using various selection or eraser tools to separate the product from its background. Only after you do this can you effectively do the following:

- Fix or replace a distracting background
- Colorize, texturize, or add motion blur to the product
- Add depth through a drop shadow or other layer effect

How hard is it to use Photoshop Elements to do this? It depends. I've been handed digital photos of products taken against a white or single-colored background and with a few clicks of the Magic Eraser tool I finished the job in a few seconds. Other times, I've been handed a shot of a product placed against a busy background and spent way too much time using many of Photoshop Elements' selection and eraser tools to get the job done right.

Don't be discouraged if your results are less than perfect or if you feel you are taking an inordinate amount of time. The whole time you are trying, you are building skills and experience that will make the job easier next time. If you become really frustrated—and that is an appropriate response—you might even consider reshooting the product against a plain-colored background, which will make your Photoshop Elements work go easier and faster.

Note: When you choose and apply one of the several selection tools to an active layer, you'll get a dotted border that looks like an army of marching ants. Technically, this dotted border is called a *selection marquee*, but I like to think of the little dots as protective ants, keeping the outside at bay. Any tool or task that you apply while the ants are in place will affect only the selected areas. For example, if you choose a Gaussian blur, the effect will apply only to the area that is bounded by the selection marquee. You can easily reverse the selection by choosing Select ➤ Inverse from the menu bar or by using the keyboard command Ctrl+Shift+I / ⌘ +Shift+I. Then, for example, when you apply a Gaussian blur, it will affect only the areas outside your original selection.

The relevant selection tools for this chapter include the Rectangular Marquee tool (⬚), the Elliptical Marquee tool (○), the Lasso tool (⌇), the Polygonal Lasso tool (⌇), the Magnetic Lasso tool (⌇), and the Magic Wand tool (✎). More details on these and the Selection Brush (⌇), which gives you a choice between viewing a selection marquee or a colored mask, are provided later in this book (☞ "Selection Tools" in the appendix).

When It's Easy

The image shown in Figure 5.1 makes me smile with joy. It's a shot taken with a digital camera of a 1940s-style film camera against a single-color background. All it needs is a few clicks with the Magic Eraser tool to remove similar pixels within a predetermined range. This will separate the vintage camera from its background, and I can then add a drop shadow, swap the background, or apply a myriad of other image effects that are possible only when there is a transparent background.

Figure 5.1: It's relatively easy to remove a background when it's a single color. It doesn't matter if the color is slightly graduated.

Here's what I did to remove the background:

1. I chose the Magic Eraser (🖌) from the toolbox. The Magic Eraser shares tool-box space with the Background Eraser (🖌) and the standard Eraser tool (⌫). You can flip through the eraser tools by using the keyboard command Shift+E.

2. In the options bar, I used the following settings:

Tolerance: 45 I came up with this number after some trial and error. The default setting is 32, but when I used this number the Magic Eraser sampled too few variations of color and erased only a part of the background. When I tried a Tolerance of 100, it sampled too many colors and actually ate away, or erased, some of the foreground object as well as the background. See Figure 5.2.

Figure 5.2: A Tolerance setting of 32 was too little (left). A Tolerance setting of 100 was too much (right).

A tolerance of 45 wasn't perfect because it still required a few clicks in different parts of the background to do the job, but it was close enough. Theoretically, if my background had been exactly one color, a Tolerance setting of 1 would have removed all of the background with one click. However, I've noticed that making a photo with no color or tonal variations in the background is difficult. Even when you use a perfectly white or single-colored background, the slightest variations in lighting result in different tonal values.

Anti-aliased: selected This keeps a smooth transition between erased and non-erased parts.

Contiguous: selected This setting, which is the default, is very important. If I hadn't kept this setting, the Magic Eraser would have assumed that I wanted to erase all similar pixels in the image and not just pixels contiguous to the one I clicked. This means that if there had been a similar color anywhere in the image, even within the boundaries of the toy figure, these colors would have been erased as well (regardless of the Tolerance setting).

Use All Layers: selected In this case I had only one layer, so it didn't matter whether I selected this option. However, it would have made a difference if I had had more than one layer and wanted to sample the erased color by using data combined from all visible layers.

Opacity: 100 percent I wanted to erase completely to transparency. A lower opacity would have erased the pixels to partial transparency. Frankly, for the purposes of erasing a background in preparation for other tasks, I can't think of a reason why you should choose anything less than 100 percent.

3. After I set my options, I clicked first on the top part of the image. As you can see on the left in Figure 5.3, this only partially erased the background. Next I reset the tolerance to 20 and clicked lower in the image, and to the left in the shadow areas, until I got what you see on the right of Figure 5.3. I lowered my tolerance to 20 because the higher setting actually erased part of the camera. I also used the standard Eraser tool (✎) to clean up some stray pixels at the very bottom of the camera that weren't erased by the Magic Eraser.

Figure 5.3: One click of the Magic Eraser erased part of the background (left). More clicks with a lower tolerance setting erased the rest of the background (right).

When you use the Magic Eraser (or Background Eraser) on a background layer, as I did, you'll notice that the name in the Layers palette is automatically changed from **Background** to **Layer 0**. That's because a background layer can't contain transparency, and by changing its name its properties are also changed.

Note: What is a *transparent layer*? It's helpful to think of an illustration in a physiology book that shows the various parts of the human body in several translucent overlays. Viewed together, the layers make up the complete human body. But lift the layers and you can view each component—skin, muscles, skeleton, and internal organs—separately as well. This is basically what's happening when you place an object on a Photoshop Elements' transparent layer. The object—or technically, the grouping of pixels—is surrounded by a sea of transparency that is designated by a translucent checkered pattern. This pattern can be removed or changed to make the transparent areas more or less obvious (Edit ➤ Preferences ➤ Transparency; in OS X, Photoshop Elements application menu ➤ Preferences ➤ Transparency). If the layer that contains transparency sits above another layer, the non-transparent areas of the lower layer show through.

In this chapter, I'll show you ways to create and use layers that contain transparency. Keep in mind that a background layer cannot contain transparency. If you cut or delete from a background layer, it will fill with the background color as defined in the color selection box located at the bottom of the toolbox. If you have a background layer and want transparency in that layer, you'll need to change the name of the background layer to something else. To do this, double-click the layer in the Layers palette and either leave the default name, **Layer 0**, or type something else and click OK. You can also choose Layer ➤ New ➤ Layer from Background from the menu bar.

By the way, what is the difference between the Magic Eraser and the Magic Wand (✎)? Not much. The Magic Eraser finds pixels of similar value and automatically *erases* them, either to transparency or—if the transparency is locked in the Layers palette—to the selected background color. The Magic Wand finds pixels of similar value and *selects* them.

In the preceding example, I could have used the Magic Wand to select the background and then pressed the Delete key or chosen Edit ➢ Cut from the menu bar and I would have gotten the same effect (↩ "Selection Tools" in the appendix). Because one click of the Magic Wand wouldn't have been enough, just as it wasn't enough with the Magic Eraser, I then would have held the Shift key while clicking on other areas, thereby adding new selections without deselecting the preceding ones. Of course, to cut to transparency I also would have had to rename my background layer.

When It's a Little More Difficult

Look at the image on the left in Figure 5.4. The designer of the wine label, Lisa Friedman, didn't want me to get rid of the background; she just wanted me to tone it down a little so she could use the image to promote her design work. Because the background is filled with texture, this image is more difficult to work with than the preceding one.

Figure 5.4: The bottles and the background aren't very distinct (left). No matter what I did, I couldn't get the Magic Wand to select just the background (right).

Just for fun, try using the Magic Wand to select the background. (Forget the Magic Eraser because Lisa basically liked the background and didn't want to replace it.) I tried various Tolerance settings, but the Magic Wand always seemed to select pixels inside the bottle as well. There were just too many similarities in tone between the bottles and the background for the tool to work efficiently. On the right in Figure 5.4 you can see the results when I chose a tolerance of 44.

Because the Magic Wand wasn't so useful, I decided to use a combination of two other selection tools, the Magnetic Lasso and the Lasso, which share a spot in the toolbox.

I started with the bottle on the right and the Magnetic Lasso tool. Because the edges of this bottle are fairly well defined, the Magnetic Lasso's selection border should easily and automatically snap into place.

This is what I did to select the bottle on the right:

1. I selected the Magnetic Lasso tool (🖉) from the toolbox and chose the following options from the options bar:

   Feather: 0 This is the default setting and I wanted the selection to tightly hug the edge of the bottle so I left the setting at 0.

   Anti-aliased: selected This is also the default setting and will produce a smooth transition between the bottle and its background.

   Width: 40 The range here is 1–40, and I chose 40 because the image is relatively simple and has well-defined edges. With this setting, the Lasso is looking in a 40-pixel radius from the cursor for edge values. In other words, I don't need to be right up close to the edge I wish to select with the cursor. I can be within a 40-pixel range, and the cursor will still find the edge. This means I can be looser with the cursor and work a lot faster. Lower width values are critical when you are working on images with soft edges that are adjacent to other soft edges. In those cases, if you used a higher value, the Magnetic Lasso would easily get "confused" and place anchor points on edges that you didn't want selected. With lower values, you need to be very precise in placing the cursor, and that definitely will slow you down.

   Edge Contrast: 30 The range here is 1–100 percent, and I chose 30 percent after some trial and error. Higher values are usually fine for very defined edges. I chose a relatively low number because the shadow areas around the top and bottom of the bottle were less defined, and when I selected a higher percent the Magnetic Lasso didn't do a good job of finding the edges.

   Frequency: 57 I left this at its default. This specifies the rate at which the Magnetic Lasso sets fastening points. A higher value anchors the selection border in place more quickly.

2. I started on the lower-right side of the bottle by clicking the mouse. This set the first fastening point, which anchored the selection border in place. Next, I moved the pointer along the edge of the bottle. As I moved the pointer, the active segment snapped to the strongest edge in the image based on my Width settings. As you can see on the left in Figure 5.5, fastening points were

periodically set based on my Frequency setting. (You can remove a previously set anchor by simply hitting the Backspace key.) I also set fastening points manually by clicking the mouse. For a close-up view, I used Ctrl+spacebar+click / ⌘ + spacebar+click to magnify my image and then held the spacebar to activate the Hand tool so I could scroll around the image.

A couple of times, as I was moving the Magnetic Lasso around a corner, my fastening point jumped way off the edge (you can see this on the right in Figure 5.5). I did one of two things: I simply hit the Delete key, which brought me back to the last fastening point, where I tried again. Or I just left the mistake alone, knowing I was going back later to fine-tune the selection.

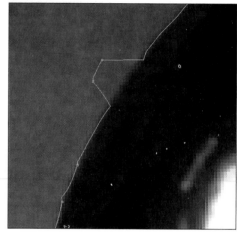

Figure 5.5: This magnified view (left) shows the fastening points and selection border of the Magnetic Lasso tool. I've increased the contrast of the image so you can see the points and border better. A more closely magnified view (right) shows a fastening point gone awry. I'll go back later and fix it with the Lasso tool.

3. After I circled the bottle and was ready to close the selection border, I double-clicked. (You can also press Enter/Return, or click anywhere outside the document window.)

4. To refine the selection, I selected the Lasso tool (◠) from the toolbox. Because I wanted to subtract from the selection, I clicked the Subtract from Selection icon (◫) on the options bar. You can also hold down the Alt/Option key. A minus sign (–) appears next to the pointer.

 Note: To add to a selection, either choose Add to Selection from the options bar or hold down the Shift key. A plus sign (+) will appear next to the pointer.

5. I then clicked and dragged the cursor around the area that I wanted to subtract, following the edge of the bottle closely. After I released the cursor, the selection was updated to reflect the boundaries of my new selection. See Figure 5.6.

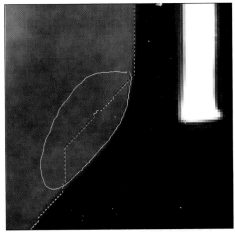

Figure 5.6: Subtract from a selection by choosing Subtract from Selection or holding down the Alt/Option key and circling the area you want deselected.

I like the Magnetic Lasso a lot, but it takes getting used to. The first time I used it, I had no trouble. I was working on an image with clearly defined edges. However, not long after that I had a really frustrating experience with it. I was working on an image that didn't have clearly defined edges, and the selection border was constantly snapping into the wrong place. I didn't seem to have any control over where it was going; I felt I had stuck my fingers into a wad of bubble gum and couldn't shake it loose. I suggest that you spend some time getting to know more about this tool in the Adobe Online Help or elsewhere in this book (◈ "Selection Tools" in the appendix).

Changing a Product's Color

With a product selected or its background deleted, changing the product's color is easy. Let's try this on the plastic toy image shown in Figure 5.7. The background of this shot was deleted using the Magic Eraser, and the plastic toy is alone on a transparent layer (◈ "Separating a Product from Its Background" earlier in this chapter).

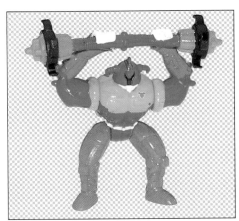

Figure 5.7: Changing the color of this toy is easy. Note that the toy is surrounded by a sea of transparency.

Changing Color via the Hue/Saturation Command

Figure 5.8 shows the effect of changing the colors via the Hue/Saturation controls (Enhance ➤ Adjust Color ➤ Adjust Hue/Saturation). All I did was slide the Hue slider until I got the colors I wanted. Obviously, this method is easy and provides immediate gratification, but it's useful only if you are trying to globally change or shift colors. If you want to change just one color or a specific range of colors, you'll find the following method a lot more useful.

Figure 5.8: Globally change color with the Hue/Saturation controls (left). Slide the Hue slider (right) to change the color.

Changing Color via the Replace Color Command

Figure 5.9 shows the effect of selectively changing the color via the Replace Color command. This method is much more precise than the Hue/Saturation command because it enables you to create a mask around specific colors and then replace those colors in the image. You can change the saturation and lightness of the masked area as well.

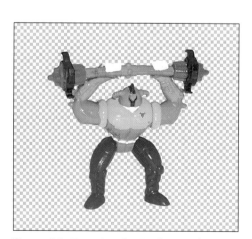
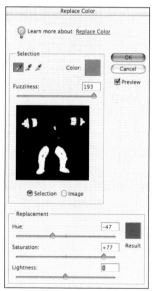

Figure 5.9: By using the Replace Color command, I could selectively replace the pink with purple (left). The Replace Color dialog box (right).

This is how I used the Replace Color command:

1. I selected the Replace Color command (Enhance ➢ Adjust Color ➢ Replace Color).

2. In the Replace Color dialog box shown on the right in Figure 5.9, I used the Eyedropper tool (✐) to select the pink colors in the legs and barbell. The black areas in the preview window are the masked areas. I expanded the tolerance of the mask slightly to include more than the sampled colors by dragging the Fuzziness slider. The black areas in the preview window expanded accordingly. (You can add distinctly different colors to your selection by clicking the Add to Sample eyedropper (✐) found in the Replace Color dialog box.)

3. When I was satisfied that I had masked the areas I wanted, I dragged the Hue slider to change the color just as I wanted. Then I added some saturation with the Saturation slider.

Changing Color via Painting

You can also selectively paint different colors with the brush tools. Before you do this, however, you must select the object so the painting or fill area doesn't spill over into the transparent areas.

To select the object in the Layers palette, on the layer containing your product and transparency, Ctrl+click / ⌘ +click the layer thumbnail. Another way to prevent color bleeding is to lock the transparent pixels. To do this, click the Lock Transparent Pixels button (▦) in the upper part of the Layers palette.

The left side of Figure 5.10 shows what happens when the plastic toy isn't selected or the transparency isn't locked. The blue paint spills all over the canvas. On the right you can see how selecting or locking the transparency confines the paint to the plastic toy.

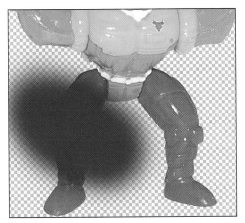 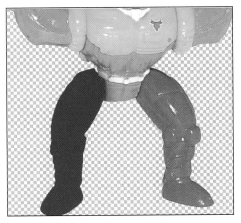

Figure 5.10: Paint spills all over if you don't select or lock the transparency of your image (left). With the object selected or transparency locked, the paint goes only where you want it to go (right).

There are many things to consider when you use a brush tool to change or alter the colors. For example, you'll probably want to experiment with different Mode and Opacity settings. If you leave your settings at their defaults (Mode: Normal, Opacity: 100 percent), you will replace an area that has tonal variations with a single, flat color, which may not be what you want. This is what happened in Figure 5.10.

Here is one simple way to use a brush to change or add colors and still maintain control over how the new paint blends with the old:

1. Assuming that the object you want to paint is already on a transparent layer, select it by Ctrl+clicking / ⌘ +clicking the layer thumbnail.

2. Create a new layer and name it **Color** (Layer ➢ New ➢ Layer). Make sure this layer sits above the layer containing the figure you want to color.

3. Select the Brush tool (✒) from the toolbox and if you wish, select the Airbrush option (✍) on the options bar. Pick a brush size from the options bar. Keep the Option settings at their defaults. Select a color to work with from the foreground color box at the bottom of the toolbox.

4. Paint on the layer called **Color**. Make sure the selection from step 1 is still visible. If it's not, your paint will spill all over the layer and not be confined to the parts of the object you want to paint.

5. When you are finished painting, while keeping the **Color** layer active, experiment with different Mode and Opacity settings in the Layers palette.

The advantage of using this method is obvious. Because you are painting on a separate layer, your original image remains intact. If you don't like what you have, just delete the **Color** layer and start over. Also, you are not confined to one Mode or Opacity setting. You can go back and change these settings at any time until you get just the right blending of new and old colors. (Remember, these are the settings accessible via the top of the Layers palette.)

Changing Color via the Paint Bucket Tool

Another simple way to replace color is via the Paint Bucket tool. Figure 5.11 shows an example of a product prototype created by product designer Marcia Briggs for L.L. Bean. Marcia made the line drawing by hand and then scanned it into her computer to create the image on the left. Because the client wanted to see the product in various colors, Marcia left the original drawing uncolored, knowing how easy it is to use the Paint Bucket tool to create several versions.

Figure 5.11: Marcia drew this product prototype and scanned it into the computer (left). She then filled the bag with color (right) by using the Paint Bucket tool.

This is what she did to color the bag:

1. She selected the Paint Bucket tool ( ) from the toolbox.
2. She left all the options in the options bar set at their defaults. Because she was working with a line drawing with basically no color variations to take into consideration, the Tolerance settings didn't matter. (The Paint Bucket tool looks for adjacent pixels that are similar in color value. The more colors you want to replace, the higher you must set the Tolerance values.)
3. She specified a foreground color from the foreground color box at the bottom of the toolbox. She clicked inside the area where she wanted the color. Then she chose another color and clicked inside another area. She did this until she got the results shown on the right.

By the way, even though Marcia was working with essentially a bitmap image, which is an image that contains only black or white, she stayed in the RGB mode (Image ➤ Mode ➤ RGB Color). Otherwise, she wouldn't have access to any other colors. Also, the Paint Bucket tool doesn't work in Bitmap mode.

Changing a Product's Texture

It's easy to change the texture of a product or add a pattern after you have selected it or separated it from its background. You can try a variety of Photoshop Elements tools, filters, and fills and see what you come up with.

Adding a Pattern via the Paint Bucket Tool

Let's go back to Marcia's bag. With her permission, I've applied a series of patterns by using the Paint Bucket tool. I also changed some of the colors (see Figure 5.12).

Figure 5.12: These patterns were created by using the Paint Bucket tool and setting the Fill option to Pattern.

Here's all I did to produce the patterns shown in this image:

1. I selected the Paint Bucket tool (✋) from the toolbox.
2. In the options bar, I changed Marcia's Fill setting from Foreground to Pattern and then chose a pattern from the Pattern menu.
3. I clicked inside an area where I wanted the first fill pattern. Then I chose another fill pattern and clicked inside another area. I did this until I had I totally ruined a perfectly good bag.

Adding a Pattern via the Fill Command

Look at the pattern shown in Figure 5.13.

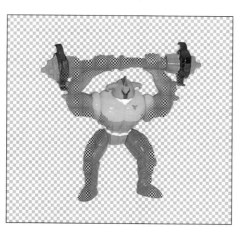
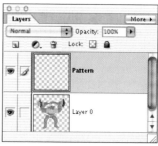

Figure 5.13: To create this pattern, I used the Fill command and selectively erased (left). With the plastic toy selected, I created a new layer, called it Pattern, and made it active (right).

To create this pattern, I first removed the toy from its background with the Magic Eraser. Then I did the following:

1. I selected the plastic toy by Ctrl+clicking / ⌘ +clicking the layer thumbnail.
2. I created a new layer and named it **Pattern** (Layer ➤ New ➤ Layer). I made sure that this layer sat above **Layer 0**, which contained the plastic toy (see Figure 5.13).

3. I chose Edit ➤ Fill Selection from the menu bar, making sure that the layer called **Pattern** was active.

4. I selected Pattern in the Use list and selected the fill of my choice in the Custom Pattern box, shown on the left in Figure 5.14.

5. I clicked OK. The pattern totally filled the plastic toy, as shown on the right in Figure 5.14.

6. To selectively remove the pattern, I selected the Eraser tool (✐) from the toolbox and selected a soft-edged brush from the options bar. On the layer called **Pattern**, I applied the Eraser to various parts of the toy where I wanted to remove the pattern.

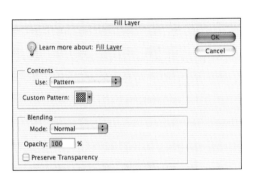

Figure 5.14: From the Use list, I chose Pattern (left). The Pattern filled the plastic toy (right). I used the Eraser tool to selectively remove it where I wanted the original colors to show through.

Another variation of this procedure is to apply a Texture or Image Effect from the Styles and Effects palette located in the palette bin. (Select Effect from the left drop-down menu, and either Texture or Image Effects from the drop-down menu on the right. Choices, represented by icons, will appear below the drop-down menus.) If you use one of these effects, follow the procedure I just outlined, but after step 1, drag and drop the effect you want from the Styles and Effects palette onto the image window. You can also double-click the effect's thumbnail. You don't need to make a new layer; a new layer will be created automatically when you apply the effect. Just remember to avoid using any textures whose name is followed by the word *layer*. For example, if you use the Sunset (Layer) effect, the effect won't fill your selection—it'll fill the entire layer.

Adding Pattern via a Fill Layer

You can also apply a pattern (or, for that matter a solid color or gradient) via a fill layer. Not only is a fill layer nondestructive, it can be easily changed at any time.

To use a fill layer for applying a pattern:

1. Select your object by Ctrl+clicking / ⌘ +clicking the layer thumbnail. This is important. If you don't select your object, the fill will completely fill a layer.

2. Choose Layer ➤ New Fill Layer ➤ Pattern (or Solid Color or Gradient). After

you follow the prompts and create a new layer, you will see the choices shown in Figure 5.15. Alternatively, you can select Pattern (or Solid Color or Gradient) directly from the Layers palette. Just click the Create New Fill or Adjustment Layer icon (⬤) at the top of the Layers palette and you'll go directly to the Pattern Fill options.

3. Choose from the various palette choices.

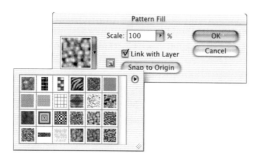

Figure 5.15: After you select New Fill Layer ➤ Pattern and you follow the prompts to create a new layer, you get the choices shown here.

4. After you select your fill, you can go back later and edit the mask to selectively apply the fill (↩ "Making Dull Images Shine" in Chapter 2). Figure 5.16 shows an image and its Layers palette. Note that Opacity is set at 62 percent, which allows only part of the fill to show through. Note also that I've erased some of the layer mask.

*Figure 5.16: Note the edited mask in the **Pattern Fill 1** layer and the Opacity setting (left). The final image after selectively applying a pattern fill and setting the layer Opacity to 62 percent (right).*

Note: When you erase by using the Eraser tool on a fill layer, or for that matter on an adjustment layer, you must make sure the foreground color—found at the bottom of the toolbar—is set to white. You can also erase from a fill or adjustment layer by using the Brush (✏) found in the toolbar. When using the Brush to erase, make sure the foreground color is set to black.

Adding a Pattern via a Filter

Many filters will create a pattern or texture effect. Especially useful are the ones found in the **Artistic, Noise, Pixelate, Sketch,** and **Texture** folders. These filters act on the actual pixels of the image, so I suggest that you create a duplicate of the layer containing the object you want to alter and apply the filter to the duplicate layer. That way, you can selectively erase or change the layer Mode or Opacity settings, as I did in the preceding example.

Here is an example of using a filter to create a pattern:

1. I duplicated the layer containing the plastic toy and called it **Stained Glass Filter**.

> **Note:** To make a duplicate layer, select the layer you wish to duplicate and either choose Layer ➢ Duplicate Layer from the menu bar or select the layer and then drag it to the Create a New Layer icon (回) at the top of the Layers palette.

2. I applied the Stained Glass filter to the duplicate layer (choose Filter ➢ Texture ➢ Stained Glass from the menu bar; or drag and drop, or double-click, from the Styles and Effects palette).

3. From the Layers palette, I set the Mode to Color Burn and the Opacity to 46 percent. In Figure 5.17, you can see my Layers palette on the left and the final image on the right.

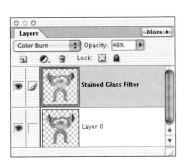

Figure 5.17: Note the duplicate layer called **Stained Glass Filter** *and the Mode and Opacity settings (left). The final image after applying the Stained Glass filter (right).*

And So On...

I think you get the idea. As you can see, there are many ways to add texture and fills to your product shot—or for that matter, to any digital image. Don't forget to experiment with different Opacity and Mode settings in the Layers palette and to use the Eraser tool to erase areas in which the fill or texture isn't needed.

Adding Motion Blur

The photo shown in Figure 5.18 is a relatively mundane shot of a very nice vintage car. By removing the background and applying the Motion Blur filter, I gave this static shot some added motion. You can apply this technique to just about any appropriate image.

Figure 5.18: The original image could use some motion.

Here are the steps for adding motion:

1. I changed the name of my background layer in the Layers palette to **Citroen**. (You can do this by simply double-clicking the layer in the Layers palette and then typing the new name. You can also do it by choosing Layer ➤ Rename Layer from the menu bar.)

2. I used the Magnetic Lasso tool (🖉) and the Lasso tool (〰) to select the car (👞 "Separating a Product from Its Background," earlier in this chapter). I wasn't precise because I knew that the Motion Blur filter would cover my sloppy work.

3. After selecting the car, I reversed the selection by choosing Select ➤ Inverse (Ctrl+Shift+I / ⌘ +Shift+I) from the menu bar. Now the area surrounding the car was selected.

4. I pressed Delete on my keyboard to remove the area around the car and replace it with transparency. If I hadn't changed the name of the layer in step 1, my selected areas would have filled with the background color—not transparency—when I deleted.

5. I deselected my selection (Selection ➤ Deselect or Ctrl+D / ⌘ +D).

6. I used the Eraser tool (✐) and the Clone Stamp tool (🖈) to touch up the edges and to remove the roof rack (see Figure 5.19). Again, I wasn't precise.

Figure 5.19: After I deleted my selection to transparency, I touched up the edges and removed the roof rack. I wasn't precise.

7. I made a copy of the **Citroen** layer and renamed it **Motion Blur** (Layer ➤ Duplicate Layer). Additionally, I made a temporary background layer so I could see the effects of my next step. I did this by choosing Layer ➤ New Fill Layer ➤ Solid Color from the menu bar and made the new layer the bottommost layer by clicking and dragging it below the layer called **Citroen**. (You can also click the Create New Fill or Adjustment Layer icon (❂) at the top of the Layers palette and then select Solid Color.)

8. I selected the layer named **Motion Blur** and ran the Motion Blur filter (Filters ➤ Blur ➤ Motion Blur) using the following values: Angle: 41, Distance: 185 pixels. (The effect of the Motion Blur filter will be unsatisfactory if you have locked your transparency in the Layers palette.) The Layers palette up to this point is shown on the left in Figure 5.20.

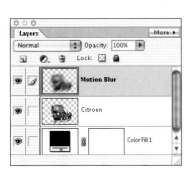

Figure 5.20: With Motion Blur on its own layer, I can selectively erase the effect (left). The final image (right).

9. I selected the Eraser tool, and on the **Motion Blur** layer I selectively erased the effect. In the final image, shown on the right in Figure 5.20, you can see why I didn't need to be precise in my selecting, erasing, and cloning.

Changing Scale and Perspective

Photographer Maggie Hallahan was in Hawaii shooting photos for a medical company, and the art director requested a shot of a man holding an oyster and pearl. He was very explicit and wanted the oyster to fill most of the bottom frame of the image with a man's hand and arm receding into the background. The shot would have been difficult even if Maggie had shot with a view camera with tilts and swings and sophisticated perspective control. Instead, Maggie shot the oyster and pearl with a Hasselblad medium format camera and got the results shown in Figure 5.21. Maggie knew the shot could be fixed later in Photoshop. She showed me what needed to be done and gave me permission to use her work as an example of the kind of perspective control you can get with Photoshop Elements' transform tools.

Figure 5.21: Professional photographer Maggie Hallahan shot this picture knowing it could be fixed later.

Here's what I did to change the scale and perspective:

1. I used the crop tool (⌗) to crop the image as shown on the left in Figure 5.22.
2. I used a combination of the Magnetic Lasso (⌇) and Lasso (⌇) to select the oyster. I copied and pasted this section (Ctrl+C / ⌘+C and then Ctrl+V / ⌘+V). I named the resulting layer **Big Pearl**. The Layers palette is shown on the right.

Figure 5.22: The cropped image (left). After selecting, copying, and pasting the oyster onto its own layer, I increased its scale (right).

3. With the **Big Pearl** layer active, I chose Image ➢ Resize ➢ Scale and, while holding the Shift key to constrain the proportions, I dragged the top corner of the bounding box to enlarge the oyster. (Don't drag the side handles; you'll distort the image.)

4. I turned off the visibility of the **Big Pearl** layer and made the layer containing the cropped image (**Background**) active. I then selected the hand and part of the arm as shown on the left in Figure 5.23. I reversed the selection (Select ➢ Inverse or Ctrl+Shift+I / ⌘ +Shift+I) and then I applied a strong feathering to the sky and the rest of the arm and body (Select ➢ Feather 10 pixels). To the feathered selection I applied a Gaussian blur. The feathering made the blur appear to recess in a more natural way.

Figure 5.23: I made a selection, feathered it, and applied a strong Gaussian blur (left). The final image (right).

5. Back on the layer called **Big Pearl**, now active and visible, I used the Clone Stamp tool (⬚) to get rid of the gum Maggie had cleverly used to hold the pearl in place. I also used the Dodge tool (●) to lighten the pearl. The edges of the oyster looked ragged, so I selected the oyster by Ctrl+clicking / ⌘ +clicking the image icon in the Layers palette, reversed this selection (Select ➢ Inverse, or

Ctrl+Shift+I / ⌘ +Shift+I), applied a 2-pixel feather (Select ➢ Feather), and hit the Delete key. This softened the edges a little and made the oyster blend more naturally into the background.

The final image is shown on the right in Figure 5.23.

Fixing Keystoning

Artist Tom Mogensen was given the photo shown on the left in Figure 5.24. It was taken by his friend Len Luke, in a bike shop in Italy. The poster was hanging high on a wall, and Len took the photo by aiming his camera nearly straight up. Because the plane of the camera and the plane of the wall weren't parallel to each other, the resulting photo has a distorted effect called *keystoning*. Keystoning occurs when lines converge rather than remain parallel. Still, Len really wanted a good copy of the poster to hang in the Bike Nook, his bike shop in San Francisco, so Tom helped him out.

Figure 5.24: Len Luke shot this distorted picture (left) of a poster hanging on a wall in a bike shop in Italy. Tom Mogensen began fixing it by expanding his canvas by 120 percent and then using the Rectangular Marquee tool to select the poster (right).

I know this isn't a product shot *per se,* but Tom did such a great job of using Photoshop Elements' Transform controls to fix the photo that I thought it would be useful to show how he did it. His method can be applied whenever you have an image, or a part of an image, that contains keystoning. I can imagine this method being used, for example, on an image of a book or rectangular package when the edges aren't parallel as they should be.

Tom straightened the poster out by doing the following:

1. He changed the name of his background layer to **Poster** and expanded his canvas 120 percent (Image ➢ Resize ➢ Canvas Size). He changed the name so the new canvas area would be transparent, rather than colored. A larger canvas gave him more room to work with.

2. He used the Rectangular Marquee tool (⬚) to select the poster (see Figure 5.24).

3. He selected Image ➢ Transform ➢ Perspective and dragged the top-right corner of the bounding box until the lines of the poster were parallel (shown on the left in Figure 5.25). Then he applied the transformation by clicking the Commit button (✔) in the options bar. He also could have pressed the Enter/Return key or double-clicked inside the bounding box.

Figure 5.25: Tom fixed the keystone effect by dragging the top corners of the bounding box until the lines were parallel (left). Now the keystoning is gone (right).

> **Note:** If you have trouble determining whether lines are parallel, create a visual crutch to help. Simply make a new layer and then select the Pencil tool (✐) from the toolbox. Select a small brush from the options bar. Hold the Shift key and drag a line near the area you are working on. The Shift key constrains the line so that it will be perfectly horizontal or vertical. Now you can use this as a reference when you apply the Perspective control. When you are finished, just trash the layer containing the vertical line.

4. Tom used the Clone Stamp tool (♒) to fill in the missing edges and applied the Levels command to correct the tonal values of the image. After he was finished, he cropped the image to its edges.

The final image is shown on the right in Figure 5.25.

Improving the Background

The background sets the mood, gives a product context, and helps add depth. Sometimes the simplest background is best. Other times a colorful, flashy background is called for. Regardless of what you use for a background, it should complement and not detract from the product.

Simplifying a Complex Background

One of the easiest ways to improve a background is to diminish its effect. Let's apply this to the wine bottles from a previous example (↪ "Separating a Product from Its Background," earlier in this chapter). As noted earlier, the art director basically liked the background but wanted it toned down.

Here's what I did after I selected the wine bottles:

1. I chose Select ➤ Inverse to make the background the active selection. I then slightly feathered this selection 2 pixels to soften the transition between the foreground and background (Select ➤ Feather).

2. The background was too dark, so I adjusted its tonal values and lightened it with the Levels command (shown on the left in Figure 5.26).

Figure 5.26: Just by applying Levels to the background, the image was improved (left). Applying a Gaussian blur made the background less distracting (right).

3. This helped, but to give the picture more depth I applied a Gaussian blur to the background (Filter ➤ Blur ➤ Gaussian Blur). I set the Radius at 13.5 pixels.

4. The label still needs selective burning and dodging, and the reflections at the top of the bottles are too harsh. I'll fix the harsh reflections later in the chapter, but as you can see on the right in Figure 5.26, simplifying the background already has significantly improved this shot.

Creating New Backgrounds

After you have isolated a product from its background, there is no reason why you can't insert any background you want. Backgrounds can come from another photograph or purely from selective Photoshop Elements' effects and a little imagination. Some of the most effective backgrounds are a combination of a real photograph and a Photoshop Elements filter or effect.

In Figure 5.27, you'll see an example of a background created using a combination of a gradient fill adjustment layer and an effect.

Figure 5.27: This background was quickly created using a gradient fill and an effect.

Here's what I did to create the new background:

1. Starting with the car that I worked on previously, I selected and removed the previous background titled **Color Fill 1** (Layer ➤ Delete Layer) and made a new gradient background by clicking the Create Adjustment Layer icon (◓) at the top of the Layers palette and choosing Gradient from the pop-up menu. (You can also select Layer ➤ New Fill Layer ➤ Gradient from the menu bar.)

2. From the various Gradient options, I chose the settings you see on the left in Figure 5.28. To find the Silver gradient, I started by clicking the drop-down arrow adjacent to the word *Gradient* in the Gradient Fill dialog box. Then, when another palette of options opened, I clicked the arrow pointing to the right. This brought up a drop-down menu with various options. I selected the one called Metals. This loaded several icons into the palette. I chose the one named Silver (the third one from the left—the name appears only when the cursor is placed on top of the icon).

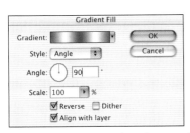

Figure 5.28: I chose the Silver gradient with the settings you see in the dialog box (left). The Layers palette (right).

3.   I clicked and dragged the gradient adjustment layer to the bottom of the Layers palette.

4.   Making sure that the **Citroen** layer was active, I applied Colorful Center from the Styles and Effects palette (choose Effects and then Image Effects from the pop-up menus). You can see on the right in Figure 5.28 that the Colorful Center effect created a duplicate layer and left the **Citroen** layer intact.

The great thing about creating backgrounds this way is that they are totally changeable. I can go back at any time and adjust the gradient adjustment layer or remove an effect (☞ "All about Layers" in the appendix). My original image remains unchanged.

Figure 5.29 illustrates how easy it is to go back and change a background created this way. I simply selected the first layer in Figure 5.28 called **Gradient Fill**; then in the Styles and Effects palette I selected Layer Styles from the pop-up menu and Complex from the other pop-up menu. Next I clicked the layer style called **Rainbow**. The Layers palette for this new image is shown on the right in Figure 5.29.

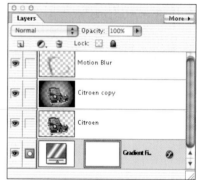

Figure 5.29: It's easy to change or add to a background if it is created with an adjustment layer (left). This is the Layers palette for the image (right).

Modifying an Existing Background

The image shown on the left in Figure 5.30 is a mistake. My digital camera fired unexpectedly. Instead of erasing the blurred image, I kept it and then used it later to create the background shown on the right.

Figure 5.30: *This was a mistake (left), but I thought the image might have potential, so I saved it. Later, I used it as the basis for this background (right).*

This is what I did to modify the image:

1. I opened the image shown on the left in Figure 5.30 and chose Enhance ➤ Auto Levels.
2. I applied the Add Noise filter (Filters ➤ Noise ➤ Add Noise). I used the following settings: Amount: 57, Distribution: Gaussian.
3. I applied the Radial Blur filter (Filters ➤ Blur ➤ Radial Blur) and used the following settings: Amount: 22, Blur Method: Zoom, Quality: Best. The results are shown in Figure 5.31.

Figure 5.31: *The image after applying the Add Noise and Radial Blur filters and with a 1368 × 1676 pixel selection.*

4. I opened a new image of a bag and noted its pixel dimensions, 1368 × 1676.

5. Now, with the **Mistake** image, I selected the Rectangular Marquee tool (⬚) from the toolbox and in the options bar I changed Style from Normal to Fixed Size. Then in the Width box I typed 1368 and in the Height box I typed 1676. I then made a selection, placing the constrained Rectangular Marquee over the area that I wanted. I made a copy of this selection (Ctrl+C / ⌘+C).

6. I pasted the **Mistake** selection into the bag image (Ctrl+V / ⌘+V). It fit perfectly. I made sure that the **Mistake** image layer was below the one containing the bag. You can easily move layers into different positions (☞ "All about Layers" in the appendix).

7. I added a drop shadow to the bag and I was done (☞ "Adding Depth," next).

Shooting Digital: Are You Sure You Want to Delete?

One of the great features of digital cameras is the capability to erase shots you don't like. A word of caution: as you've seen throughout this book, there are many ways to use a digital photo. Think before you erase an accidental shot of the pavement, because it could be used as an interesting background. Think before you erase a picture that is inherently boring but could conceivably be used in a collage. Think before you erase a bad photo of Uncle Jimmy, because the good shot of Aunt Annie next to him could be used for something else. Instead of always erasing, consider investing in more memory for both your camera and computer and building a digital library of those potentially useful "throwaways."

Adding Depth

After you've found a background, you need to give your image a sense of depth. An easy way to do this is to make a clear distinction between the foreground object and the background. Assuming you've isolated your object from the background, you can do this by creating a drop shadow or other layer style.

Drop Shadows

Drop shadows are commonly used to create a sense of depth. Here's what I did to replace the background, rotate, and add a drop shadow to the image shown in Figure 5.32.

Figure 5.32: The original digital camera shot.

1. I selected and removed the background by using the Magic Eraser (✍)
   (☞ "Separating a Product from Its Background," earlier in this chapter). I
   rotated the image to the right (Image➢ Rotate ➢ 90° Right).

2. I created a new background by clicking the Create Adjustment Layer icon (●)
   at the top of the Layers palette and choosing Solid Color from the pop-up
   menu. I chose white. (Alternatively, you can choose Layer ➢ New Fill Layer ➢
   Solid Color from the menu bar.)

3. With the layer called **Bag** selected, I chose a drop shadow from the Styles and
   Effects palette (Layer Styles from the first pop-up menu and Drop Shadows
   from second pop-up menu). I applied a drop shadow called Soft Edge by simply
   clicking its icon. After the drop shadow was applied, an *f* symbol appeared in
   the **Bag** layer in the Layers palette. I double-clicked the *f*, which opened the
   Style Settings dialog box. (Choosing Layer ➢ Layer Style ➢ Layer Settings also
   brings up this dialog box.) From this box, I tweaked the drop shadow by using
   the settings shown on the left in Figure 5.33. The Layers palette is shown on the
   right. The final image is shown in Figure 5.34.

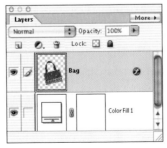

*Figure 5.33: These are the settings I used for my drop shadow (left). The Layers palette
shows the new background and layer with the drop shadow layer style attached (right).*

Figure 5.34: The final image.

Outer Glow

You can use other layer styles such as Outer Glow to also make a distinction between a product and its background, as you can see on the left in Figure 5.35.

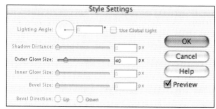

Figure 5.35: Use Outer Glow styles to add depth to your image (left). These are settings I used for my Simple Outer Glow (right).

To add depth with Outer Glow, I started with the previous example and then did the following:

1. I changed the color of the background from white to black by clicking on the layer thumbnail in the **Color Fill** layer and choosing black from the Color Picker.

2. I deleted the drop shadow effect from the layer called **Bag** by selecting that layer and then choosing Layer ➤ Layer Style ➤ Clear Layer Style from the menu bar.

3. I applied an Outer Glow from the Styles and Effects palette to the layer called **Bag** (choose Layer Styles from the first pop-up menu, then Outer Glows from the second pop-up menu). I chose the Outer Glow called Simple. I used the settings shown on the right in Figure 5.35.

Creating Lighting Effects

Effective lighting can give a product shot dimension and drama. If the interesting lighting isn't there to begin with, you can use Photoshop Elements' Lighting Effects filter to create it. Figure 5.36 shows how lighting effects can alter an original shot.

Figure 5.36: The lighting is even but uninteresting (left). With the help of the Lighting Effects filter, the image is more dramatic (right).

This is what I did to create the effective lighting:

1. I selected the Lighting Effects filter (Filter ➢ Render ➢ Lighting Effects).
2. I applied the settings shown in Figure 5.37 and clicked OK.

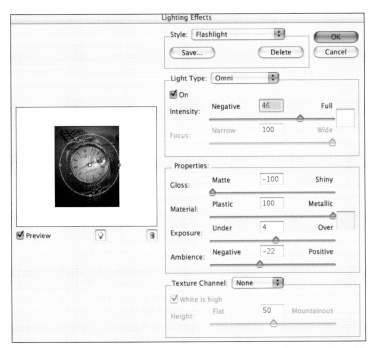

Figure 5.37: These are the settings I used for the Lighting Effects filter.

Softening Highlights and Glare

On the left in Figure 5.38 is a close-up of the wine bottles from a previous example (☞ "Separating a Product from Its Background," earlier in this chapter). You can tell that the light source for the photograph was direct and harsh and not the soft, diffused lighting often used by professional photographers. Fortunately, it is easy to fix this in Photoshop Elements.

Figure 5.38: The reflections are harsh and need to be softened (left). With the help of the Blur tool, the reflections are softer, more diffused (right).

All I did to get the results shown on the right in Figure 5.38 was select the Blur tool (◊) from the toolbox and then click and drag it several times over the spots of light. (The Blur tool shares the same spot on the toolbar as the Sharpen and Smudge tools. Shift+R will cycle through the three tools.) I selected a soft-edged brush in the options bar and left the Pressure set at 50 percent. The Mode was Normal.

Adding a New Label

Will Rutledge is a professional photographer and the manager of QVC Inc.'s photo studio. QVC is an electronics retailer mostly known for its cable-shopping channel. As you can imagine, Will shoots a lot of products. He mostly uses a high-end digital camera and he often uses Photoshop to fix a photo because something isn't quite right with the product. Take, for example, the photo shown on the left in Figure 5.39. One of the lipstick cases didn't have a label. However, Will had another, similar shot of a different lipstick case that did. He used Photoshop to copy and paste the label from one photo to the other. Although he used Photoshop to do the job, everything he did can be done in Photoshop Elements as well.

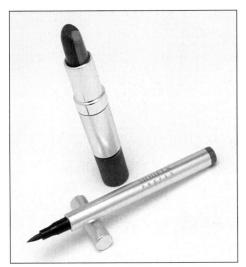

Figure 5.39: The vertical lipstick case didn't have a label and it needed one (left). Will used the Polygonal Lasso tool to select the label from an image of another case (right).

Here's what Will did to fix the photo:

1. With both images open, Will used the Polygonal Lasso tool ( ) to select the label from the image that had one. The right side of Figure 5.39 shows a close-up of the lipstick case and Will's selection.

> **Note:** The Polygonal Lasso tool is similar to the Magnetic Lasso tool; however, you manually set endpoints for each straight segment ("Selection Tools" in the appendix).

2. He then copied (Ctrl+C / ⌘ +C) and pasted (Ctrl+V / ⌘ +V) the selection onto the second image. He used the Move tool ( ) from the toolbox to position the label in place. (See Figure 5.40.)

3. Will then used the Eraser tool ( ) to erase parts of the pasted label so it blended nicely.

The final image is shown on the right in Figure 5.40.

Figure 5.40: Will copied and pasted the label on this image (left) and then used the Move tool to put it in place. The pasted label blended nicely after Will erased parts of it (right). (Photo by Will Rutledge. Copyright 2000 QVC. Courtesy of Stacey Schiefflin of Models Prefer Cosmetics.)

Making a Product Smile

Will Rutledge also took the product shot shown on the left in Figure 5.41, this time for QVC's annual report. He was given creative license to make the image fun, and that is what Will did to make the image shown on the right.

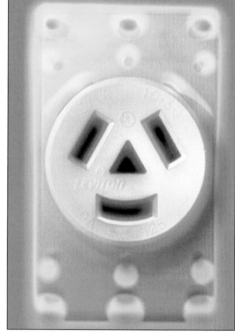

Figure 5.41: A typical shot of an electrical outlet (left). A not-so-typical shot of an electrical outlet, helped along by the 3D filter (right). (Photo by Will Rutledge. Copyright 2000 QVC.)

1. Will used the Lasso tool (🔵) to select one of the rectangular slots.

2. He copied and pasted his selection onto a separate layer. He rotated the slot until it was horizontal by choosing Image ➤ Transform ➤ Free Transform (see Figure 5.42).

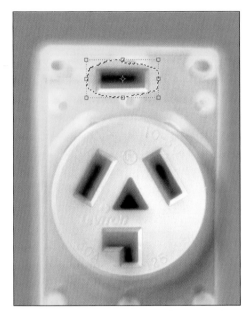

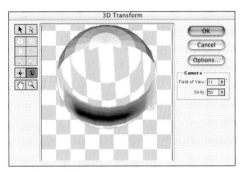

Figure 5.42: After copying and pasting the vertical slot, Will used a Transform command to rotate it to a horizontal position (left). The 3D filter mapped Will's selection to a sphere. When he rotated the sphere, he got a smile (right).

3. With the layer containing the pasted, rotated slot selected, he opened the 3D filter (Filter ➤ Render ➤ 3D Transform).

4. In the 3D Transform filter dialog box, Will selected the Sphere tool (⊕) and drew a circle tightly around the rectangular slot in the preview window. He then clicked the Trackball tool (⊛) and in the preview window rotated the ball until he got a smile. Then he clicked OK. The result is shown on the right in Figure 5.42.

5. Will used the Move tool (➤⊹) from the toolbox to position his smile in place. He then used the Eraser tool (✐) and Clone Stamp tool (⚖) to make the smile completely replace the old slot.

Who says life always has to be so serious?

Simplifying a Product Shot

Converting a complex product shot into a simple line drawing can be useful for brochures or instructional material. To simplify the shot shown on the left in Figure 5.43, I applied the Photocopy filter with the foreground color set to black (Filter ➤ Sketch ➤ Photocopy). I also set the Detail at 14 and the Darkness at 33. The result is shown on the right.

 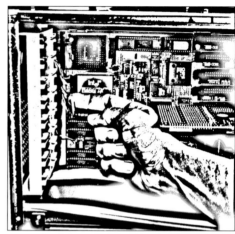

Figure 5.43: The original photo (left). A much simpler image after applying the Photocopy filter (right). (Photo by Maurice Martell)

Shooting Digital: Creating Your Own Mini Photo Studio

It doesn't take a lot of money or equipment to set up a mini photo studio in your office or home. With the following setup, you'll be able to shoot perfect photos of small objects such as books, coins, jewelry, small appliances, or other objects that you want to place on an online auction or prepare for a flyer or ad:

- A digital camera
- A white, seamless backdrop and a means to hold it
- Two diffused light sources

Look at the following diagram. The seamless paper is draped over a table. It's important for it to drape smoothly, or it will catch light and create unwanted shadows. Also notice how the object to be photographed is set away from the edge of the paper. This also keeps shadows at a minimum. Two diffused lights are enough for most situations. You can diffuse a light source with a sheet of thick, translucent plastic or a window screen. Move the lights around and try to make the light fall as evenly on the product as possible.

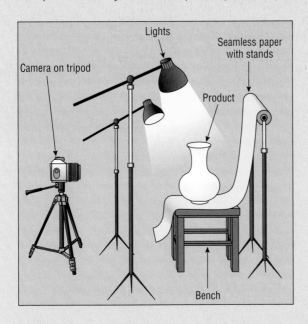

When you shoot, experiment with different angles. But remember to show as much of the product as you can. The shot should be informative as well as interesting.

Where can you find the equipment for this mini studio? Professional photography supply houses all carry the seamless paper, lights, and stands. Go to my website (**www.shooting-digital.com**) for more resources.

Making Photo-Realistic Composites

Composites are like tapestries woven together from the fabric of more than one source. They can be relatively simple to create (adding a missing person to a group shot) or complex (combining many images from many sources). Creating a photo-realistic composite tests nearly all of your Photoshop Elements skills, from selecting to transforming, from cloning to managing multiple layers. But when you're finished, you'll have a single image visually richer than the sum of its individual parts.

6

Chapter Contents

Adding Yourself (or Anyone) to a Group Shot

I'm not in the shot shown on the left in Figure 6.1, but I wanted to be. It was one of those typical situations when old friends gather and suddenly someone says, "Hey, let's get a group shot of *everyone!*"

Figure 6.1: I wanted to be in this shot (left), but someone had to take the picture. My wife took this second shot with me in it (right).

I had my digital camera but no tripod and I couldn't find anything high enough to place the camera on for a self-timer shot. Instead, I took a shot of the group and then my wife took a shot with me in it (shown on the right in Figure 6.1).

I left my spot open in the first shot so I could simply copy and paste myself from one image into the other. Here's how I did it:

1. I opened both digital images. Starting with the one that didn't include me (I'll call this Image 1), I adjusted Levels to make the image look lighter, using Enhance ➢ Adjust Lighting ➢ Levels.

2. I turned to the second shot, the one with me in it. I'll call this Image 2. I wanted the exact same Levels settings applied to Image 2 so the tonal values of my upper body would match those of the other people in Image 1. I could have noted my Input Levels settings in my Levels controls in Image 1, and with Levels open for Image 2, typed them into the Levels Input boxes. Instead, I used a neat shortcut that I learned from Will Rutledge at QVC, Inc. With Image 2 active, I pressed Ctrl+Alt+L / ⌘ +Option+L. This shortcut automatically applied the same adjusted Levels setting from Image 1 to Image 2, and I got exactly the results I wanted. Cool. I could have continued applying Levels this way to an entire batch of similar images, which would have been a real time-saver. Another simple way to do this—suggested by my trusty assistant Ed Schwartz— is to use an adjustment layer for Levels in Image 1 and then drag the adjustment layer over to Image 2 to get the same adjustment (➣ "Adjustment and Fill Layers" in the appendix).

3. OK, now on Image 2 I used the Lasso tool (⟨⟩) to make a loose selection, as shown in Figure 6.2. At this point I wasn't precise, and in fact, I purposely included other areas of the image to help me position my pasted selection.

Figure 6.2: I made a loose selection with the Lasso tool and copied the selection.

4. I pasted my selection (Ctrl+V / ⌘+V) into Image 1, and Photoshop Elements placed it automatically into its own layer. From the Layers palette, I set the Opacity to 50 percent so I could see part of the underlying image. I then used the Move tool (✥) to position the selection into place. I used part of my friend Joe's shoulder that I had included in my pasted selection as a reference (Figure 6.3).

Figure 6.3: I set my layer Opacity to 50 percent so I could see the underlying image.

> **Note:** What is the difference between the Paste and Paste Into Selection commands found on the main menu bar under Edit? Let's say you select an expanse of sky by using the Rectangular Marquee selection tool ([⬚]) and then copy the selection. If you Paste this copy into another layer or image, the entire rectangular selection will be pasted. In contrast, using Paste Into Selection enables you to set different boundaries. Before you paste, say you make a selection on the layer or image with, for example, the Elliptical Marquee selection tool (○). Then when you paste the rectangular selection from before by using the Paste Into Selection command, the rectangular selection will appear bounded and defined by the selected circle. You can use any of the selection tools and make any shape. Paste Into Selection will use that selection as the parameter—or mask, if you will—for your paste.

5.   Next came the tricky part. I reset my layer Opacity to 100 percent and used the Eraser tool (⬠) with a Hard Round 19 pixels brush to remove the superfluous areas around my head and shoulders. Then I magnified my image from 100 percent to 300 percent and used a Hard Round 9 pixels brush to erase any leftover tidbits. At one point, when I was working on the area to my left, I momentarily changed the layer Opacity back to 50 percent so I could tell where the face of the man in front of me ended and my neck and shoulder started. I finished with a Soft Round 13 pixels brush, brushing the edges of my pasted selection lightly to make them blend into the background.

6.   I didn't bring my legs over from Image 1, so I just used the Clone Stamp tool (⬠) to clone the shadow that was already there in Image 2. The final image is shown in Figure 6.4.

Figure 6.4: Now the group is complete.

This composite was easy to make because Image 1 and Image 2 were so similar. Creating a realistic composite is more difficult when you are working with shots taken at different times, with different lighting, with different film, or at different pixel resolutions. The next section shows you how to work with images of different resolutions. Also, later in this chapter you'll learn more about keeping composites in mind while taking pictures (⬠ "Shooting Digital: Creating Realistic-Looking Composites").

Note: Copying, pasting, and other tasks associated with creating composites can take up a lot of memory, and at some point the performance of Photoshop Elements could become noticeably compromised. If this happens, you can free up more memory by using the Clear command (Edit ➤ Clear). You'll have a choice of which item type or buffer you want to clear: Undo History, Clipboard Contents, or All. If the item type or buffer is dimmed, it just means it is already empty. You should use the Clear command only as a last resort because it can't be undone.

Combining Different Resolutions

Look at Figure 6.5. You can't easily tell by looking at the printed page, but the image on the left was taken with a 6 megapixel digital camera that produced an image with a pixel resolution of 2000 × 3008. The image on the right has a pixel resolution of only 1000 × 1504. Figure 6.6 shows what happens when I select the girls from the larger file and paste them into the smaller one. The selection from the larger image "swamps" the smaller target image.

Figure 6.5: The image on the left has a pixel resolution of 2000 × 3008, while the target image on the right has a resolution of only 1000 × 1504.

Figure 6.6: This is what happens when a selection from the larger file is pasted on the smaller one.

How can I scale the selection to fit? Here are two ways:

A. Scale the entire larger image file down *before* selecting and pasting to the smaller image.

B. Use the Resize command (Image ➢ Resize ➢ Scale) *after* selecting and pasting part of the larger image into the smaller one.

I'll get to option B in a minute. If you choose option A, here are the steps:

1. With both images open, select the smaller, target image by clicking anywhere on the image window with your cursor.

2. Determine the pixel resolution of the smaller, target image. Do this by choosing Image ➢ Resize ➢ Image Size from the menu bar and noting the Width *or* Height in the dialog box. Figure 6.7 shows the Image Size dialog box. (You need only the width or the height, not both. And you don't need to note the number next to Resolution; this is relevant mostly when printing.) You can also get the image size by right-clicking the top outside edge of the image window (Windows) or by Option+clicking in the box next to the percentage readout, at the bottom left of the image window (Mac). You can also get the image size by going to the Info palette (Window ➢ Info).

3. Select the larger image. Choose Image ➢ Resize ➢ Image Size from the menu bar. Enter a Width *or* Height value as determined by the smaller image. If Constrain Proportions is selected, Photoshop Elements will automatically calculate the corresponding width or height. Make sure the Resample Image check box is also selected in the Image Size palette. If you leave the sampling method at its default Bicubic setting, you'll get good results. You might get better results if you select Bicubic Sharper from the pop-up menu. Bicubic Sharper preserves crisp edge transitions and works best when you are resampling *down*. Bicubic Smoother, another option, suppresses image noise and is a good choice when you resample *up* to a larger pixel resolution.

4. Click OK in the Image Resize dialog.

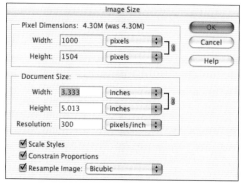

Figure 6.7: The Image Size dialog box. Make note of the Width or Height dimensions. When resizing, make sure the Resample Image check box is selected.

After your larger image has been resampled to match the target image, you can use any of the various selection tools to select the part of the image you want to copy and paste. (I used the Lasso tool to select the two girls.) Next you can copy (Ctrl+C / ⌘+C) and paste (Ctrl+V / ⌘+V) onto the target image. Alternatively, you can Ctrl+click and hold (⌘+click and hold on Mac) and drag the copied selection to the target image. Either way, a copy of the selection will appear on a layer of its own. You can use the Move tool (⊕) or arrow keys to precisely position the selection. If you need to tweak the size of the selection to get it just right, use the method described next (Image ➤ Resize ➤ Scale). Just be sure the layer containing the pasted image is selected. Figure 6.8 shows the final composite.

Figure 6.8: The final composite after matching resolutions.

A word of warning: don't inadvertently close and save the resized image. You'll end up throwing away a lot useful image data.

If you choose option B, use these steps:

1. On the larger image, select and copy (Ctrl+C / ⌘ +C) the desired element(s).

2. Paste (Ctrl+V / ⌘ +V) or Ctrl+click / ⌘ +click, hold, and drag the copied selection to the target image. It's likely, because of the discrepancy in image size, that your pasted selection will block most or all of the target image, as it did in my example in Figure 6.6.

3. Choose Image ➢ Resize ➢ Scale from the menu bar. Normally you could simply point your cursor to one of the bounding boxes located at the corners of the selection and click, hold, and drag the selection to a desired size. Because the pasted selection is so large relative to the target image, the bounding boxes are often not visible. Instead, go to the options bar (Figure 6.9). Point your cursor to the space between the Width and Height boxes and click on the linked chain. This will lock the width and height together, maintain a fixed aspect ratio, and thereby prevent distortion. Now type in a percentage in either box. Start with 25 percent. Because you've locked the width and height together, you need to type in only one box. You might need to type in a lower percentage depending on the size of the pasted selection.

4. At some point, with enough reduction, the bounding boxes at the edges of the selection will become visible. You can now point your cursor at one of the boxes and click, hold, and drag the selection to the desired size. Hold the Shift key when you drag to constrain the dimensions. You can also move the selection into place by placing your cursor in the middle of the selection and then clicking, holding, and dragging. After you are finished, select the Commit button in the options bar or hit the Enter/Return key.

Figure 6.9: The Scale options bar. Note the chained link between the Width and Height boxes. Select this link to maintain a fixed aspect ratio and prevent distortion when you enter percentage values.

Swapping Kids

Children will be children. Some children like to be tossed up in the air, and others
don't. Photographer Maggie Hallahan couldn't get the kid on the left in Figure 6.10 to
be thrown in the air, look at the camera, and smile all at once. What a surprise! But
everything else about the picture was fine, so Maggie tried another tack. She shot the
other photo shown in Figure 6.10, this time with an older child who smiled but wasn't
keen on being thrown in the air. Maggie's client was PJA, an advertising and marketing
agency in San Francisco.

*Figure 6.10: Everything about this picture was fine, except for the kid (left), who was great
but didn't like being thrown in the air. A second picture (right) provides a replacement child
for the composite. (Photos by Maggie Hallahan)*

Back at the computer, PJA Photoshop pro Bretton Newsom went to work with
Photoshop, putting the best parts of Maggie's two shots together. I talked with Bretton
before he finished the final composite, and he agreed to walk me through the steps
he'd taken so far on a low-resolution file. It should be noted that Bretton, like most
pros, works with the full version of Photoshop. However, just about everything he did
in this example can be duplicated in Photoshop Elements.

Here are the steps Bretton took to create the composite:

1.   He used the Clone Stamp tool (⚒) to remove the child in the first image (shown
     on the left side of Figure 6.11).

2. He went to the image of the smiling older kid and created a precise selection around the child by using a Quick Mask—a function not available in Photoshop Elements. Fortunately, the program has a roughly equivalent tool: the Selection Brush tool (⟋). For more on using the Selection Brush tool and other selection tools, see the appendix. After the kid was selected, Bretton copied the selection and pasted it into its own layer in the first image, as shown on the right in Figure 6.11. He used the Move tool (⤢) to position the pasted selection into the outstretched arms of "mom."

Figure 6.11: Bretton used the Clone Stamp tool to remove the first child (left). After selecting and copying the second child, Bretton pasted the smiling child into the outstretched arms of "mom" (right).

3. As you can see in Figure 6.11, the woman's arm is covered by the pasted image of the child. So Bretton copied and pasted part of the woman's arm and shoulder, as shown on the left in Figure 6.12. He placed the layer containing the arm and shoulder above the layer containing the smiling child, which put the arm and hand in the correct position relative to the child. You can see Bretton's Layers palette in Figure 6.12. (Alternatively, he could have selectively used the Eraser tool on the child to reveal the woman's left arm.)

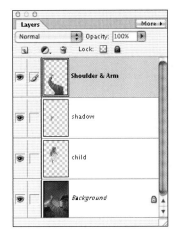

Figure 6.12: Bretton made a copy of the woman's arm and shoulder and pasted it onto its own layer (left). Bretton's Layers palette is shown to the right. Note that the arm and hand layer is above the layer containing the child.

4. As a final step, Bretton added a slight shadow on top of the child's dress, as if it came from the outstretched arm. The "final" image is shown in Figure 6.13.

Figure 6.13: The final composite.

After the client approved this low-resolution "comp," Bretton worked on a high-resolution copy of both images to make a perfect version suitable for print.

Note: Photo-realistic composites make compelling narratives. Mark Ulriksen, a freelance illustrator for *The New Yorker* magazine who is best known for whimsical portraits often derived from photo composites, says that when creating such a composite, you should think of your Photoshop Elements' image window as a stage and all the images you want to use as your props. Let's say you just came back from a family vacation to the Grand Canyon. Your "props" might include shots of the Grand Canyon, the kids, a red-tailed squirrel, and your favorite hamburger stand. You might start by using the Grand Canyon shot as the background. Then pick another image (or prop, if you will) that represents the most memorable part of your vacation. That great meal, the squirrel that ate from your kids' hands, whatever. Place that image in front of the background and make it big so it takes on significance and importance. Now place the other images, or props, in relationship to the dominant image or prop. Use Photoshop Elements' transform tools to play with the size of each image, and use the Move tool to change the relationships between the objects. Experiment and, most importantly, have fun.

Expanding Your Image

Figure 6.14 is also Maggie's work. This image is another composite consisting of two shots taken in Hawaii for PJA: the man in one photograph, and the beach in another. Once again it was Bretton Newsom who did the Photoshop work of copying and pasting the man onto the beach.

Figure 6.14: To extend the edge of a composite such as this one, you'll need special techniques to make the addition look realistic. (Photo by Maggie Hallahan)

I'd like to use this image to illustrate a couple of techniques that Bretton uses when he needs to extend the edge of an image and make it look realistic. This situation comes up often when creating photo-realistic composites, so these techniques are very useful:

1. He uses the Rectangular Marquee tool (▢) to select an area that's equivalent to the size of the needed addition. To see the size of your selection, use the Info palette (Window ➤ Info). The numbers in the lower-right corner actively display the measurements as you adjust the marquee. Using the Info palette's More pop-up menu, you can change the measurements to display in pixels, inches, centimeters, points, picas, or as a percentage. You can also change the measurements by clicking the crosshair icon next to the X Y cursor coordinates in the Info palette. Figure 6.15 shows the rectangular selection, as well as the Info palette indicating that the selection size is 1 × 6.480 inches. You can also set the size of the marquee in the selection tool options bar. Just choose Fixed Size from the Style list box and type the numerical values in the Width and Height boxes.

Figure 6.15: Start with a rectangular selection of the area you want to extend (left). Use the Info palette (right) to see the size of the selection marquee.

2. He then copies (Ctrl+C / ⌘+C) and pastes (Ctrl+V / ⌘+V) the selection. It is automatically placed onto its own layer.

3. To expand the canvas area, he chooses Image ➤ Resize ➤ Canvas Size. This opens the dialog box shown in Figure 6.16. He moves the Anchor point to the leftmost center position and adds an inch (or whatever is needed) to the Width box. For this example, he left the Height alone. Generally, he adds a little more area than is called for and crops away the extra when he is done.

4. Using the Move tool (▶+), he slides the pasted selection over, as shown in Figure 6.17.

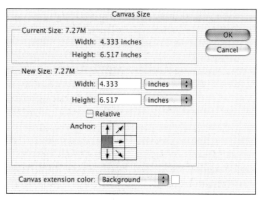

Figure 6.16: Use the Canvas Size dialog box to extend the edges of your canvas.

Figure 6.17: Use the Move tool to slide the selection over.

5. At this point, he uses either of these two methods to finish the image:

- He uses the Eraser tool (⌀) with a small, soft-edged brush to shave a small amount off the edges of the adjacent sides. He doesn't drag the Eraser tool by hand along the edge as you might imagine; the tool is only as precise as your hand is steady. Instead, he holds the Shift key and then clicks and releases with the Eraser tool on one of the edges at the very top of the image. Next he moves the cursor straight down to the bottom of the image and, still holding the Shift key, clicks once again. The Eraser tool erases everything between the two clicks in a straight line the width of the selected brush. Then he does exactly the same thing to the adjacent side, remembering to select the layer that contains that side (Figure 6.18). When he uses the Move tool or, for more precise control, the arrow keys, to slide the two sides together, they fit like a hand in a glove. In the spots where the blend is noticeable, he uses the Clone Stamp tool (⎙), cloning and stamping in horizontal sweeps to spread pixels of similar values (Figure 6.18).

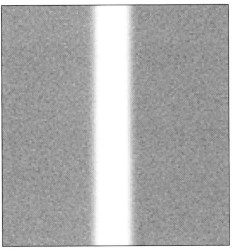

Figure 6.18: Slightly erasing the edges with a soft-edged brush makes them fit together seamlessly (left). Now the edges slide together like a hand into a glove (right). In spots where the match isn't perfect, the Clone Stamp tool will finish the job.

- His alternate method is to flip the pasted selection horizontally using Image ➤ Rotate ➤ Flip Layer Horizontal. Then the edge of the pasted selection mirrors the edge of the original image and lines up almost perfectly (Figure 6.19). Again, where the match isn't perfect, he uses the Clone Stamp tool to fix it.

Figure 6.19: When the pasted selection is flipped horizontally, the edges are mirrors of each other and fit almost perfectly. Again, the Clone Stamp tool fixes anything that isn't perfect.

Seamlessly Pasting

One of the biggest challenges in composite making is pasting a selection seamlessly into another image so it looks natural without a halo or jagged edges. It's a lot easier when you are pasting a selection into a busy background, as I did in the first example in this chapter, but more difficult when you are pasting to an area of continuous tone, such as a sky.

I use one method with pretty good success. I'll demonstrate by selecting, copying, and pasting the Doggie Diner head from the image on the left in Figure 6.20 to the shot shown on the right.

Figure 6.20: The two components of my composite.

Figure 6.21 shows a close-up of what happens if I simply make a selection, copy it, and paste it into the street shot.

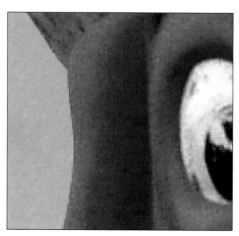

Figure 6.21: By using a simple copy and paste, I get the jagged edges shown here.

Now I'll try something different:

1. I make a selection just as before, using the Magic Wand selection tool (✎). One click on the white background with a Tolerance of 15 pretty much does it, except I'll use the Lasso tool (⚲) to select some of the white areas in the Doggie Diner's hat that were missed by the Magic Wand.

2. I reverse my selection by using Select ➤ Inverse (Ctrl+Shift+I / ⌘ +Shift+I) and shrink it by 2 pixels (Select ➤ Modify ➤ Contract). This tightens up my selection and reduces the chance that I'll copy unwanted background areas.

3. I add a 3-pixel feather (Select ➤ Inverse, then Select ➤ Feather), as shown in Figure 6.22.

Figure 6.22: The Feather Selection dialog box

4. I copy (Ctrl+C / ⌘ +C) and paste (Ctrl+V / ⌘ +V) the selectionon on top of Telegraph Hill. I use the Move tool (➤) to position it where I want. Because I slightly shrank my selection and feathered it, the edges of the Doggie Diner head now blend more naturally into the new background.

5. As you can see in Figure 6.23, the paste is almost seamless. Where it is not, I can use the Eraser tool (⌀) with a combination of both hard-edged and soft-edged brushes to make it perfect.

Figure 6.23: Now the Doggie Diner head looks like it's always been on top of Telegraph Hill. Even on closer examination (right), the deception is barely visible.

Cloning Elements from Multiple Images

Up to now, I've shown you mostly select, copy, and paste techniques to combine images. With some images it's just as effective to use the Clone Stamp tool to create photo-realistic composites. For some people, "painting" images with this tool is more intuitive and satisfying than pasting.

Take the screen shot in Figure 6.24. The images were all taken with the same camera, around the same time of day, against a similar background. Using the Clone Stamp tool to combine parts of these images is easy because I don't need to be precise. It would be more difficult if the backgrounds were significantly different. In that case, selecting, copying, and pasting would be the way to go.

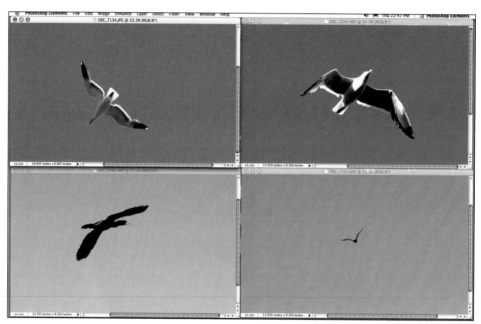

Figure 6.24: Combining birds from similar shots is easy with the Clone Stamp tool.

This is what I did to come up with the composite:

1. I opened the four image files. (To view all your images side by side, choose Window ➤ Images ➤ Tile.)

2. I selected one of the bird photos as a target image. Because I wanted each cloned bird to go on its own layer, I created three new layers: Layer ➤ New ➤ Layer.

3. Next I selected one of the other three bird images and selected the Clone Stamp tool from the toolbar (⚓). I picked a Soft Round 100 pixels brush from the options bar and placed my cursor over the bird. Then I held the Alt/Option key and clicked on the bird. This defined my source point.

4. After I had my source point defined, I selected my target image. In the Layers palette I made sure I was working on one of the new layers. Then I placed my cursor over the target image window, roughly in the area I wanted to add the new bird. I clicked, held, and painted. After I was finished, I selected another

image, containing another bird, and repeated the process. On the target image, in the Layers palette, I made sure to select yet another new layer, thereby keeping each bird on its own layer.

5. After I finished cloning the birds, I went back and fine-tuned my composite. I used the Eraser tool to define the edges of some of the birds. I used a Transform command to slightly reduce the size of one of the birds (Image ➤ Resize ➤ Scale). I slightly rotated the orientation of one of the birds (Image ➤ Transform ➤ Free Transform). I could easily do all this because each bird was on its own layer. Figure 6.25 shows the final version.

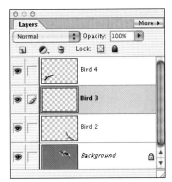

Figure 6.25: The resulting composite (left); the Layers palette (right). Note each cloned bird is on its own layer.

> **Note:** If you want to clone within the same image, it's often useful to clone onto a separate layer. To do this, first create a new layer (Layer ➤ New ➤ Layer). Select the layer containing the pixels you want to clone. Select the Clone Stamp tool from the toolbar and—this is very important—go to the options bar and select the box next to Use All Layers. Define your source point by holding the Alt/Option key and clicking. Then, in the Layers palette, select the new layer. Now when you click and hold while painting the image window, the cloned part will appear on its own layer. You can move it around separately, or remove it without damaging the original underlying image. This also holds true with the Healing Brush tool. Select "Use All Layers" from the Healing Brush tool's option bar to "heal" onto a separate layer.

Pre-visualizing a Scene

Photo-realistic composites are extremely important in the world of architecture. Architects can use a composite not only to show a client what a potential building or remodel will look like, but also to help convince a design review board to approve a project by showing the effect that it will have on a neighborhood.

David Mlodzik is one of those rare architects who is not only versed in design but is also computer-literate and adept with high-end digital imaging. A significant part of his business is providing other architects and the construction community with design visualization and graphic services.

Figure 6.26 shows one of his projects for a Hilton hotel. At the time David started work on the project, the hotel didn't even exist. He took the design done by the San Francisco firm RYS Architects, and used a 3D rendering and animation program to create several views of the hotel. Then he turned to Photoshop. Although he worked in the full version of Photoshop, everything he did is possible using Photoshop Elements.

Here are the steps he took to create an image of the hotel:

1. He scanned the site photograph shown in Figure 6.26.

Figure 6.26: The site photograph. (Photo by David Mlodzik)

2. He copied and pasted the hotel into a layer with the site photograph. The rendering had a black background, which David removed by using the Magic Wand selection tool (✎) and then cutting to transparency.

3. David applied a slight Gaussian blur to the hotel rendering to make it look more realistic (Filters ➤ Blur ➤ Gaussian Blur).

4. As you can see on the left in Figure 6.27, the hotel sits in front of the McDonald's in the site photograph. David created a copy of the background layer containing the site photo, and in that layer he erased the areas shown at the right in Figure 6.27 by using the Eraser tool (✐) and various selection tools to select and delete.

Figure 6.27: When it's pasted in (left), the hotel sits in front. David used various erasing techniques to make room for the hotel (right).

As you can see on the left in Figure 6.28, the hotel looks like it has always been there.

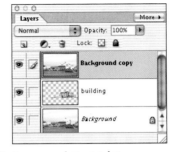

Figure 6.28: The final composite (left). David's Layers palette (right).

Note: If you want to create a composite from several images and are willing to give up some control, try using Photomerge: File ➤ New ➤ Photomerge. It's fast, it's easy, and it's fun. I'll tell you more about this Photoshop Elements plug-in later in the book (☜ Chapter 8).

Shooting Digital: Creating Realistic-Looking Composites

A while back I got a call from a company in Sweden that wanted a group shot of their board of directors for an annual report. The only problem was that one of the directors, futurist Paul Saffo, lived in California and wasn't about to make the long trip just for a photo opportunity. Would I shoot a picture of Saffo here, and they'd Photoshop him into the group later?

When you attempt to come up with a photo-realistic composite as I did for this one, there are several things to consider. Ideally, all the images should be shot with the same kind of camera and lens and from the same perspective. In my case, I had to rent the same kind of lens they used in Sweden. Unless you want to spend a lot of time trying to match the film grain or the resolution of the digital file, use the same type of film, or if using a digital camera, use the same resolution. As you can see in the following picture, it worked out just fine. And neither Saffo nor, for that matter, I, had to endure a long plane ride.

Exteriors and Interiors

If you are selling, renting, or swapping a building, you'll be amazed at all the things Photoshop Elements can do to help bring out desirable features and diminish or remove detractive ones. Even if you aren't in the real estate business and just appreciate a good picture, the techniques you learn in this chapter will be extremely useful.

7

Chapter Contents

Straightening a Slanted Looking Facade

Look at just about any real estate magazine or newspaper section and you'll see photos of buildings with sides that appear to converge rather than remain parallel. This is an effect called *keystoning*, and it occurs when the plane of the camera and the plane of the building are not parallel to each other. You already encountered a variation of this phenomenon earlier in the book, in Chapter 5, when you saw a poster on a wall that was shot at an angle.

You can avoid keystoning by positioning your camera so that it is level with the plane of the building. However, this isn't always possible, and Figure 7.1 illustrates my point. I shot it with a Canon Digital Rebel aimed up from the sidewalk. Notice how the pillars appear to converge when in reality they are parallel. In some photographs keystoning isn't bothersome. But in others it can be so extreme that disorients the viewer and leaves an impression that something is profoundly wrong with the building. Fortunately, it's not hard to fix shots like this with Photoshop Elements and the Perspective command (Image ➤ Transform ➤ Perspective).

Figure 7.1: The pillars of this building appear to converge.

Here's what I did to straighten the building:

1. I copied the background layer containing the building (Layer ➢ Duplicate Layer). I turned the visibility of my original background layer off so it wouldn't confuse me later when I applied the Perspective command. (You can turn a layer's visibility off by deselecting the eye icon in the leftmost side of the Layers palette.) I created a copy for a couple of reasons: first, I wanted to keep my original image intact, and second, Transform commands aren't an option when you are working on a background layer.

2. After duplicating the layer, I made sure all of my image fit on the screen and was visible by double-clicking the Hand tool ().

3. I then selected View ➢ Grid to give me a series of 90-degree vertical references. The grid makes it a lot easier to determine when the lines of the building are straight. Figure 7.2 shows the grid, which I customized (as described in the following Note). Using the grid is an alternative to another method I described earlier in the book, when I used the Pencil tool to draw a 90-degree reference line on a separate layer (➣ "Fixing Keystoning" in Chapter 5).

Figure 7.2: A grid provides a series of 90-degree lines, which I can use as reference points when I try to straighten the building.

Note: To change the pattern and color of the grid, choose Edit ➢ Preferences ➢ Grid (in OS X, choose Application ➢ Preferences ➢ Grid). You can select a preset color or a custom color. You can choose solid, dashed, or dotted lines. You can also vary the spacing of the major grid lines and the frequency of minor grid lines.

4. I selected the Perspective command (Image ➤ Transform ➤ Perspective) and kept the default Transform settings found in the options bar. In the Transform options bar, Rotate ( ) selects the Rotate transform, Scale ( ) selects the Scale transform, and Skew ( ) selects the Skew transform. You can also select Transform commands from the Transform pop-up menu. To display this menu in Windows, click the right mouse button anywhere in the image window. On a Mac, hold down the Control key and click anywhere in the image window.

5. I dragged the top right corner of the bounding box outward until the pillars were parallel.

6. When I was finished, I clicked the Commit button (✔) in the options bar. You can alternatively press Enter/Return.

To better illustrate how the Perspective command works, I'll give you an example of using it in the wrong way. On the left in Figure 7.3, you can see what happens when I place the pointer on the bounding box handle in the upper right and click and drag it inward. On the right, you can see what happens when I change the perspective by dragging the opposite way.

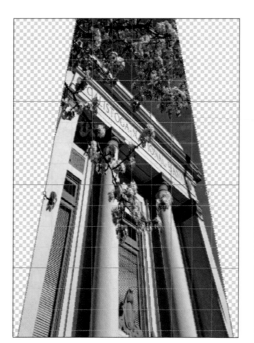

Figure 7.3: The image on the left shows what happens when I drag the bounding box inward. The image on the right shows what happens when I drag the bounding box too far the other way. Notice that I've expanded the image window, as signified by the gray. Now the bounding boxes are visible.

Figure 7.4 shows the correct adjustment, as confirmed by the vertical grid lines. In the second and third attempt it was necessary for me to slightly expand my image window. I did this by placing my cursor over the lower-right corner of the image window and clicking and dragging to the right. This made it possible to see the perspective control bounding boxes even as I dragged them beyond the edges of my image.

Figure 7.4: By aligning the sides of the pillars with the grid lines, I can see that this is about right.

Transforming a Kitchen

When the real estate market is hot, Jeanne Zimmermann shoots hundreds of photos a month with a digital camera. She documents property from both an indoor perspective and an outdoor one. She shoots big buildings and small buildings, commercial and residential. As soon as she is finished shooting, the images are quickly downloaded into her computer and prepared for newspaper ads, flyers, and the Web. (Her website is **www.loftsunlimted.com.** You'll also find her work under the name Sally Rogers.) Jeannie's job is demanding because it requires attention to both quality and speed. She does her best to get the shot right in the first place, but that's not always possible considering her schedule.

Figure 7.5 shows a not-so-uncommon mistake: the picture wasn't framed properly. In the days before Photoshop Elements, Jeannie would have had to live with the mistake, reshoot, or decide that the kitchen wasn't that important after all. Nowadays she just starts up her computer and gets to work.

Figure 7.5: This kitchen looks like it was in an earthquake. (Photo by Jeanne Zimmermann)

Note: Just about all real estate shots will benefit from the basic image-processing techniques found earlier in this book (↩ Chapter 2 and Chapter 4). Another relevant topic is how to make panoramas from a sequence of photos (↩ Chapter 8). Chapter 11 contains several useful advanced digital photography techniques such as extending exposure latitude.

Here is what Jeannie did to straighten the kitchen:

1. She made a copy of the background layer, turned off the visibility of the original layer, and turned on the grid, just as I did in the preceding procedure.

2. She then selected Image ➢ Transform ➢ Free Transform (Ctrl+T / ⌘ +T) from the main menu bar.

3. As she positioned the pointer in the upper-right bounding box, it turned into a curved arrow (↻). She rotated the image until the lines in the cabinet lined up with the vertical lines of her grid. Rotating some images like this will rotate parts of the image off the edge of the canvas. If this happens, you can enlarge your canvas area (Image ➢ Resize ➢ Canvas Size) before applying the Transform command or, even easier, use Image ➢ Resize ➢ Reveal All *after* you apply the Transform command.

4. When she was finished, she clicked the Commit button (✔) in the options bar. You can alternatively press Enter/Return.

5. As you can see on the left in Figure 7.6, the rotation fixed the kitchen but created a skewed image frame. She used the Crop tool to crop the image, as shown on the right in Figure 7.6.

Figure 7.6: After using the Free Transform command, the kitchen appears mostly level (left). Jeannie used the Crop tool (right) as a final step.

Note: Nowadays most real estate photographs end up shared on the Web. In Chapter 10 I'll show you ways to optimize images destined for the web. In Chapter 12 I'll show you how to automatically create a web photo gallery of images.

Removing a Construction Sign

Jeannie does her best to shoot around clutter or objects that detract from the property. In the case of Figure 7.7, she couldn't avoid the bright red construction sign in front, which gave the false impression that the building was still under construction.

Figure 7.7: The red construction sign is distracting. (Photo by Jeanne Zimmermann)

Here is what she did to remove the sign:

1. She created a duplicate of her background layer. She'll work on the duplicate and save the original layer for future reference.

2. She selected the Clone Stamp tool (🖈) from the toolbox and magnified her image 400 percent. She positioned the red construction sign in the middle of her image window. (If an image is larger than the image window, you can move it around by holding down the spacebar. The cursor turns into a hand. Then, when you click and drag, the image moves with your cursor.)

3. She used a Soft Round 13 pixels brush and started on the red cones, sampling or "cloning" parts of the road and sidewalk by holding the Alt/Option key while clicking on them, and then painting the sampled areas over the cones (shown on the left in Figure 7.8). Then she sampled parts of the wall and the sidewalk and painted them over the sandwich sign, this time using a Hard Round 5 pixels brush because the work in this area required her to be more precise. Next she turned to the sign itself, sampling and using parts of the window and window frame to cover it. At times, the clone didn't look quite right. Ctrl+Z / ⌘+Z quickly reverted the step. As a final step in removing the sign, Jeannie selected a Soft Round 35 pixels brush and a Soft Round 9 pixels brush and cloned the intact tree trunk over what remained of the sign (shown on the right in Figure 7.8).

Figure 7.8: Jeannie started with the red cones, using the Clone Stamp tool to replace them with parts of the sidewalk and street (left). She then cloned the tree on the left side of the image over the area where the red sign used to be (right).

4. She then zoomed back to 100 percent magnification (by double-clicking the Zoom tool) and tightly cropped the image. Using the Levels controls, she adjusted the contrast of her image by choosing Enhance ➤ Adjust Lighting ➤ Levels or by pressing Ctrl+L / ⌘+L.

5. She then used the Hue/Saturation controls to increase the saturation by choosing Enhance ➤ Adjust Color ➤ Adjust Hue/Saturation or by pressing Ctrl+U / ⌘+U until she got what she wanted, as shown in Figure 7.9.

If you zoomed in tightly, you'd see that the clone job isn't perfect. Zoomed out, however, most people wouldn't notice.

Figure 7.9: The final image after cropping, applying Levels, and increasing saturation.

Note: The secret to using the Clone Stamp tool is not to get too caught up in the details. Zoom in to see what you are doing. But then periodically zoom out to see how your work looks in a normal view. It's also useful to turn away from the monitor from time to time. When you look back, you'll have a different perspective. The fact is, after spending so much time working with the Clone Stamp tool, you'll be tuned into every tiny imperfection—things that most people probably won't even notice.

Smart-Blurring a Background

In the photo shown on the left in Figure 7.10, Jeannie wanted to highlight the staircase, not emphasize the view out the windows. Shooting-wise, there wasn't much Jeannie could do except cover the windows completely. At first, Jeannie tried selecting the entire window area and applying a Gaussian blur (Filter ➤ Blur ➤ Gaussian Blur). She got what you see on the right in Figure 7.10. The Gaussian blur blurred everything, including the window frame. She considered selecting each glass part of the window individually and applying the Gaussian blur, but that would have taken too much time. Instead she turned to the Smart Blur filter, which gave her a lot more control over the blur, enabling her to blur the background and leave the window frame alone.

Figure 7.10: Jeannie wanted to diminish the view out the windows (left). A Gaussian blur blurred everything, including the window frame (right). (Photos by Jeanne Zimmermann)

To use the Smart Blur filter, she did the following:

1. She used the Polygonal Lasso tool ( ) to select the window areas on both sides of the staircase. (Remember, you add to a selection by selecting the Add to Selection icon in the options bar.)

2. She selected the Smart Blur filter (Filters ➤ Blur ➤ Smart Blur). By playing with the relationship between the Radius and Threshold settings, she got the effect she was looking for.

Jeannie's Smart Blur settings are shown on the left in Figure 7.11. The final effect is shown on the right.

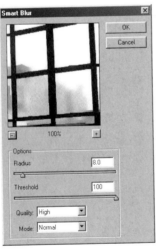

Figure 7.11: Jeannie's Smart Blur settings (left). The result after applying the Smart Blur filter (right).

If you look closely at the staircase, specifically at the handrail and the wire mesh below it, you will see that this image isn't perfect. The Smart Blur actually blurred the thin wire mesh as well as the background. Because this particular image was destined to run small on a website, this imperfection was acceptable. It's possible to be more precise by first selecting the area around the wire mesh and choosing a smaller Smart Blur Radius such as 1.0. The smaller Radius protects the thin wire mesh and still slightly burs the background. After applying the Smart Blur to the selected area, deselect the first selection (Ctrl+D / ⌘ +D) and then select the other window areas with the Polygonal Lasso. Finally, apply the Smart Blur and stronger settings shown in Figure 7.11.

Note: The Smart Blur filter's Radius setting specifies the area the filter covers when looking for pixels of dissimilar values. In some cases, a higher number doesn't produce more blur as you might expect. It all depends on the value of adjacent pixels and your Threshold setting. Increasing or decreasing the Threshold setting determines how different the pixel values must be before they are affected by the Radius setting. You can also choose between speed and quality with the Quality setting. The High setting will slow the processing but produce a better result. Normal mode is the default, but for special effects you can also choose Edge Only and Overlay Edge.

Balancing the Light

Figure 7.12 shows a dark living room with a lot of light pouring in from a window. Getting a proper exposure in this kind of situation is tricky—especially considering the limits of the relatively inexpensive digital camera Jeannie was using. To balance the light and bring out the details of the room, Jeannie used one of the most useful commands in Photoshop Elements 3: Shadows/Highlights (Enhance ➢ Adjust Lighting ➢ Shadows/Highlights). This command replaces—and improves on—the Fill Flash command found in previous versions of Photoshop Elements. Not only can you lighten the darkest areas of an image independent of the light areas, but you can use the Highlights control to darken the lighter colors independent of the dark ones.

Figure 7.12: The light needs balancing. (Photo by Jeanne Zimmermann)

Note: Architects use "before and after" photomontage techniques to help create visual references for clients and approval boards. An example of these kinds of composites appears in the preceding chapter (☞ "Pre-visualizing a Scene" in Chapter 6).

This is what Jeannie did to balance the light:

1. She chose Enhance ➢ Adjust Lighting ➢ Shadows/Highlights.
2. She used the settings shown on the left in Figure 7.13. Note that she adjusted only the Lighten Shadows slider. She left the Darken Highlights slider at 0 percent, and the Midtone Contrast slider at 0.

The results are shown on the right in Figure 7.13.

Jeannie, of course, could have adjusted the lighting of this image by using other methods. For example, she could have used a selection tool to select the brightly lit window area, then inverted the selection (Selection ➢ Invert) and used Levels controls to adjust the tonal values of the dark areas only. This would have worked fine; however, it would have taken more time than simply using the Shadows/Highlights command.

Figure 7.13: The Shadows/Highlights settings (left) and the results (right).

Creating a Warm and Inviting Atmosphere

Figure 7.14 shows a living room photographed by Jeannie. The cold blue cast is the result of an improper white balance setting and doesn't show the room as it really is. It is easy to apply a warm cast to this image, making it much more inviting to a potential buyer.

Figure 7.14: The original photo has a cold, blue cast. (Photo by Jeanne Zimmermann)

Here is what Jeannie did to produce the effect shown in Figure 7.15:

1. She chose Filter ➤ Adjustments ➤ Photo Filter. (You can also apply Photo Filter as an Adjustment Layer. Just click on the adjustment layer icon located at the top of the Layers palette and select Photo Filter from the pop-up menu.)

2. She selected Filter: Warming Filter (85) from the dialog box shown in Figure 7.15.

3. She set the Density slider to 85 percent.

4. She selected OK.

Figure 7.15: The Photo Filter's warming filter makes the room more inviting (left). The Photo Filter's settings (right).

That's all. It's that easy to apply a warm tint to just about any image. If you look at the Photo Filter's pop-up options, you'll also find a collection of other photo filters loosely based on traditional film camera filters. Warming Filter (81), for example, will produce a slightly less warm effect, while Cooling Filter (80) will produce a pronounced blue, or cool, cast. (Jeannie uses the Cooling Filter on some images when she wants to produce a more industrial or high-tech effect.) You can also customize the Photo Filter by selecting Color from the dialog box and clicking on the color swatch to the right. This brings up a color picker, and any color you choose will form the basis for the effect. Sliding the Density slider to a greater percentage increases the effect of the filter.

Sure, there are other ways to use Photoshop Elements to change the tint of any image. Choose Enhance ➢ Adjust Color ➢ Remove Color Cast, for example, or Enhance ➢ Adjust Color ➢ Color Variations. I suggest you start with Photo Filter—it's so easy—and if that doesn't work, try one of the other methods.

Removing Wires

Telephone or electric lines are just about everywhere, and it's nearly impossible to shoot a home or building in such a way as to avoid them. Sometimes these lines can be removed easily by using the Clone Stamp or Healing Brush tool, or by using a "Nudge" technique that I'll explain shortly. I say "removed easily" with the following qualification: our eyes are very sensitive to horizontal lines. Take a telephone line that runs horizontally in an image and rotate it so it is vertical, and it's less likely that you'll even notice it. Our innate sensitivity to horizontal lines also means that if you try to remove such a line from your image, you must do it carefully, in a way that leaves no trace. I suggest that if you have a choice between doing the job poorly and leaving a vestige of our modern life, choose the latter.

Having said all this, let's look at two simple techniques for removing the pair of horizontal wires shown in Figure 7.16.

Figure 7.16: Power and telephone lines are hard to avoid but easy to remove.

The first method requires either the Clone Stamp tool or the Healing Brush tool. I'll start with the wires on the left side of the image and use the Clone Stamp tool to remove them. If you choose to use the Healing Brush tool, the method is basically the same. However, with the Healing Brush tool, you are blending, not replacing, pixels and the results are more unpredictable. You can make the Healing Brush tool act like the Clone Stamp tool by selecting Replace from the Mode's pop-up menu in the option bar.

Note: I don't recommend using the Spot Healing Brush tool for this kind of job. It's easy to use because it doesn't require establishing a sampling area, only a target. However, the results are often unpredictable, especially with larger targets.

Here are the steps for the first method:

1. I selected the Clone Stamp tool ( ) from the toolbox and kept the default settings in the options bar.

2. I started with a Hard Round 19 pixels brush and then changed to Hard Round 5 pixels as I worked on the wire near the windowsill and the wire near the top of the roof. I chose a hard-edged brush because I wanted to keep the texture of the stucco intact. A soft-edged brush would have diffused the edges and blurred some of the details.

Remember, both the Clone Stamp tool and the Healing Brush tool require you to first place your cursor over the area you wish to clone from. Alt+click / Option+click then establishes the sampling point. After establishing the sampling point, move the cursor to the target you wish to clone to, click, and paint with your cursor. With the Clone Stamp tool, the results are almost immediate. With the Healing Brush tool, the results are somewhat delayed because the Healing Brush tool does more than just replace pixels; it actually blends texture, lighting, and shading of the sample and target areas.

When working with the Clone Stamp tool (or any other brush tool), get near-instant access to the brush palette by right-clicking anywhere in the image window area. On a Mac, hold down the Control key and click anywhere in the image window. The palette will appear on the screen, and you can choose a new brush. This method is especially handy because you can easily match the size of your brush to the area you are working on.

The Clone Stamp tool worked great, as you can see in the close-up in Figure 7.17. I could have kept using it—or the Healing Brush tool—to remove the rest of the wires. To demonstrate a slightly faster alternative, however, I'll use the Nudge method to remove the rest of the lines.

Figure 7.17: I used the Clone Stamp tool to remove the wires that crossed the building.

To use the Nudge method, I followed these steps:

1. I selected both wires by using the Polygonal Lasso tool. I feathered this selection 5 pixels (Select ➤ Feather or Ctrl+Alt+D / ⌘ +Option+D), as shown on the left in Figure 7.18. I used the arrow keys on my keyboard to move just the selection outline slightly below the power lines, as shown on the right.

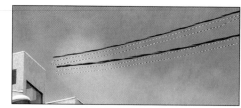

Figure 7.18: I made a selection by using the Polygonal Lasso tool and feathered it 5 pixels (left). Then I used the arrow keys to move the selection down (right).

2. While holding the Ctrl+Alt / ⌘ +Option keys, I used the arrow keys to nudge up the selection of the sky. This copied my selection and offset the duplicate by 1 pixel (shown on the left in Figure 7.19). I kept nudging the selection until the power lines were replaced by sky. There was a little streaking in the clouds, but after deselecting my selection, I went back and quickly fixed it with the Clone Stamp tool. The final image is shown on the right in Figure 7.19.

Figure 7.19: Holding the Ctrl+Alt or ⌘+Option keys while using the arrow keys duplicates a selection and offsets it by 1 pixel (left). On the right, the final results.

The Nudge method works especially well when the line to be removed crosses areas of continuous tones. It doesn't work so well in complex areas, where the copying and shifting of pixels are more noticeable.

Shooting Digital: Focus on Marketable Features

You can do a lot with Photoshop Elements to fix a photograph that is lacking. However, you can save time by shooting interiors or exteriors with certain points in mind in the first place. Here are a few tips:

- If you are using a typical digital camera, you can avoid keystoning by shooting a building straight-on level. This may require the use of a ladder or it may mean scouting out a higher vantage point, such as the roof of another building or a hill.

- When shooting, focus on desirable aspects of the property, such as hardwood floors, new appliances, a beautiful deck, or a view.

- To avoid window glare, use a polarizing filter. You'll need to rotate the filter until the glare is gone. Remember that polarizing filters are most effective when used at a 90-degree angle off axis to the sun. This means the lens is less effective if the sun is directly behind you or in front of you, and most effective when the sun is to the left or right. Polarizing filters can also help increase color saturation in many outdoor shots.

- Shoot around clutter or just remove it before shooting. If your camera has manual aperture and focus controls, you can control the depth of focus and blur a distracting background or foreground.

- Because you are shooting with a digital camera and film costs are not an issue, shoot the same scene from several angles. You can edit the best shot later.

Creating Panoramics with Photomerge

8

Until recently, it took an expensive camera or a time-consuming cut-and-paste procedure to produce images that offered a field of view beyond 90 degrees. That's all changed with Photomerge. All you need are two or more sequential, digital images taken with just about any kind of camera, and Photomerge will automatically blend and stitch them together into a panoramic that is both beautiful and informative. This chapter shows you how to use Photomerge to create panoramics and other types of photomontages as well.

Chapter Contents

Photomerge Dos

Photomerge does a very good job of creating panoramics on certain sequenced photographs, especially ones that were shot with the capabilities of Photomerge in mind. To avoid a lot of frustration and to help you manage your expectations about what Photomerge can and cannot do well, I suggest you keep the following tips in mind:

- Do follow some simple shooting rules and suggestions for better, quicker stitching (☞ "Shooting Digital: Planning for Photomerge," later in this chapter).
- Do expect mixed results depending on the content of your image.
- Do expect better results from images that contain a modest amount of edge detail, such as a building with windows.
- Do expect to spend time later in Photoshop Elements using the Clone Stamp tool (⚖), Healing Brush tool (✐), and the Burn and Dodge tools (☜) (☜) to clean up areas where the merge wasn't perfect.
- Do keep an open mind for lucky mistakes that occur when Photomerge doesn't do what you expect it to do.
- Do use Photomerge for things other than panoramics—for instance, collages. (I'll show you how to make collages in the last project of this chapter and how to extend latitude with Photomerge in Chapter 11.)

Now let's get into the actual work of using this tool.

Note: The Photomerge feature in Photoshop Elements version 3 is similar to the one found in Photoshop Elements 2. However, the newer version is more robust and works with larger files. It also features the ability to save individual images used for the composite on their own layers for more blending control. Both versions are significantly better than the one found in Photoshop Elements 1.

Creating a Precious View

To create the panoramic shown in Figure 8.1, I mounted my Nikon D100 digital camera on a tripod and zoomed in on the scene using a long focal length, I chose a long focal length purposely. I wanted to compress the perspective and at the same time create a wider angle of view. If I had used a wider focal length to create the images for my panoramic, it would have required me to shoot fewer frames to cover the same angle of view, but the picture would have been totally different. The buildings would have seemed much farther away, which isn't how it looks to the naked eye.

Figure 8.1: This view was created by stitching together several sequenced frames.

To maintain a consistent exposure for each frame, I selected a Nikon function button that locked my auto-exposure. If the exposure doesn't vary from frame to frame, Photomerge creates a smoother stitch. I shot one frame, then rotated the camera and took another, then rotated the camera and took another, repeating this until I covered the scene. I used visual references to overlap each shot by about a third but I wasn't particularly precise, and the variations didn't seem to affect the final Photomerge results.

After transferring my digital files to the computer, I did the following:

1. I opened Photomerge from the File menu (File ➤ New ➤ Photomerge Panorama).

2. I chose Browse from the Photomerge dialog box and then navigated to my source files. On the Mac, I selected all image files by Shift+clicking each one individually; you can do the same in Windows by Shift+clicking consecutive files or Ctrl+clicking nonconsecutive ones. Figure 8.2 shows the Photomerge dialog box after I selected the files. (Photomerge will automatically add any files that are saved and open on the desktop. You can selectively remove them or any other files by using the Remove button.)

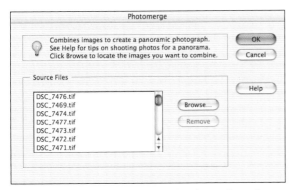

Figure 8.2: The Photomerge dialog box after selecting the sequenced images.

Note: On a Mac—but not on a Windows PC—you can apply the Photomerge maker directly from the File Browser window. Simply select the images you want to merge—Shift+clicking for multiple selections—and then select Automate ➤ Photomerge from within the File Browser menu. If your images are not oriented properly, I suggest you use the File Browser rotate controls before applying the Photomerge command.

3. In the dialog box, I clicked OK, and then I waited while Photomerge went through an automatic process of opening, transforming, and stacking images into layers. When the merge was done, the window shown in Figure 8.3 appeared.

At this point I could click OK and Photomerge would automatically render a perfectly useable, full-resolution version of my panoramic. However, for the sake of this exercise I'm going to explore some of the Photomerge options available.

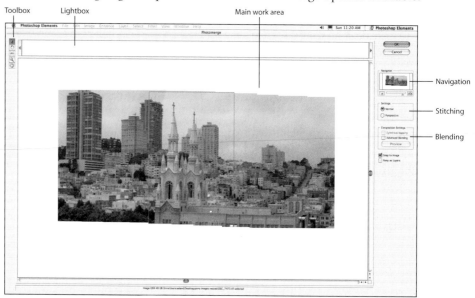

Figure 8.3: The work area in this Photomerge window consists of a toolbox, a lightbox, a main work area, and various navigation, stitching, and perspective options.

Note: You can stop the Photomerge process at any point by simply pressing Esc (Windows) or ⌘+period (Mac).

Shooting Digital: Planning for Photomerge

You'll get better results with Photomerge if you shoot with the following suggestions in mind:

- Use a tripod and keep the camera level. If you can't use a tripod, plant your feet firmly and keep the camera as level as possible as you turn from your waist. If your camera has one, use the optical viewfinder rather than the LCD. Holding the camera firmly to your eye helps maintain consistency.
- If you are using a zoom lens, don't zoom while you shoot your sequence. Keep a consistent focal length.
- If your camera has an exposure lock, use it to maintain a consistent f-stop and exposure between frames. If you have only an automatic setting, avoid scenes with wide variations in lightness and darkness.
- Don't use a flash in one frame and not in the others.
- Consider rotating your camera 90 degrees into a vertical (or portrait) orientation, which will give you a larger view vertically (up and down) than if you held the camera horizontally.
- Avoid using filters, especially polarizing filters. Filters can cause slight vignetting, or fading, on the edges of the image, which will result in noticeable banding when images are merged together.
- Use the camera's viewfinder to pre-visualize the panoramic before shooting. Turn your head slowly and imagine how the panoramic will look. Pay attention to the way the light changes from the start of the panoramic to the end. Avoid extreme fluctuations of light and dark.
- When you shoot, allow a one-third to slightly less than one-half overlap between frames. Use a visual reference to imagine a spot one-third to one-half of the way into the viewfinder, and then rotate the camera so that spot is at the opposite edge of the frame in the next shot. Then find your next visual reference before rotating again. If you overlap more than one-half of an image between frames, the blending will suffer.
- Use your camera's "Stitch assist mode," if it has one, to help you line up the images in the LCD viewfinder. Some cameras, such as the Canon PowerShots, have this feature.

Applying Perspective Control

Look at the Settings box in the Photomerge work area shown in Figure 8.3. You'll see that Normal is selected and Perspective is not. Normal is the default setting, which works fine for most landscape and scenic shots. However, at times applying a perspective improves a panoramic and makes it look more natural. Often you won't know unless you try.

To apply a perspective to my panoramic, I selected Perspective from the Settings box; Figure 8.4 shows the results. The perspective didn't look right to me but I can try to fix it by setting a different vanishing point. By default, if Perspective is selected, Photomerge makes the middle image the vanishing point, and outlines it in a light blue border when it is selected.

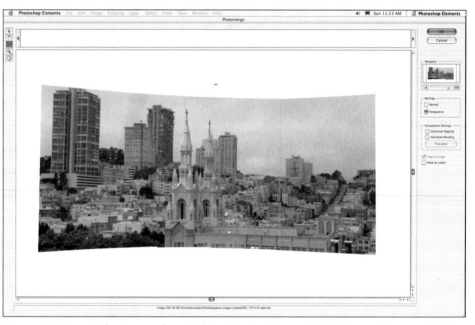

Figure 8.4: Here is the image after applying Perspective control. The vanishing point, by default, is set to the middle image, outlined in blue.

What is a vanishing point? It's helpful to think of the *vanishing point* image as a base image, or one that sets the perspective for all the others. For example, if the vanishing point image is in the middle, as it is in this example, the images on either side are transformed so that they lead the eye toward the center. If you look again at Figure 8.4, you'll see the bow-tie configuration that I found objectionable.

To try another vanishing point, I simply selected the Set Vanishing Point tool (⌖) and clicked another image in the work area. In Figure 8.5, I made the image on the left the vanishing point. See what happens to the perspective? In an attempt to correct the perspective to the new point of view, the images to the right of the vanishing point are transformed in size and shape. To deselect the vanishing point completely and start over, I simply clicked the Normal radio button. Undo works for this as well.

Figure 8.5: *This is the result after I applied Perspective control and set the vanishing point to the image on the far left, outlined in blue.*

After experimenting with different vanishing points, I decided to turn Perspective off and go with the Normal setting.

Manually Arranging Images

In this example, Photomerge automatically arranged my images. But what happens if your images are shot in such a way that they don't easily match up and Photomerge cannot automatically arrange them? If this happens, you'll see the dialog box shown in Figure 8.6. Then you will need to arrange the images yourself.

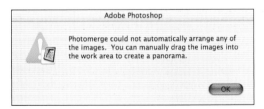

Figure 8.6: *This dialog box appears if Photomerge can't automatically arrange your images. If this happens, you can still try to arrange them manually.*

You do this by dragging images from Photomerge's lightbox into the main work area. Figure 8.7 shows how I have started this process by dragging two of the six thumbnail representations from the lightbox into the main work area. (I placed my images into the lightbox by holding the Alt/Option key and clicking Reset, but Photomerge will automatically place images there if it can't arrange them.) I then dragged the other thumbnail representations from the lightbox to the main work area, placing each one adjacent to the next. Because parts of the underlying image showed through, it made alignment easier.

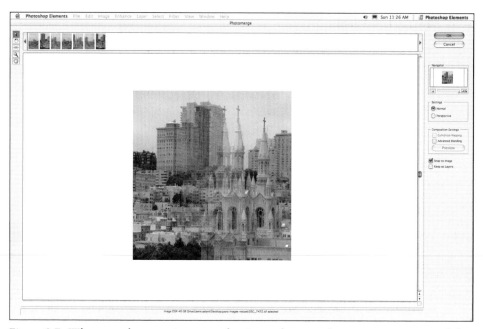

Figure 8.7: When you drag one image so that it overlaps another, you can see part of the underlying image and therefore more easily line up the images.

As similar parts of the adjacent images overlapped, something remarkable occurred. When Photomerge detected similar areas, it automatically snapped them together. The more edge detail it had to work with, the easier it was for Photomerge to line up the adjacent images. (If you have Perspective selected, the program will automatically correct perspective and attempt to compensate for the natural distortion between images. If you have Perspective turned off, Photomerge still looks for similar edges and snaps the images together, albeit without any perspective compensation.)

Note: Just because Photomerge can't find and snap edges of different images together doesn't mean it can't do perspective compensation. If you are trying to arrange your images manually and Photoshop Elements is still having trouble aligning your images, try the following: While clicking and dragging one image on top of another, hold down the Ctrl / ⌘ key. When you release the mouse, Photoshop Elements will bypass the attempt to find similar-edge pixels and go right to the perspective algorithm.

It's easy to forget where your vanishing point is. To find it, simply hold down the Alt/Option key and roll your mouse over the frames. The vanishing point image has a light blue border, and all the other images have red borders.

> **Note:** To move your images from the work area back into the lightbox, you can drag them one by one. To move all the images at once back into the lightbox, hold the Alt/Option key. The Cancel button changes to Reset. Click Reset and start editing your composition again.

Setting Advanced Blending

Next, I tried different blending options. Advanced Blending differentiates between areas of detail and areas of similar tones or colors. When it detects a lot of detail, Advanced Blending applies a sharper blending transition. When it detects similar tones or colors, it applies a more gradual blending transition. In some cases, Advanced Blending can compensate for different exposures in adjacent frames. On these types of images, if you don't use Advanced Blending, you'll see obvious diagonal banding.

In my image, Advanced Blending added several sharp shafts of light shooting down from the top of the image. The shafts of light didn't make any sense, so I attributed the flaw to a bug in the software. I turned Advanced Blending off, and the artifacts disappeared and the blending was just fine. (You can see a preview of the effect of Advanced Blending by selecting the Preview button from the Photomerge window.)

> **Note:** If you select the Keep as Layers check box, Photomerge keeps individual images that make up the panorama on separate layers. (If you select Keep as Layers, Advanced Blending is no longer an option.) Use this option if you are not satisfied with the way Photomerge blends images. With each image on its own layer, you can use a combination of the Eraser with either the Clone Stamp tool or Healing Brush tool to blend the images manually. In Chapter 11, "Extending Dynamic Range with Photomerge," I'll show you a way to use Photomerge and the Keep as Layers option to extend the dynamic range of a digital camera by merging two or more images with different exposures.

Rendering the Final Panoramic

I clicked the OK button and waited while Photomerge merged the higher-resolution versions of my images. Up to this point, Photomerge had worked on and displayed only screen resolution versions of the images. The time it takes for this transformation depends on the size of the final image and the computer's processing speed. With the final panoramic open as a new Photoshop Elements file, I adjusted the Levels controls and used the Healing Brush tool ( ) to clean up some of the background. Then I cropped the irregularly shaped image into a rectangle and I was done.

Creating an Interior Panoramic

How many times have you tried to shoot an interior photo and couldn't get back far enough to fully capture the room? Cutting a hole in the wall behind you might help, but that solution is not practical. Using an expensive super-wide-angle lens might help, but many of these lenses create a fish-eye look. If you are shooting with a digital camera, forget it. At this time, the widest available lenses for digital cameras aren't very wide.

Professional photographer and panoramic/virtual reality expert Scott Highton encounters logistical problems like this all the time. It's his business and passion to push the boundaries of photography, to take it places it could never go before the advent of the computer. The shot in Figure 8.8 is an example. (The three images that make up this panoramic are not available on the CD.) Scott created the panoramic of a large satellite control room of a major telecommunications company by stitching together three sequenced images with Photomerge. By doing this, he got a fully corrected shot that would have been virtually impossible otherwise.

Figure 8.8: This interior panoramic is made up of three images stitched together with Photomerge. (Photo by Scott Highton)

Here are the steps Scott took to shoot the images:

1. He set a 35mm camera on a tripod and used an 18mm rectilinear lens. (The *rectilinear lens* is a corrective lens that makes straight lines appear straight in wide-angle images.) He used a medium-speed print film, which gave him a lot of exposure latitude.

2. Using a specially marked tripod head, he shot a sequence of 12 consecutive images at 30-degree intervals, going well beyond the 120-degree view you see in Figure 8.8. Scott used all 12 images and another software program to stitch together a 360-degree panorama for a QuickTime VR presentation, but that's another story. (To see Scott's virtual reality work, go to **www.highton.com**.)

3. He processed the film and had the images digitized onto a Kodak Photo CD.

Scott then took three of the images that covered the field of view he wanted and in Photoshop Elements he did the following:

1. He selected Photomerge (File ➤ New ➤ Photomerge Panorama).
2. He clicked the Browse button in the dialog box.
3. He selected the three images.
4. Scott started with the central image by dragging and dropping its thumbnail into the main work area. With Perspective selected, this image automatically became his vanishing point image. He then placed the other images on either side of the vanishing point image. As you can see in Figure 8.9, the images came in sideways.

Figure 8.9: When an image comes in like this, use the Rotate Image tool to correct it.

5. Scott used the Rotate Image tool (⟳) to turn the images 90 degrees. Holding down the Shift key while turning constrained the move to 45-degree increments. Because the images could be rotated only one at a time, turning them was time-consuming and Scott wished Photomerge offered some way to turn all the images with one command. The images also came in out of order. That's because the Photomerge Panorama command doesn't follow the sequence of the images in the first Photomerge dialog box but attempts to sequence the images based on their filenames or numbers. Although this may be annoying, you can always rearrange the order of the thumbnails in the lightbox by clicking and dragging.

Note: Photoshop Elements offers several useful Photomerge keyboard shortcuts. You can use the Zoom tool by pressing Z, and holding down the Alt/Option key toggles Zoom In to Zoom Out. You can also nudge your images around with the arrow keys, and you can click and drag your work around the window. Ctrl+Z / ⌘ +Z will step backward, and Ctrl+Shift+Z / ⌘ +Shift+Z will step forward in the Undo history.

6. Because the images contained a lot of edge detail, they snapped right into place. The perspective transformation worked well also, and even matched up the lines in the ceiling. Scott used Advanced Blending with good results (see Figure 8.10).

Figure 8.10: Photomerge corrected the perspective and blended the three images together nicely. The light blue box shows the vanishing point image. (Photos by Scott Highton)

7. Scott then clicked OK.
8. The final panoramic was nearly perfect. Scott had to only crop, apply the Levels command, apply a slight Unsharp Mask, and he was done.

Creating an Epic Panoramic

Only a very expensive panoramic camera could have matched the results that Scott Highton got with a conventional camera and Photomerge, shown in Figure 8.11. A fish-eye lens would have covered the same field of view but with a huge perceived distortion. (The five images that make up this panoramic are not available on the CD.)

Figure 8.11: This is actually five images stitched together (Photo by Scott Highton)

Figure 8.12: The vanishing point is in the middle. (Photo by Scott Highton)

Scott created this moving panoramic of the Lincoln Memorial in much the same way that he created the interior shot described in the preceding section. His shooting technique was basically the same, and once again, he shot this as a 360-degree panoramic that could be turned into a QuickTime VR as well. His Photomerge settings were also the same; he kept the Perspective and Advanced Blending settings on. As you can see in Figure 8.12, he set his vanishing point directly in the middle.

Although this image looks great at first, on closer examination it reveals some of the limitations of Photomerge on this type of image. If you look on the left in Figure 8.13, for example, you can see where Photomerge had trouble matching a column. This is because of the lack of edge contrast that Scott had so much of in the previous example. You can also see on the right in Figure 8.13 where Photomerge had trouble correcting the perspective. Still, even with its flaws, it's a dramatic image.

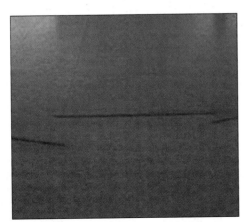

Figure 8.13: Photomerge had trouble aligning the column because of the lack of edge detail. It also had trouble correcting the perspective.

Making a Handheld Vertical Panoramic

I don't want you to get the impression that the only way to use this cool tool is by shooting very carefully in a controlled way. You also don't have to shoot horizontally; you can shoot up and down and create vertical panoramics. Driving past a mountain pass in Norway, I stopped and snapped three quick shots, holding the digital camera by hand. As you can see in Figure 8.14, Photomerge did a fine job stitching the images together. I didn't select Perspective because adding a perspective gave the image a distorted look that I wasn't happy with. I also didn't select Advanced Blending because Photomerge worked fine without applying that option.

Figure 8.14: This is actually three handheld shots, stitched together with Photomerge.

Showing Baseball's Big Picture

Until recently, illustrator Mark Ulriksen spent a lot of time kneeling on the floor, trying to assemble batches of 3 × 5 inch prints with tape and scissors to create a panoramic. After he was finished, he'd use the patched work as a basis for many of his illustrations that appear in *The New Yorker* magazine.

I talked Mark into trying Photomerge on a series of eight images he took of the San Francisco Giants at spring training in Arizona a couple of years ago. He shot the images with a 35mm film camera and used a normal focal length. He didn't shoot with Photomerge in mind, and in many cases the images don't overlap at all. Still, as you can see in Figure 8.15, he managed to create a fun panoramic that could easily be used as a basis for one of his illustrations. Now that Mark has tried Photomerge, I don't think he'll ever use tape and scissors again. Figure 8.16 shows one of Mark's attempts at changing the vanishing point and his Photomerge settings.

Figure 8.15: Mark Ulriksen created this panoramic from eight images by using Photomerge. It's not perfect, but creating it with this command was a lot easier than using tape and scissors.

Figure 8.16: Mark played with different vanishing point settings until he got the image he liked.

Photomerging a Collage

There is no reason why your images need to be in sequence to use Photomerge. I brought several images into Photomerge and played with different arrangements until I got the Hockneyesque image you see in Figure 8.17. Sure, I could have created the montage by cutting and pasting the images into their own Photoshop Elements layer. If I had done this, though, the process wouldn't have been nearly as much fun. Every time I'd want to move a particular image, I'd have to go to its layer, select it, and then move it. Using Photomerge was much faster and more satisfying.

Figure 8.17: This Hockneyesque collage was created in Photomerge.

In this case, I chose Normal instead of Perspective (there was no vanishing point to speak of). To help create a smooth overlap between images, I selected Snap to Image and Advanced Blending.

Scanning Digital: Creating Scanograms with a Flatbed

Flatbed scanners are mostly used to scan flat art, but there is no reason why the boundaries can't be stretched to include inanimate objects such as flowers, coins, and jewelry. If the cover of the flatbed doesn't completely close, you may have to play around with different scanner color and brightness controls. Also, be careful when placing hard objects on the scanner glass so you don't scratch it. The following image is a beautiful example created by photographer Michelle Vignes. She simply placed a whole head of garlic on her flatbed scanner and scanned.

Aa Bb C
cDd E
e FfG
gHh I

Taking Type Further

Many times you'll want to add type to your digital image. In some cases, type takes a relatively minor role, such as a small photo credit or caption in the corner of your digital image. Other times, as in a poster or a flyer, the type is big, bold, colorful, and dominant. Creating all kinds of type is easy with Photoshop Elements' Type tool, which makes type that is fully editable so you can go back to your layered PSD file at any time and make changes. This chapter covers the basics of this powerful tool and shows a few of the myriad ways you can take type further. It also introduces the Shape tool, which can be used to set type apart from a background image.

9

Chapter Contents

Adding a Photo Credit

Let's start with the relatively simple task of creating a photo credit (see Figure 9.1). By walking step-by-step through the process, you'll see how the Type tool actually works. It's a fairly intuitive tool to use, especially if you are familiar with word-processing software. However, please take a minute to read the sidebars that accompany this otherwise simple step by step example. Until you've grasped some of the basic concepts behind the Type tool and used it a few times, it won't always work the way you might expect it to.

Figure 9.1: To create a photo credit, find an area with similar tones and then use a contrasting color and an easy-to-read font.

Here's how I made the photo credit text:

1. I selected the Type tool (**T**) from the toolbox. If I click and hold the Type tool icon, or right-click it, four choices appear: Horizontal Type Tool, Vertical Type Tool, Horizontal Type Mask Tool, and Vertical Type Mask Tool. I chose Horizontal for this example, but the choice is not critical because I can always go back and change the orientation later in the options bar.

Note: Type is fully editable as long as it remains as a type layer. If you simplify the type layer, the type becomes rasterized and has the same properties as any other bitmap element in your image. You can simplify a layer via the Layers palette pop-up menu or by selecting Layer ➤ Simplify Layer from the menu bar. Why simplify a type layer? There are certain things you can't do to a type layer, such as apply Perspective and Distort commands or use any of the filters or paint tools. I suggest that you make a copy of your type layer and simplify the copied layer. That way, you can always go back to the original type layer and make changes.

2. Before I typed, I had to choose a font and a font style, size, and color from the options bar. I also checked that the other options in the Type tool options bar were appropriate. For example, I wanted to be sure that I didn't inadvertently select the Horizontal or Vertical Type. (Photoshop Elements 3 also offers control over the amount of space between lines of type. This is called *leading,* and most of the time the Auto setting in the pop-up menu is the way to go. Generally, the higher the leading value—measured in points—the greater the distance between the baseline of one line of type to the baseline of the next line.)

Choosing Fonts and Styles

You must have the bold, italic, and bold italic versions of your font loaded in your system for these options to be available. You can always choose a faux bold or faux italic from the options bar. Keep in mind that these faux fonts are only crude approximations of actual fonts and are machine-made without considering nuances such as spacing and aesthetics.

Before adding type to your digital image, consider your choice of fonts. If you plan to use small type, say as a photo credit or caption, use a font that holds up and is still readable when small. Usually, so-called *sans serif* fonts are best for this because they are simpler and don't contain decorative flourishes, or *serifs*, at the top or bottom of a character. Two popular and commonly available sans serif fonts are Arial and Helvetica. If you are using type as a headline for a poster or flyer, the font can be either serif or sans serif as long as it is readable from a distance. Latin Wide and Copperplate are popular headline fonts. If you plan to fill your type with an image or texture, use the bold version of a heavy font such as Verdana, Myriad (both sans serif), or Georgia (serif). It's a good rule of thumb not to mix more than two fonts on a single image. If you've chosen an appropriate font, you also won't need to embellish it with too much color or gaudy effects. Photoshop Elements uses the fonts installed in your system folder. The actual fonts that are available to you will vary.

Font: Arial. This is a sans serif type that is legible even when it's small.

Font Style: Regular. I want the type to be readable but not necessarily dominant. The other options—Bold, Italic, and Bold Italic—draw more attention to the type

Font Size: 14pt. The size you use depends on the size of your image. As a rule of thumb, 72pt type is approximately 1 inch high in an image that is 72dpi. My image is 144dpi, so the pixels are packed relatively tighter, which reduces 72pt type to about half an inch. Having said this, the fact is I'm never exactly sure how big my type will look. I experiment until I get the size I want.

Font Color: Black. I chose a contrasting color to the underlying tonal values. You can change the color at any time by clicking on the color swatch located in the options bar. (In earlier versions of Photoshop Elements, you couldn't change colors while typing without changing the color of the previous type.)

Anti-aliased: Selected. This smoothens the edges of the type. It also adds more colors and therefore adds file size. The increased file size is inconsequential unless your image is destined for the Web.

3. After selecting my options, I placed my cursor on the upper-right side of the image and clicked. I chose an area consisting of light, flat tones so my black type would be easily visible. When I clicked my mouse, an insertion bar in the shape of an I-beam appeared at the point of clicking. I then typed in my letters. The baseline of my type lined up with the small line through the bottom of the I-beam. The I-beam also marked a point of reference for any alignment choices I made in the options bar.

4. As you can see in Figure 9.2, when my letters came to the edge of the image, they didn't automatically wrap to another line. They continued off the edge. I could have pressed the Enter/Return key when I got to the edge of the picture, which would have created a new line, but instead I continued typing. When I was finished, I pulled the cursor away from the type until it turned into the Move tool pointer (⊹), at which time I dragged the type into position. You can also move type in 1-pixel increments by using the arrow keys. To move the type in 10-pixel increments, hold down the Shift key while using the arrow keys.

Photo by George Washir

Figure 9.2: Type will not wrap to the next line as it does with conventional word-processing software. It will continue off the edge of the image unless you press the Enter/Return key. In this case, I just dragged the single line of type into position.

Understanding Type States

Photoshop Elements type can exist in one of three basic states: edit, committed, and simplified. When type is in the *edit* state, all you can do is edit it; you can't use other Layer commands from the Layer menu. After type is *committed*, you can edit and apply just about any Photoshop Elements tool or command, including a layer effect. However, in order to use any of the painting tools or filters, you must first *simplify* the type layer.

If you have committed your type, you can quickly change the color of your type by double clicking on the **T** in the type layer in the layer palette or selecting the Type tool from the toolbar and the layer containing the type you wish to change, and clicking on the color swatch found in the options bar. Click a new color, and the type will change accordingly. You can also use either of these shortcuts: Alt+Backspace / Option+Delete will fill the type with the foreground color. Ctrl+Backspace / ⌘ +Delete will fill it with the background color.

After type has been committed, you can drag it at any time into different positions. Just select the Move tool (⊹) from the toolbox and click on the type to automatically select the type layer. A bounding box appears around the selected type. Clicking outside the bounding box deselects the type. Place the pointer inside the bounding box and drag the type into position. Be sure that the Auto Select Layer and Show Bounding Box options are selected in the Move tool options bar.

How do you know which state your type is in? One way is to look at the Layers palette. If the layer thumbnail contains a *T*, the type is in either edit or committed state. If the layer thumbnail doesn't contain a *T*, it is a simplified layer. If the Cancel and Commit buttons are showing in the Type tool options bar, the type is in the edit state. If not, it has been committed. If your type has been simplified and you try to use the Type tool on it, the Type tool will just create a new type layer. You can't edit simplified type.

Moving the type automatically committed it. I could have committed it before this, however, by clicking the Commit button (☑) in the options bar. I also could have clicked the Cancel button (⊘), which would have discarded the type layer. Clicking the Cancel button discards a type layer only if the type has not been previously committed.

What do you do if you want to go back and change your type? Here's what I did to add a copyright symbol and date to the photo credit in Figure 9.1:

1. I made sure the Type tool was selected.
2. I placed the cursor over the type I wished to edit. The cursor turned into an I-beam insertion point. I placed the insertion point at the end of the word *Washington* and clicked. This automatically selected the type layer and put me back into the edit state. I then typed a copyright (©) symbol and 2004. (On Windows the copyright symbol is typed by pressing Num Lock on the numeric keypad, holding down the Alt key, and typing 0169 on the numeric keypad. On the Mac OS, it's entered by pressing Option+G.) At this point, I could have selected all my type and chosen a new font or font style or even changed the color of the type in the options bar. I also could have changed the orientation from horizontal type to vertical by selecting the Text Orientation button (T⁺) from the options bar, but I didn't. (Only selected type will change if you choose a new font, size, or color. You do not need to select any type to change the orientation.)

Note: To select all the type on a type layer, either triple-click anywhere on the type itself or use the keyboard shortcut Ctrl+A / ⌘+A or, in the layers palette, on the type layer, double-click on the **T**. Additionally, double-clicking on a word will select all the letters in that word. You can select individual characters by clicking and dragging the cursor over them, or by using the Shift+arrow keys. To delete individual characters, position the insertion point in front of the character you wish to delete, click, and then press the Delete key. You can also select one or more characters and press Delete.

3. When I was finished, I moved the cursor away from the text and moved the type into position. Doing this automatically committed my new type. The edited text is shown in Figure 9.3

Photo by George Washington © 2004

Figure 9.3: Edit your type by selecting the Type tool and clicking on the type.

As I said, the basics of the Type tool are pretty simple. Let's move on.

Grabbing Digital: Taking Screen Captures Further

Both the PC and the Mac have built-in commands that create a snapshot of your entire desktop window and save the image to the clipboard or, on a Mac, as a PDF file as well. On the PC, press Ctrl+Print Screen for the entire screen, or Alt+Print Screen for the focused window. To quickly paste the screen capture into Photoshop Elements, you can select File ➤ New ➤ Image from Clipboard. On the Mac, you also have a few choices. Pressing ⌘+Shift+3 creates a picture file of your entire desktop and saves the file to your desktop in the PDF format. Pressing ⌘+Shift+4 captures a rectangular section of your screen: you can adjust its size. If you press ⌘+Shift+4, and then, before doing anything else, press the spacebar, your cursor turns into a tiny camera. As you move the camera around the screen, different sections are highlighted. When you get what you want, click, and only the selected screen element will be captured. If you hold the Ctrl key when you click to capture a selection, regardless of which selection method you use, the screen grab is saved to the clipboard, ready for pasting, rather than saved as a document on your desktop. Third-party alternatives give you much more control over your screen captures. Check out SnagIt by TechSmith for the PC, or Snapz Pro X by Ambrosia Software for the Mac. Both enable you to capture the entire screen, a dialog box, a menu, or a selection of your choice. They give you the capability to capture video frames as well. Mac OS X ships with the Grab utility, which enables you to save a selection, a window, or the entire screen in the TIFF file format.

Adding a Copyright Watermark

To guard against unwanted commercial usage of an image, photo agencies and professional photographers often imprint a faint, but noticeable © symbol over an entire image. This imprint lives with the image in print or electronic form, telling the viewer not to use the image for commercial purposes without getting permission—and an unaltered version of the image—from the photographer.

Here's how to create a copyright watermark:

1. With the image open, select the Shape tool (▶).

2. In the Shape tool options bar, click the Custom Shape tool icon (⬭). Keep the Custom Shape option set to Unconstrained. Then click the arrow next to the word *Shape* to call up the Custom Shape Picker.

3. Click the arrow at the top right of the Custom Shape Picker, and from the resulting list select Symbols. This brings up the choices shown in Figure 9.4. (I've circled the icons and arrows to click.)

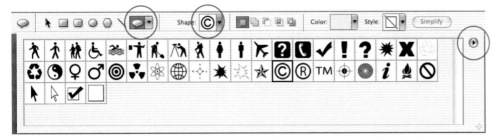

Figure 9.4: In the Shape tool options bar I selected Custom Shape and Symbols, which brought up what you see here.

4. Choose the shape to create; I selected the © shape.

5. Drag across your image to define the area you'd like the shape to appear in. I held the Shift key to constrain the scale and then clicked in the upper-left corner of my image and dragged my cursor all the way to the bottom of the image, filling the screen with the © shape.

6. In the Layers palette, set the blend mode to Soft Light and opacity to 50 percent. These settings allow most of the image to show through the shape, as illustrated in Figure 9.5. You can choose other blending modes and opacities depending on how obvious you want to make the symbol.

Figure 9.5: A copyright watermark will help prevent unwanted commercial use of your image.

Making Headline Type

Headlines are meant to be bold and catchy, and often they consist of just one or two words that reinforce the theme or message of the underlying image. The secret to a good headline is readability and simplicity. This is how I created the headline shown in Figure 9.6:

Figure 9.6: You can create very large type (here, 120pt) by typing the point size directly into the Set Type Size box in the Type options bar.

1.   With my target image open, I selected the Type tool from the toolbar and set the following options in the options bar:

     Font: Helvetica.

     Font size: 120pt. The secret here is not to feel restricted by the 72pt maximum displayed in the pop-up window; you can type in any number you want.

     Font color: Black.

2.   I then clicked the sky and typed *California*.

3.   I moved the cursor outside the type area, and it turned into the Move tool pointer. I dragged the headline into place, which also committed it.

     That's it for now. In the next section, I'll show you ways of making the headline even more readable.

Making Type More Readable

Sometimes type needs a little help to make it stand out from a busy or colorful background. Photoshop Elements has as many techniques to distinguish type from the background as there are stars in the galaxy. Here are a couple of examples that should spark your imagination.

Adding a Drop Shadow and Embossment

Figure 9.7 shows the result of adding two layer styles to the word *California*, making it easier to read and more interesting.

Figure 9.7: By adding a drop shadow and emboss layer style from the Layer Styles palette, the type is more readable.

To create this effect, I did the following:

1. In the Layers palette, I selected the type layer containing the word *California*. (The *California* type is in the committed state.)

2. I selected the Type tool from the toolbar. In the Type options bar, I clicked the arrow next to the Style box, which brought up a pop-up menu. In this menu, I clicked the arrow on the right side and chose Drop Shadows (see Figure 9.8). I then chose the Low drop shadow. You can see the effects so far on the left side of Figure 9.9. (You can also find the layer style Drop Shadows in the Styles and Effects palette.)

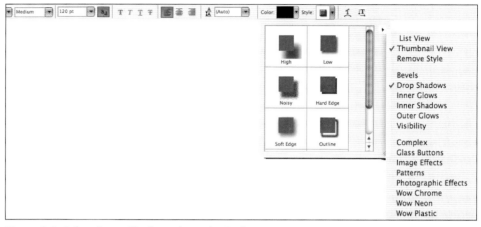

Figure 9.8: Select Drop Shadows from the Style pop-up menu.

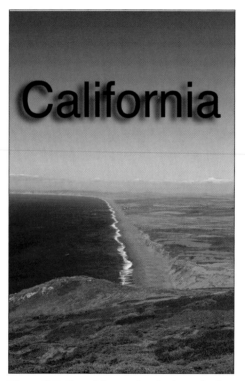 

Figure 9.9: By adding a simple drop shadow, the type is already more readable (left). The embossment makes it look even better (right).

Note: You can remove a style by selecting the Undo button (↶) from the shortcuts bar, or by choosing Layer ➤ Layer Style ➤ Clear Layer Style.

3. Next, from the Style box pop-up menu, I chose Bevels; I then chose Scalloped Edge (see Figure 9.10). The right side of Figure 9.9 shows the effects so far.

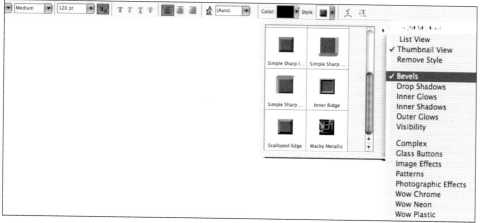

Figure 9.10: Select Bevels from the Style pop-up menu.

Note: Layer Styles effects are cumulative. Attributes of a second style are added to the attributes of the first style, and so on. Unfortunately, you can remove layer styles only sequentially. You can't, say, remove the third of five layer styles and keep the rest. Furthermore, you have to use the Undo command to remove the last layer style, then remove the next-to-last layer style, and so on. If you upgrade to the full version of Photoshop, layer styles are more manageable.

4. In the Layers palette, on the type layer containing the word *California*, I double-clicked the *f* with a circle around it. This brought up the dialog box shown in Figure 9.11. I slightly increased the Shadow Distance but kept the Bevel Size. (You can also access the style settings by choosing Layer ➤ Layer Style ➤ Style Settings from the main menu bar.)

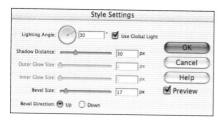

Figure 9.11: In the Style Settings dialog box, you can control the fine points of a layer style.

Using a Gradient

As you can see on the left in Figure 9.12, when you place type with a single color against an area containing a similar color or contrast, part of the type becomes unreadable. You can use a Gradient fill to make your type readable across a wider spectrum of color and contrast (as shown on the right).

Figure 9.12: Black type disappears in the shadow area (left). By applying a Gradient fill to the type, it is more readable (right).

This is what I did to make the type more visible:

1. I needed to fill my Foreground and Background boxes on the toolbox with contrasting colors so that I could use those colors later to make the Gradient tool work properly. To do this, I used the Eyedropper tool ( ) to select a dark area from my image. When I clicked the cursor, that dark color became my foreground color. I then clicked the Switch arrows ( ) to swap the foreground color on the toolbox with the background color. (You can also set the background color by holding down the Alt/Option key and clicking the Eyedropper tool on a color.) I then used the Eyedropper tool again to find a contrasting tone, clicked, and it became the foreground color, which is what I wanted.

2. On the text layer, I held down the Ctrl/⌘ key and clicked on the Layer thumbnail. This selected the type. If I didn't select the type and then applied the Gradient fill, the fill would fill an entire layer and not just my type.

3. I selected Gradient from the pop-up menu that appeared when I clicked the Create Adjustment Layer button ( ) at the top of the Layers palette. (Don't confuse the Gradient adjustment layer with the Gradient tool in the toolbar. The Gradient tool will work only on a simplified layer, which is not what you want.) From the Gradient dialog box that appeared, I selected a linear gradient type and chose the Foreground to Background gradient fill from the Gradient Picker pop-up palette. (Now you see why I needed to go through step 1.) Before selecting OK, I positioned my cursor on the words *Photo by Ana Mikaela*, clicked, and while holding down the mouse button, dragged back and forth across the text until the gradient looked right. Dragging like this across the type sets the starting and ending points of the gradient.

4. I linked the two layers together so that if I moved my type layer, the gradient would move with it. To link the two layers, I selected the type layer in the Layers palette. Then, in the gradient layer, I clicked in the column immediately to the left. As you can see in Figure 9.13, the link icon now appears in the column next to the gradient layer.

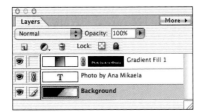

Figure 9.13: My Layers palette showing the linked Gradient Fill layer.

Using a gradient like this requires a little work, but after you get the hang of it, it really opens a lot of possibilities. You can choose different colors or different gradients and get completely different looks for your type. Just keep in mind when you're ready to print your work that some printers might not capture the fine detail of the gradient. If you are having trouble, merge your gradient and type layers, and then apply a very slight Add Noise filter (Filter ➤ Noise ➤ Add Noise). Use the Monochromatic and Gaussian settings, and this should help.

>
> **Note:** Sometimes if you open an older PSD file or a file you received from someone else that contains a type layer, you will see this warning: "Some text layers might need to be updated before they can be used for vector based output. Do you want to update these layers?" Don't freak out. What this means is you don't have the proper font loaded on your computer system. If you choose to update the layers, Photoshop Elements will substitute a font for the missing one. Sometimes the substitution is hardly noticeable. Other times the change is radical. Adding matching fonts to your system will prevent this from happening. You can also delete the type layer and start over.

Using Shape Tools to Accent Type

Shape tools provide an easy and quick way to create a simple background that will help make your type stand out from the rest of the image. Shape tools include the Rectangle, Rounded Rectangle, Ellipse, Polygon, Line, and Custom Shape tools. They are all found in the same spot in the toolbox, along with the Shape Selection tool.

When you use a shape tool, Photoshop Elements places the shape of choice onto its own layer by default. You can go back at any time and edit a shape's color in the options bar. You can also apply layer styles to a shape as well as apply transformations to it. However, with one exception, a shape layer is similar to a type layer in that you must simplify it before you can paint or apply filters to it. With a shape layer, you can use the Paint Bucket tool to change the color before simplifying.

On the left in Figure 9.14, you can see examples of different shapes that are particularly useful for placing type against. As you can see on the right, the shape layer must reside under the type layer, or the type won't be visible.

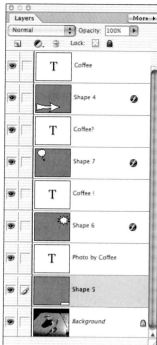

Figure 9.14: Here are just a few of the ready-made shapes that can be used to make your type stand out (left). In the Layers palette on the right, note that the type layers must be above the shape layer; otherwise, the type won't be visible.

The yellow shape This was created by using the Rectangle tool filled with yellow. I didn't use any layer styles.

The green shape This was created by selecting the Custom Shape tool and navigating to the Thought 2 shape found in the Talk Bubbles category. (You access this category—and all categories—by clicking the down arrow button next to the word Shape in the options bar. Then click the right arrow in the upper-right corner of the new window.) I flipped the shape to a horizontal position (Image ➤ Rotate ➤ Flip (Layer Horizontal), and applied a Glass Button: Lime Green Glass layer style.

The blue shape This was created by selecting the Custom Shape tool and navigating to the Arrow 21 shape found in the Arrows category. I applied a Bevels: Simple Shape Inner Layer effect. (Be sure to turn off the Glass Button layer style used in the previous example. Remove layer styles via the Style pop-up menu in the Custom Shape options bar or from the main menu, Layer ➤ Layer Style ➤ Clear Layer Style.)

The red shape This was created by selecting the Custom Shape tool and navigating to the 10 Point Star shape found in the Default category. I applied a Drop Shadow: High Layer effect.

Warping Type

I can't believe how easy it is to warp type. In the old days, you'd never consider using a bitmap program such as Photoshop Elements to do this. You'd use a vector program such as Macromedia FreeHand or Adobe Illustrator. Now, in just a few simple steps, you can distort type into an arc or a wave and make it conform to a particular shape. That's what I did to create a 50th wedding anniversary card for my parents, as shown on the left in Figure 9.15. The Warp dialog box is shown on the right.

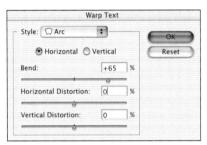

Figure 9.15: The type in this image (left) was warped to conform to the shape of the photograph. Warped type is completely changeable. On the right is the Warp Text dialog box and options.

Note: When you warp type, you warp all the characters in a particular type layer. You cannot warp individual characters within the same type layer.

To get this effect, I did the following:

1. I selected the Type tool and typed in the text.

2. I committed the type and then applied a drop shadow and bevel from the Style options found in the Type tool options bar. (The Style option will appear only if your type is committed, the Type tool is selected, and you have selected the layer containing your type.)

3. With the Type tool selected, I clicked on the type and selected the Create Warped Text button (𝕋₎) from the options bar.

4. In the Warp Text dialog box, I selected Arc from the Style options. I slid the Bend slider until the type assumed the general curve of my photograph. I didn't touch the Horizontal Distortion or Vertical Distortion sliders.

Filling Type with an Image

You can blur the distinction between type and image by creating type out of an image. To do this, follow these steps:

1. Open an appropriate image, such as the one shown on the left in Figure 9.16.

Figure 9.16: Choose an image with lots of color and texture (left) as fill for your type. When you type, a red background appears (right), showing you the selected areas.

2. Select the Horizontal Type Tool Mask in the options bar or from the toolbox.

3. Choose a bold font wide enough to adequately show your fill. For this example, I chose Myriad Bold as the font style and 500pt as the font size.

4. Type in the area you wish to use as fill. A red background will appear, showing the selected areas (as shown on the right in Figure 9.16).

5. Commit your type, and the text will appear as a selection. Now make a copy of the selection (Ctrl+C / ⌘+C), and paste the selection to its own layer (Ctrl+V / ⌘+V) or paste into a new file (File ➤ New). If you paste into the same image, turn off the visibility of the original layer to view the final image-filled type.

Note: You can save a selection (Select ➤ Save Selection), name it, and retrieve it later (Select ➤ Load Selection). This feature comes in handy when you want to save a selection for future use, such as to create an outline for another image. As long as you save your work in the PSD format, the selection is always available until you delete it (Select ➤ Delete Selection). You can save as many selections as you wish. To share a saved selection between files, you'll need to open multiple files, load the selection (Select ➤ Load Selection), and then copy and paste the selection into another open file.

6. At this point, your type is simplified, meaning you can't use the Type tool to change it. However, you can use just about any other tool or filter to further enhance the type. For the type shown in this example, I applied a drop shadow and bevel from the Styles and Effects palette and got the final results shown in Figure 9.17.

Figure 9.17: Fill your type with an image.

Adding Effects to Type

Photoshop Elements has several effects that can enhance your type. Effects, unlike layer styles, are not changeable. They also simplify your type layer, so it's best to always create a copy of your type layer before applying an effect. (In order to see certain effects, you'll need to turn off the visibility of your original layer. Turn off visibility of a particular layer in the Layers palette by clicking its eye icon.) Type effects are found in the Styles and Effects palette. Select Effects and then Text Effects from the pop-up menus. Figure 9.18 shows a few examples of type treated with effects.

Figure 9.18: Type treated with different type effects, which are found in the Styles and Effects palette.

Applying Liquify to Type

If you really want to have fun with your type, use the Liquify filter. You'll need to simplify the type layer before doing so, but after your type is in the Liquify filter work area, you'll have trouble deciding when to stop.

Artist Tom Mogensen used about every technique outlined in this chapter to create the wine label shown in Figure 9.19 for his friend Ellen Deitch. I won't go into all the details of what he did, but I was particularly impressed with his treatment of the word *Champagne* and how he used the Liquify filter to create a ripple with the letter C.

Figure 9.19: Tom Mogensen used a variety of type tricks to create this wine label.

This is what he did:

1. He duplicated the type layer containing the warped word *Champagne* (Layer ➢ Duplicate Layer).

2. He flipped the duplicate type layer and moved the flipped *Champagne* to a position below the original warped type (Image ➢ Rotate ➢ Flip Layer(Vertical), as shown on the left in Figure 9.20.

3. He used the Type tool to create a large C and applied an Outer Glow layer style to it. He positioned the C over the C in *Champagne*. He duplicated the C type layer and positioned the duplicate C over the C in the flipped copy of the word *Champagne*, as shown on the right in Figure 9.20.

Figure 9.20: Tom flipped a copy of the word **Champagne** *and dragged it below the original type (left). The bottom* **C** *will soon get liquified (right).*

4. He simplified the layer containing the duplicate C and selected the Liquify filter (Filter ➢ Distort ➢ Liquify).

5. With the Liquify filter Reflection tool (✏), he lightly brushed the letter to get the effect shown in Figure 9.21. As a final step, he played with his Layers palette Opacity settings to make the reflected word *Champagne* and the liquified letter C look right.

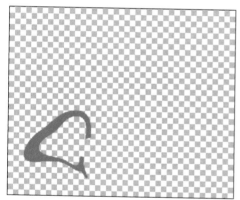

Figure 9.21: The Liquify filter Reflection tool distorted the letter **C** *as shown.*

By the way, as discussed earlier, there is a Text Effect called Water Reflection. If Tom had used this effect, he would not have had as much control over the final look of his work.

Note: If you want type to be visible outside the image area, you'll need to expand the canvas. To do this, choose Image ➢ Resize ➢ Canvas Size and enter the desired dimensions in the Width and Height boxes. Give yourself plenty of room; you can crop later. If you want an equal amount of extra canvas surrounding your image, leave the Anchor set in the middle position. You can also choose a canvas extension color directly from the pop-up menu.

Preparing Images and Graphics for the Screen

There is a big difference between preparing images and graphics for the Web and other electronic presentations and preparing images for print. DPI, for example, is not an issue when you are display on an electronic screen, but choosing an appropriate file format is. This chapter focuses on using Photoshop Elements to prepare visual content that not only looks great on as many display systems as possible but downloads or displays quickly as well. It'll also walk you through the creation of essential Web design components, such as navigational buttons and web page backgrounds.

10

Chapter Contents

Choosing a File Format

Before you begin optimizing your digital images for the Web or for other electronic presentations created using applications as PowerPoint or Keynote, you'll need to decide on a file format. Photoshop Elements, not surprisingly, offers many choices of file formats, available when you choose File ➢ Save or File ➢ Save As from the menu bar (Windows users should save files from within the Editor workspace).

Note: Windows users can save files in different formats via the Organizer workspace by choosing File ➢ Export from the Organizer menu bar. However, you'll have more options—and more control over the final image—if you save files from within the Editor workspace.

File formats organize data in different ways. How they do this will affect the way you prepare the image. Preparing an image for, say, the JPEG format differs from how you'd prepare it for the GIF format.

So which file format should you choose? Let's take a look at the most relevant formats and decide. After that I will get into the nitty-gritty of using Photoshop Elements to prepare and save to the file formats most useful for the Web and other types of onscreen display.

Note: Photoshop Elements will automate the entire process of preparing images for the Web. It'll even choose an appropriate file format, build a background, and create and place navigational graphics on a web page (✐ Chapter 12).

JPEG

It's remarkable that the term *JPEG* has made it into the popular vernacular. "Just JPEG it to me" has become almost as common as "send me an e-mail" or "just Photoshop it." Its popularity is for good reason. The JPEG (Joint Photographic Experts Group) file format shrinks full-color or grayscale digital images to a manageable size. And just as Visa and MasterCard are household names in the financial world, JPEGs are universally accepted by most applications and web browsers.

The JPEG file format supports millions of colors and compresses an image much more than a GIF ever could. However, with the JPEG file format you don't have precise control over the individual colors, and because data is actually thrown away (this is known as *lossy compression*), there is some reduction in quality. The loss of quality is especially noticeable in images that contain a lot of detail. That's why the JPEG format is generally not used on images that contain type or where precise detail is critical.

GIF

The GIF (Graphics Interchange Format) file format supports only up to 256 colors. It can simulate more colors through a process called *dithering*, but this often results in a grainy or rough-looking image. Most digital images consist of millions of colors, so you can see right away that GIF is not necessarily the best choice for a photograph or continuous-tone image. On the other hand, GIF gives you precise control over which colors you choose to use. This can be important, for example, if your image is a graphic containing large expanses of color that you want to blend seamlessly into an HTML-designated background color. It's also possible with the GIF file format to define selected areas as transparent, which can make an irregularly shaped graphic or image appear to float without a rectangular border on a web page. Finally, you can use the GIF file format to create simple animations. I'll get into both transparency and animation later in this chapter.

TIFF

TIFF (Tagged Image File Format) isn't supported by web browsers so is it not a viable format for the Web. However, the TIFF format is capable of saving millions of colors and is supported by most presentation and slide show applications. TIFF is cross-platform, which means you can view it on both Mac and Windows computers. It is also a *lossless* format, which means no data is lost or pixels altered when you save your image file. File size is primarily controlled by resizing your image, but some lossless compression is also possible. In terms of capabilities, there really isn't that much difference between the TIFF and PSD file format. In fact, an advanced TIFF format can even save layers.

Advanced Formats

Photoshop Elements 3 opens and generates PNG (Portable Network Graphics) and JPEG 2000 formatted files. Both formats combine the best of JPEG (24-bit color support) and the best of GIF (transparency and lossless compression) without the drawbacks. They also fix the gamma problem that exists between platforms, so images look the same on any monitor. With JPEG 2000 it is even possible to create 24-bit animations.

PNG and JPEG 2000 are slowly gaining acceptance, and most web browsers will display them. However, most browsers and image presentation software don't yet take advantage of these formats' advanced features such as transparency and gamma control.

The Bottom Line

For the sake of simplicity, I'll say this:

- Use JPEG for photographic images and continuous-tone art destined for the Web or other electronic format via just about any imaginable application.
- Use GIF when you want universal support for graphics that contain type or a limited number of colors, or for those special situations when you want transparency or an animation.
- Use TIFF for applications such as Microsoft's PowerPoint, Apple Computer's Keynote, and Simple Star's PhotoShow when file size isn't such a big issue and quality is. (PNG and JPEG 2000 are other lossless options that would work fine in a supported, closed-loop environment.)

Even though Photoshop Elements supports and saves images in many formats, I'm going to focus on JPEG, GIF, and TIFF—the most popular file formats used for onscreen viewing —and show you ways to prepare and save your images in these formats.

Making Great JPEGs

Bear with me for a moment and suffer through a brief technical discussion about the JPEG file format. The more you know about this format, the easier it will be to use Photoshop Elements to create great JPEGs.

To start, keep in mind that the JPEG file format—and, for that matter, all file formats—organize digital data. The JPEG file format compresses data as well. However, unlike some graphics file formats, JPEG compresses data by sampling images in 8 × 8 pixel squares. It looks for similarities in tone and contrast and then transforms each block by using mathematical equations representing the relevant color and brightness values. You can actually see these blocks by magnifying a highly compressed image (see Figure 10.1). The JPEG file format also "intelligently" selects and throws away high-frequency data that it determines unimportant; as I said earlier, this is why the JPEG file format is called a *lossy* technology. Other file formats, such as the PSD, TIFF, or PNG file formats, are called *lossless* because they compress images without throwing away data. (The JPEG 2000 format offers a choice of lossless or lossy compression.)

Figure 10.1: This image has been magnified 1200 percent to show the 8 × 8 pixel squares that result from JPEG compression.

With Photoshop Elements, you can control the amount of JPEG compression by a ratio as high as 70:1. Lossless file formats typically compress by a ratio of only 2:1 or 3:1. The more compression, the smaller the file size, and the more data is thrown away. The secret is to find the right balance between quality and file size, and I will discuss that a little later in this chapter.

Note: When preparing images destined just for the Web, consider setting your Photoshop Elements preferences to reflect the special requirements of that medium. Choose Edit ➤ Color Settings and make sure your option is set to No Color Management. Choose Edit ➤ Preferences ➤ Saving Files and turn off the image preview options, especially if you are creating JPEG files. By doing this you'll make the File Browser work more slowly, but you'll also reduce the file size and eliminate the chance of creating a corrupt file. Choose Edit ➤ Preferences ➤ Units & Rulers and select Pixels, the preferred measurement unit of the Web's bitmap world. (Remember that Mac OS X Preferences are found on the Photoshop Elements menu.)

Saving JPEGs

There are two main ways to create JPEGs when using Photoshop Elements: File ➤ Save As and File ➤ Save for Web. The method you use will depend on where your digital image is headed. Use the File ➤ Save As method for most general purposes.

Use the Save for Web plug-in if you are optimizing a digital image destined for the Web or for other purposes where file size is critical. Because a slight delay occurs between the moment you select the plug-in and the moment it is ready to use, this method is a little slower than the File ➤ Save As method. However, the Save for Web plug-in enables you to view and compare your original image alongside an optimized version of your image and determine precisely the optimal JPEG compression and format settings.

Grabbing Digital: Images from the Web

It's easy to grab digital images directly from the Web and then use them as reference material or even components in a composite. Just remember that many of these images are copyrighted, meaning that if you use them for anything but personal use you must obtain written permission. Although some images are considered public domain, such as the images on the Library of Congress website (**www.loc.gov**), you should still make sure that no special restrictions are attached to their use.

The method you use to grab these images will vary slightly depending on which computer platform (Windows or Mac) and web browser you are using. If you are using Netscape Navigator or Internet Explorer on Windows, right-click the image and save the image to the destination of your choice. On the Mac, just click and hold on the picture (or Control+click), and choose Save This Image or drag the image to your desktop.

Many Web images use the GIF file format. (You can tell it's a GIF file by the **.gif** extension.) If you are saving these GIFs for whatever reason as JPEGs, you can learn all about that later in this chapter (↪ "Converting GIFs to JPEGs").

Save As Options

To create a JPEG by using the Save As method, choose File ➤ Save As. After the dialog box shown in Figure 10.2 appears (Windows on the left, Mac on the right), select JPEG from the Format list box. Make sure that the ICC Profile (Windows) or Embed Color Profile (Mac) option is turned off. If it isn't, Photoshop Elements will include color profile settings and thereby add file size to your JPEG image.

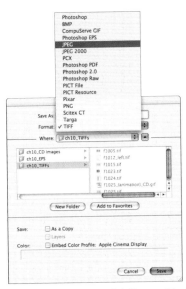

Figure 10.2: When you select File ➤ Save As, you have a choice of different file formats (the Windows version is on the left, and the Mac OS X version is on the right).

Now click the Save button and you'll see a dialog box much like the one shown in Figure 10.3. Here you can choose compression settings, JPEG format, and, if your original Photoshop files include transparent areas, even add a colored matte. If Preview is selected, you get a real-time view of the effects of your JPEG settings on your original image. You can zoom in and out by using the standard Photoshop Elements Zoom commands to get a better view of the effects (Ctrl/⌘ +click enlarges, and Alt/Option+click reduces). An approximate file size is also provided.

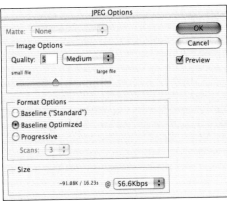

Figure 10.3: Choose JPEG and then you can specify the JPEG file options. When an image includes transparent areas, the Matte option is available.

Creating a "Transparent" JPEG

Later in this chapter I will show how to create a transparent GIF graphic that appears to "float" on a web page without showing any rectangular edges. The JPEG file format doesn't support transparency, but you can create a pseudo-transparent look.

If your Photoshop Elements file contains transparent areas (as signified by the gray and white checkerboard pattern) and you don't have a background layer, the Matte option is available, both in the Save for Web plug-in and in the JPEG options box that appears when you choose File ➤ Save or File ➤ Save As. Choose the Matte option and then select a matte color that matches the color of your web page background. Photoshop Elements then fills the transparent areas with this color, blending the edges with variations to make a smooth transition. When you view your graphic on a web page, it will seem to float against the background. Of course, it's not really floating, and if you have a complex background, or you change your mind and use another background color, what seemed transparent will stand out.

Another point to keep in mind is that there is no such thing as a web-safe color in the JPEG file format. (*Web-safe* refers to the common hexadecimal colors read by all browsers regardless of platform.) Colors shift unexpectedly when JPEG compression is applied. Even if you carefully choose a web-safe matte color for your JPEG, the color, once compressed, will never exactly match another web-safe background color.

You also need to choose one of the following options:

Baseline ("Standard") This is Photoshop Elements' default setting. If you have any doubts about what program will be used to open your image, choose this option.

Baseline Optimized I suggest that you choose Baseline Optimized, because you'll get an image that is slightly smaller in file size with better color fidelity. Most programs and web browsers support this standard. However, some (mostly older) programs have trouble opening a baseline-optimized JPEG.

Progressive I generally don't recommend using this option. The Progressive format contains the same data as the Baseline ("Standard") and Baseline Optimized formats and creates a JPEG with about the same file size. However, the data is displayed in a series of scans, and the first scan appears quickly because it is equivalent to a low-quality setting. With each subsequent scan, more data is provided. When you choose Progressive, you can choose the number of scans it takes for the entire image to appear (three, four, or five scans). A Progressive JPEG could be useful if you are creating really large images destined for a web page and you want something to appear on the page immediately. However, Progressive JPEGs are not fully compatible with all web browsers or applications, and using them is therefore risky.

The next step is determining which JPEG quality setting to use. I suggest that you start with the Medium setting from the pop-up list. This often produces a good compromise between quality and file size. Keep in mind that when I say *Medium*, I am referring to a range of 5–7, as reflected in the slider. Each of these Medium numbers will produce a slightly different sized JPEG. You'll need to fine-tune your choice. If Preview is selected, the results of your choice will be reflected in the image. Use Photoshop Elements' Zoom In command and look for loss of detail or for compression artifacts. Keep in mind that viewers will ultimately see your work at 100 percent, so don't get too hung up on how the magnified image looks. If Medium isn't good enough, try a slightly higher setting.

If you want your digital image viewed at its best, you'll probably settle for only the highest-quality settings. But keep in mind that even when you choose Maximum, there is some loss of image quality that can never be replaced—because, as I mentioned earlier, you always lose some data when you compress with JPEG.

If you must use JPEG on images with sharp-colored edges, such as text, you'll get better results if you choose the Maximum, or 12, setting. At this setting, Photoshop Elements automatically turns off Chroma downsampling, a process that works well with photographic images but causes fuzziness or jaggedness around the edges of hard lines. Chroma downsampling samples color areas at a rate of 2×2 pixels rather than 1×1 pixel. This relatively coarse method of throwing away color data results in smaller file sizes but creates 2-pixel jaggies around sharp color boundaries.

Believe it or not, depending on the image, you can produce very good quality at the Low setting. Even the 0 setting can be used on some images. You can adjust the setting to 0 by using the compression slider or by typing a zero in the Quality box.

Compare the images in Figure 10.4 to see the difference in quality between the Low and Maximum settings. The original image was 1.7MB. The Low setting produced a file size of only 44KB, while the Maximum setting produced a file size of 726KB.

Whatever setting you ultimately select, you'll quickly learn that creating the smallest possible file size without sacrificing image quality is a matter of trial and error.

Figure 10.4: An image at the Low setting—44KB (left). An image at the Maximum setting—726KB (right).

Save for Web Options

To create a JPEG by using the Save for Web plug-in, choose File ➤ Save for Web. (For Windows users, this option is available in the Editor workspace, not the Organizer workspace.) When you do this, the Save for Web dialog box shown in Figure 10.5 appears. You'll notice that the Save for Web plug-in loads and then starts to optimize your image by using either the default or the last-saved settings. If you want to stop this sometimes time-consuming process, wait until the image has loaded (as indicated by the status bar at the bottom of the work area) and then, when the image starts to be optimized (again, as indicated by the status bar), press Esc or ⌘+period.

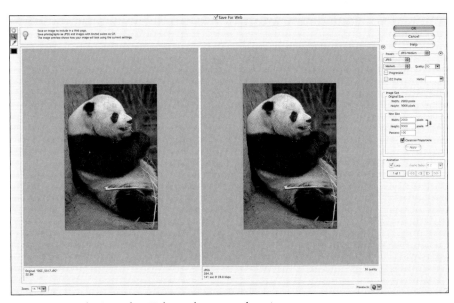

Figure 10.5: The Save for Web work area and options.

Now you are faced with several options. I suggest you do the following:
If it's not selected already, select the JPEG format from the pop-up list.

- Make sure that the Progressive check box is not selected. As I said before, Progressive creates a JPEG that downloads in increments but isn't read by all browsers. Optimized creates a better and smaller JPEG file.

- Unless you've made a strong commitment toward color management, be sure that the ICC Profile box is deselected. If it is selected, you will be adding data of dubious value and increasing your file size. This will be an option only if your Photoshop Elements color preferences are set to include ICC color profiling.

With two views of your image, one showing the original image and the other showing the effects of the compression, it's easy to compare them and choose the optimal setting. As I mentioned in the preceding section, start with the Medium setting and experiment.

You may notice that both the Save for Web and Save As options include Low, Medium, High, Very High, and Maximum settings. However, the Save for Web numerical quality values are different, ranging from 1–100 rather than 1–12. Unfortunately, these numbers do not have that much in common. A Save for Web Quality 50, for example, doesn't create a similar-sized JPEG as a Save As 6. However, the process of starting at a Medium setting and experimenting until you get the optimal setting is the same for both methods.

If your image is larger than the image window, you can use the Hand tool ($\textrm{\small 🖑}$) in the Save for Web dialog box to navigate around various parts of your image, or you can hold down the spacebar and drag in the view area to pan over the image. To zoom in with the Hand tool selected, hold down Ctrl/⌘ and click in a view, or choose the Zoom tool ($\textrm{\small 🔍}$) and click in a view. To zoom out with the Hand tool selected, hold down Alt/Option and click in a view, or choose the Zoom tool and click in a view. You can also select a magnification level—or type one—in the Zoom box at the bottom left of the dialog box.

If you hold down the Alt/Option key, the Cancel and Help buttons change to Remember and Reset. If you click the Remember button, the next time you open the Save for Web plug-in it will open with the current settings.

The Save for Web dialog box has two other relevant options: Preview Menu, which offers a variety of monitor compensations and modem download rates (found by clicking the little arrow at the top right of the image window), and Preview In, which gives you a choice of which web browser to use for previewing your work.

Photoshop Elements also gives you the option to resize your image within the Save for Web plug-in. This is especially useful when you are trying to optimize an image for the Web or for e-mail transmission, and compression alone isn't enough to make your image a manageable size. To resize, simply type in a new width or height value in the New Size section of the dialog box. If you've selected the Constrain

Proportions check box, you'll need to select only one aspect value and the resized image will retain the original image's proportions. You can also resize by typing in a percentage.

After you enter the new values, click Apply. When you are finished, click OK and save your JPEG.

Optimizing Digital Images for JPEG Compression

Some digital images compress more efficiently than others. If you understand why this is true, you'll understand why it is possible to optimize any digital image so it JPEGs more efficiently.

Look at the image on the left in Figure 10.6. It's 1000 × 1000 pixels, and uncompressed its size is 2.87MB. I saved it by using the Save for Web Medium 50 JPEG setting, and the file size shrunk to 98.14KB.

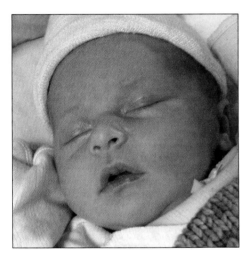 

Figure 10.6: The left image compresses better because it contains smooth, gradual tonal variations. The right image doesn't compress as well because it contains lots of high-frequency data.

Now look at the image on the right. It has exactly the same dimensions as the image on the left, and uncompressed it's also 2.87MB. I applied the same JPEG settings to it and got a file size of 207.6KB, a whopping 110KB bigger than the first image! Why?

The first image (left) is smooth, with gradual tonal variations. This kind of data is easier for the JPEG algorithms to handle, hence the smaller file size. The second image (right) contains lots of high-frequency data in the form of thin strands of hair. It takes a lot more work to compress this kind of data; therefore, the file size is higher.

Now let's take this knowledge and apply it to other digital images.

Global Blurring

As you've seen, JPEG compression works more efficiently on images that contain fewer details. It follows, then, that if you slightly blur an otherwise sharp image, you'll get a JPEG with a smaller file size. The more blurring, the smaller the file size. Fortunately, this is a realistic option, because for many digital images a small amount of blurring won't affect the perceived quality of the image.

Let's apply a small amount of blurring to the image on the left in Figure 10.7, which is 1800 × 1800 pixels for a 9.28MB file. Before blurring, I compressed the image by using a Save for Web JPEG Medium 50 setting and got a file size of 530.7KB. After globally applying a Gaussian blur of 0.7 pixels with a Radius of 0, the same image weighed in at only 374.6KB. See, even slight blurring will suppress some of the higher spatial frequencies enough to reduce the JPEG file by 156KB. If you look at the image on the right in Figure 10.7, you'll see that the slight blurring didn't noticeably affect the image quality. If I apply more blurring, I'll get even more reduction in file size.

Figure 10.7: Before applying a Gaussian blur, this image (left) compressed to 530.7KB. After applying a slight Gaussian blur (right), it compressed to 374.6KB. (Photo by Maurice Martell)

Granted, your results will depend on the type of image you are working with and the size of the original file. Sometimes this method saves you only a few kilobytes, but even that can make a difference if you are hindered with a slow modem or are optimizing images for the Web.

Selective Blurring

Let's take this blurring thing further. What if parts of your image really need to remain sharp, and other parts could be blurred with little or no consequence? In this case, you can apply a Gaussian blur selectively only to the parts that aren't critical.

Figure 10.8 shows an image with a large expanse of background area (sky and clouds) and details in the foreground (the human artichoke). The original Photoshop file (left) is 1200 × 1802 pixels, for a file size of 6.19MB. Saved by using a Save for Web Medium 50 setting (right), it comes down to 398.5KB.

Figure 10.8: Saved with no optimizing, this image (left) compressed to 398.5KB. By applying a strong Gaussian blur (right) to the areas where detail isn't so important, this image JPEGed down to 354.6KB.

Next I selectively blurred the image before compressing it. I selected only the background and then blurred it by choosing Filter ➣ Blur ➣ Gaussian Blur and setting the Radius to 3.6 pixels. When I compressed the image by using the same Save for Web setting, the file size reduced to 354.6KB, a savings of 44KB with no loss of important details.

To push the benefits of blurring a little further, I applied a Gaussian blur of 0.5 to the entire image—in addition to the 3.6 Gaussian blur applied to the sky. This resulted in a file size of 295.1KB, a savings of nearly 100KB. This final image is shown in Figure 10.9.

Figure 10.9: After selectively and globally applying a Gaussian blur, this image now compresses to 295.1KB.

Resize to Optimize

Earlier in this book, I warned you about the consequences of resizing a digital image too radically in one step (🖙 "Resizing" in Chapter 2). I showed that if you didn't resize incrementally, you'd end up with a soft, mushy looking image. Well, I am going to contradict myself. There are times when resizing radically can work in your favor.

What did I say about blurring an image to optimize for JPEG compression? The more blurring, the more efficient the compression, right? OK, let's resize an image and see what happens when you apply the JPEG compression.

Figure 10.10 shows an image taken with a digital camera. The original image, shown on the left, is 2240 × 1680 pixels, and uncompressed it takes up 10.8MB. On the right is the same image reduced to 300 × 225 pixels. I've resized as I suggest in Chapter 2, no more than 50 percent at a time, applying an Unsharp Mask between each step. After applying a Save for Web Medium 50 JPEG setting, it weighed in at 15KB.

Figure 10.10: The original image (left) is 2240 × 1680 pixels. Resizing down to 300 × 225 pixels incrementally and then applying a Medium JPEG setting (right) created a 15KB file.

Figure 10.11 shows the same image resized in one swoop with no Unsharp Mask applied. With the same JPEG settings, it's 11KB. I know 4KB may not sound like much, but when it comes to optimizing an image for the Web, every kilobyte counts.

Figure 10.11: Resizing in one swoop to 300 × 225 and then applying a Medium JPEG setting created an 11KB file.

The neat thing about this method is how quick it is. There is no need to apply a Gaussian blur or make a selection. Still, this technique isn't for every image. Some images suffer too much in quality when you resize them radically. Also, this method works only if you have a large enough image to begin with and need a much smaller image.

In any case, now you know three ways to use Photoshop Elements to optimize a JPEG: global blurring, selective blurring, and resizing. You can choose the technique or combination of techniques that work best for your image.

Converting GIFs to JPEGs

Sometimes, for the sake of file size or compatibility, you'll want to turn a GIF into a JPEG. You can do it, but do it smartly.

In the process of reducing and indexing colors, a GIF image often becomes choppy or coarse because fewer colors are available to create smooth transitions. Dithering, while fooling the eye into believing that the image has more colors, actually introduces even more noise at a subpixel level.

Because the JPEG file format doesn't handle high spatial-frequency noise well, the result can be a larger file size than you started with, as well as a lousy-looking image.

If you must turn an indexed file such as a GIF into a JPEG, first convert your file to RGB and then apply a Gaussian blur to soften the image as much as possible without noticeable visual degradation. When JPEG compression is applied, there will be less noise to interfere with the compression process.

Note: Avoid JPEGing a JPEG. Every time you open, manipulate, and save an image in the JPEG format, you lose data and increase the risk of creating a larger file size. Those distinct blocks of pixels that you saw in Figure 10.1—the ones that resulted from applying high JPEG compression to an image—add high spatial frequency to the image. The more high spatial frequency information in an image, the less efficient the JPEG compression. Save your original in the Photoshop format (or another 24-bit format), and save subsequent JPEG files from the original.

Making TIFFs

Before you save a file to the TIFF format for screen viewing, you'll need to size your images. To ensure maximum compatibility, it's best not to apply image compression to a TIFF file, so the best way to manage file size is through resizing. If you don't resize, a needlessly large image file can choke or slow down an application such as PowerPoint or Keynote. Resizing is done through the Resize dialog box (Image ➢ Resize ➢ Image Size). Be sure you keep the Resample check box selected. A good rule of thumb for images destined for the screen is to set the Pixel Dimensions in the Image Size dialog box to 800 pixels (width) or 600 pixels (height). To ensure sharpness on larger monitors, try 1600 pixels (horizontal) or 1024 pixels (vertical).

After you've optimized the image size, saving to the TIFF format is easy:

1. Choose File ➢ Save or File ➢ Save As from the Photoshop Elements menu bar.
2. In the Save dialog box Format pop-up menu, select TIFF.
3. In the dialog box that follows (shown in Figure 10.12), select None for Image Compression and select IBM PC for Byte Order. Macs will read an "IBM PC" TIFF, but Windows computers are more fickle with Macintosh TIFFs.

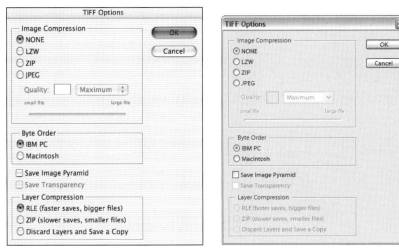

Figure 10.12. TIFF options for the Mac (left). TIFF options for Windows (right).

Making GIFs

The secret to making great GIF images lies in your choice of a color table, the number of colors you use, and how much dithering, if any, you apply.

Before I show you how to do this by using the Save for Web and the Save As methods, let me take a moment to illustrate how critical color tables are to the GIF file format. Look at Figure 10.13(a), a graphic created by Valerie Robbins. Its color table shows exactly which of the 256 possible colors are present. Believe it or not, Figure 10.13(b) shows the same exact image (left), but this time I've applied a different color table to it (right). As you can see, the image changes accordingly.

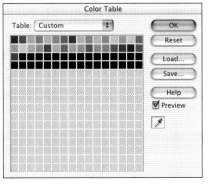

Figure 10.13(a): This image (left) works well as a GIF because it contains fewer than 256 colors. On the right is the color table showing the colors contained in the image. (Illustration by Valerie Robbins for the site **www.philanthropyroundtable.org**)

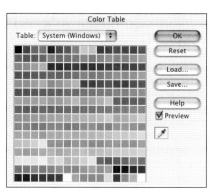

Figure 10.13(b): With a different color table (right), this is a totally different image (left).

Keep this example in mind as you proceed through the next steps.

Using Save for Web

Let's work on an appropriate image for the GIF file format. Figure 10.14 shows a headline that designer Valerie Robbins created for one of my websites, **www.shooting-digital.com**. The graphic contains text and colors that Val wanted to precisely control. I'll use the Save for Web method to convert it to the GIF file format. The Save for Web plug-in features side-by-side viewing capability so I can easily compare my original with the optimized version. It also gives me several other preview options that I'll discuss later.

Figure 10.14: I'll make this PSD graphic a GIF by using the Save for Web plug-in.

First, I'll prepare the graphic in a quick and simple way that will result in a GIF that is ready to be placed on a website and displayed by just about any web browser in the world. Afterward, I'll use the Save for Web palette, Dither, and Color options to "tweak" the same image and create a GIF that takes up fewer kilobytes but still looks great.

Keep in mind that after a graphic is open in the Save for Web plug-in, most of Photoshop Elements' regular tools and commands are not available. Although you can change the pixel dimensions from within the Save for Web plug-in, for the sake of simplicity, I resized Valerie's graphic to the desired dimensions before selecting the Save for Web plug-in and proceeding.

After the graphic was properly sized, I did the following:

1. I chose File ➢ Save for Web. (Windows users will find this command only in the Editor workspace, not the Organizer workspace.) This opened a new dialog box, as shown in Figure 10.15. As soon as my image appeared in the dialog box, the plug-in automatically began optimizing it for the Web. It applies the last-used settings, or the default setting if you are using it for the first time. You can stop the optimizing by pressing Esc or ⌘ +period.

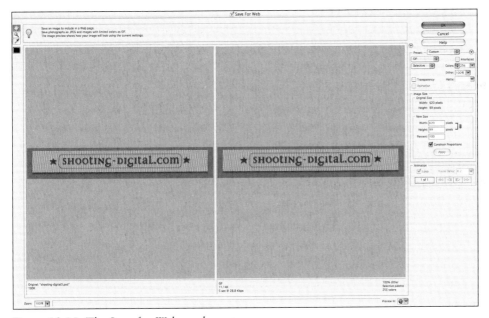

Figure 10.15: The Save for Web work area.

Shooting Digital: Lessons from Shooting Sequenced Stills

In one of my earlier lives, I was hired to shoot sequences of still images for a major CD-ROM multimedia project. The script included 50 social dilemmas that the producers needed to establish visually. Instead of shooting with a single image in mind, I needed to shoot many images that helped build narrative sequences. When I shot a curtain, I shot it in different positions. When I shot a door, I shot it open and closed. When I shot people, I tried to capture their eyes both open and shut. It sounds like film, but the model that inspired me was the comic strip, which uses a few related frames to tell a story. The comic strip also taught me that if you give viewers a chance, most of them will fill the space between images with their imagination, so you don't need to show them everything. I shot mostly horizontal images because vertical images didn't fit as well on the screen. I also centered the action and kept the images simple because of the limited resolution of most monitors. Because I was shooting digital, I learned to shoot a lot of images, because developing cost wasn't a factor and many times my outtakes became useful as transition images.

2. For this example, I made sure GIF was selected as my optimized file format and kept the default GIF settings:

   Color reduction algorithm (or Color Table) Selective

   Colors 256

   Dither amount 100 percent

   Interlaced I left this check box deselected. Interlacing creates a GIF that loads on a browser window gradually, in successive passes. However, it also adds file size, so it is best avoided.

   Transparency Because my graphic didn't contain any transparent areas, this option was not available. (Again, I'll get to the whole issue of GIF transparency and choosing a matte color later in this section.)

3. By zooming in, I could see that I had an optimized image that looked just as good as the original. I could also see by the numbers below the optimized version that the file size was 11.08KB. This number is accurate, unlike the file sizes found in Photoshop Elements' Info palette, which are approximations.

Note: You can zoom in for a closer examination of your optimized image by selecting the Zoom tool (🔍) and clicking the image. You can also zoom in by selecting a percentage from the Zoom pop-up menu. You can display a menu of view controls in Windows by right-clicking in the Save for Web dialog box. On a Mac, hold the Control key and click anywhere in the window. To preview your graphic as it would look in a browser window, click the browser icon or select a browser from the Preview In drop-down list at the bottom of the Save for Web dialog box.

4. I clicked OK and saved my image as a GIF file (the default file extension in the Save for Web dialog box). The dialog box closed, and I returned to the main Photoshop Elements window.

If you duplicate what I've just done in this example with just about any GIF-appropriate image, you'll be fine. But for now, let's talk about how you can fine-tune this image and optimize it even more.

This requires some experimentation and understanding of the various color reduction (or color table) and dither algorithms. If you click the Color Reduction Algorithm drop-down list, you'll see several other choices in addition to Selective:

> **Perceptual** This is much like Selective, in that it creates a custom color table based on the colors in your image. Selective favors web-safe colors, and Perceptual gives priority to colors that are more visible to the human eye.
>
> **Adaptive** This also creates a custom color table based on the colors found in the image.
>
> **Restrictive (Web)** This, on the other hand, creates a color table containing only the 216 colors common to both Windows and the Mac. Frankly, there are very few cases when this palette is appropriate, and I'll get into those later.

Note: To have your Save for Web settings for a particular file remembered, hold down the Alt/Option key. The Help button turns into a Remember button. If you click Remember, the next time you open this Photoshop Elements file with the Save for Web plug-in, it will open with the same settings that were applied at the time you chose Remember. If you don't do this, the next time you open your Photoshop Elements file, it will apply the most recently specified settings.

The three relevant choices, then, are Selective, Adaptive, and Perceptual. I suggest you try each one on your image and see what it does. The results vary from image to image depending on the content and colors contained in the image, so I can't give you any other advice except to experiment. In the case of Val's graphic, the Selective color reduction algorithm turned out to be the best option for my image.

The next optimization you can make is to choose from different Dither percentages. Dithering is an issue only if your original image contains more than the maximum 256 colors supported by the GIF format. In this case, dithering creates a smooth gradation between adjacent colors by using the existing colors to create patterns that the eye merges into a single new color. This gives the appearance of extending the color table beyond 256 colors. Up close, however, the patterns become obvious, and the image looks grainy or speckled. Without dithering, the sharp contrast between colors will result in banding, which is not very attractive. Dithering always increases the file size.

You can control the amount of dithering with the Dither option. The default is 100 percent, but you can lower that number. As you do, the file size will be reduced accordingly.

I chose 0 percent Dither because Val's graphic contained fewer than 256 colors, so dithering wasn't necessary.

The next choice is Colors, and this is where you can get some real file-size reduction. If you leave the default set to 256 colors, a color table that contains 256 colors will be created, regardless of whether you need that many. If you have chosen the Web or Custom color reduction algorithm, then you can choose the Auto option from the Colors drop-down list to have Photoshop Elements determine the optimal number of colors in the color table. Or with any of the color reduction algorithms, you can simply incrementally reduce the number of colors until your image just becomes unacceptable, and then go back up one increment before saving the file. That's what I did with Val's graphic. I started with 256 colors, stepped down to 128 colors, and compared the optimized version with the original. Because there was no difference, I kept going, down to 64 colors. Still no difference. At 32 colors, I began to notice some degradation in the drop-shadow areas, so I went back to 64 colors, confident that I had optimized my file size as much as I could. The final file size? I went from 11.08KB to 7.49KB, a 30 percent reduction.

Note: When you view the same image on a Mac and a Windows computer, the image will look different. This means if you create a graphic or image that looks good on a Mac, it will look too dark in Windows. If you create an image or graphic in Windows that looks right, it will look washed out on a Mac. If you are interested in having your work look good on both platforms, consider adjusting your brightness settings accordingly. In the Photoshop Elements work area, choose Enhance ➢ Adjust Lighting ➢ Brightness/Contrast. If you are working in Windows, try reducing your brightness by -15. If you are working on a Mac, try increasing your brightness by +15. Back in the Save for Web plug-in, you can preview your work to see what it will look like on either platform. Click the small right arrow in the upper right of the Save for Web dialog box, and a drop-down preview menu appears. Choose the platform in which you wish to preview your work. You can also choose Browser Dither, which shows how your graphic will look if it is forced to dither by a browser.

Using Save As

Another way to create a GIF is to use the Save As method. You'll lose certain preview capabilities but you'll gain more in the way of options and control.

As with the Save for Web method, there is a quick and easy Save As method in addition to a way that takes more time but usually results in a smaller file size.

To use the quick and easy method:

1. While in RGB mode, size your image to the desired size (Image ➢ Resize ➢ Image Size). To make sure you are in RGB mode, choose Image ➢ Mode ➢ RGB Color. (If you are working on a 16-bit-per-channel file, be sure to select Convert to 8 Bits/Channel from the Mode menu before proceeding.)

2. Choose File ➤ Save As. In the dialog box, choose CompuServe GIF from the pop-up menu. After you select Save, the Indexed Color dialog box shown in Figure 10.16 appears. (If your file contains layers, a dialog box appears asking, "Flatten layers?" To proceed, answer affirmative. If you want to keep your layers intact, work on a copy: File ➤ Duplicate.) You can also open this dialog box by going directly to Image ➤ Mode ➤ Indexed Color. Again, you must start in the RGB mode.

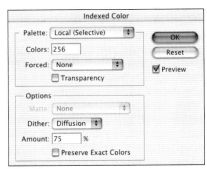

Figure 10.16: When you choose Save As ➤ CompuServe GIF ➤ Save, you access this dialog box. You need to start from the RGB mode.

3. The following settings will give you perfectly acceptable results:

Palette Local (Selective)

Colors 256

Forced None

Dither Diffusion

Amount 100 percent (75 percent is the default, and that works fine, too)

Preview By leaving this check box selected, you can see the effect of your choices on the image. You won't have the advantage of the Save for Web side-by-side comparison, and to view your original you'll need to deselect the Preview box. Using common Photoshop keyboard commands—Ctrl/⌘ +click zooms in, and Alt/Option+click zooms out—you can carefully examine the effects of your settings.

4. After you are finished, click Save.

Now for some details that will help you further optimize your image. You'll see more Palette options in the Indexed Color dialog box than you will in the Save for Web plug-in, including the following:

Exact This is an option only if the image contains 256 or fewer colors.

System (Mac OS) This uses the Macintosh default 8-bit palette.

System (Windows) This uses the Windows system default 8-bit palette.

Uniform This is used in scientific work, and I won't even try to describe it.

Custom This creates a custom palette by using the Color Table dialog box.

Preview This uses the custom palette from the previous conversion.

For most digital images, the three relevant palettes are Adaptive, Selective, and Perceptual, which I'll explain in more detail in the preceding section. You'll notice the words *Local* and *Master* in front of these three choices. Master is an option only if more than one image is open in the Photoshop Elements window at a time. If you select a palette with the word *Master* in front of it, Photoshop Elements averages all the colors in all the images that are open and creates a "master" palette that it then applies to your image. If this isn't what you want, just be sure to use the palette with the word *Local* in front of it. That way, you'll know you are getting a palette specifically tailored to the image you started with.

As I described in the preceding "Using Save for Web" section, you can experiment with the different palettes, dithering, and colors to come up with an even more optimal image. The only drawback is you won't know your file size until after you save your image.

Paying Special Attention to Web Colors

The 216 colors that can be read by both Windows and Mac computers are called *web-safe*, or *browser-safe*, colors, as noted earlier in the chapter. Web-safe colors are an issue only if a display system is not capable of displaying more than 256 colors.

If your digital image or graphic contains colors that are not web-safe, and they are viewed on a web browser running on a limited display system, the browser will either replace the color with one that is web-safe or simulate the color through dithering.

When it comes to using web-safe colors for your work, you have three choices:

- You can ignore the whole issue and say good riddance to those viewers who don't have display systems capable of displaying at least thousands, if not millions, of colors. If you choose this option, move on and skip the rest of this section entirely.

- You can get really obsessive and use only web-safe colors, in which case you should read one of my earlier books, *Photoshop for the Web* (O'Reilly & Associates, 1999), in which I devote many chapters to ways to do this.

- You can take a more reasoned approach and use web-safe colors only in areas of large expanses of solid color, such as backgrounds, and don't worry about the other areas where it won't matter if your image dithers or if the colors are slightly changed.

If you decide on the last option, which I think is a good choice, you'll need to start with web-safe colors when appropriate or swap existing non-web-safe colors with ones that are.

You can select browser-safe colors to work with from the Color Swatches palette, or from the Color Picker, accessed by double-clicking the foreground or background color boxes (▪) in the toolbox. Figure 10.17 shows the Web Spectrum found in the Swatches palette (left), and the Color Picker with the Only Web Colors option selected (right).

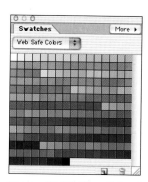
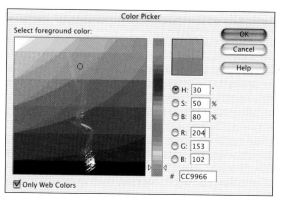

Figure 10.17: The Color Swatches palette with the Web Spectrum loaded (left). The 216 displayed colors are considered web-safe. Holding the cursor over a swatch displays the color's hexadecimal value. On the right, the Color Picker with the Only Web Colors box selected. Now only web-safe colors can be selected. Hexadecimal values are also shown.

There are several ways to swap non-web-safe colors with ones that are. One way is to follow these steps:

1. Fill the foreground color box with a web-safe color from the Color Swatches palette or from the Color Picker set to Only Web Colors.

2. Use Photoshop's Magic Wand (✎), Magnetic Lasso (🔏), or manual selection tools to select the area of the image that you want to change.

3. Fill the selected area with the foreground color that you chose from a browser-safe palette (Edit ➢ Fill Layer, and then Use: Foreground).

4. To ensure that your browser-safe colors don't shift when you apply the Indexed Color command (Image ➢ Mode ➢ Color Table), select the Preserve Exact Colors check box in the Indexed Color dialog box. This will be an option only if you choose a Dither pattern.

> **Note:** You can "force" non-web-safe colors to the nearest color-safe color by using the Color Picker "cube" (🎲) found just to the left of the Help button in the Color Picker dialog box. Access the Color Picker by double-clicking the foreground or background color boxes (▣). The cube is visible only if a non-web-safe color is selected. To shift to a web-safe color, simply click the cube or the color box underneath it.

Another way to ensure web-safe colors is to use the color table to swap out the non-web-safe color. This works only if you are in the Indexed Color mode. Here's how:

1. Choose Image ➢ Mode ➢ Color Table.

2. Choose the Eyedropper tool (✐) from the Color Table dialog box.

3. Click the area in your image that you wish to alter. The color box in the Color Table dialog box will be highlighted, and your selected color will be deleted from the box and from the image. Now deselect the Eyedropper tool.

4. Click the highlighted color box in the Color Table dialog box to bring up the Color Picker. Choose the web-safe color of your choice and click OK. That color will now replace your old, non-web-safe color.

5. You can repeat this process on other flat colors that you don't want to dither. Click the OK button when you are finished. Test your image by using the Save for Web preview options.

Of course, you can always apply the Web palette to the entire graphic palette by using the Save As or the Save for Web method. This might or might not produce acceptable results, depending on the colors in your image. With an image that contains more than 256 colors, the results generally are not good.

If you do decide to apply the Web palette to a graphic, you'll end up with an indexed image that contains 216 browser-safe colors. But what if you don't need 216 colors? What if your image contains only 64 colors, or, for that matter, 16? By saving your file with 216 colors, you have created an unnecessarily large file. What to do now? You can get rid of the unused colors by following these steps:

1. Switch from Indexed Color to RGB mode (Image ➤ Mode ➤ RGB).

2. Without doing anything else, switch back to Indexed Color mode. If your image has fewer than 216 colors, the Exact palette should be selected, and the number of colors in the image will be displayed.

3. Click the OK button and save the indexed image as a GIF.

The new image will look exactly the same as the original GIF, but the file size will shrink.

Making Transparent GIFs

By using the GIF file format, you can designate a color as transparent. This means you can make a non-rectangular object appear to float against a background.

You can do this with either the Save for Web or Save As methods. Both methods require that you start in the RGB mode and create transparent areas as indicated by the gray and white checkerboard pattern—or whatever pattern or color you've set in your Transparency preferences.

Figure 10.18 shows another graphic created by designer Valerie Robbins for another one of my websites. If I convert her graphic to the GIF format "as is" with its white background and place it on my web page with a gold background, the graphic will float in a rectangular patch of white. If I remove the white background and replace it with transparency, then the graphic will appear to float atop the gold background.

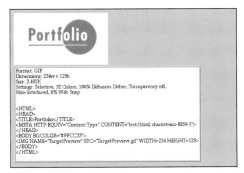

Figure 10.18: Placed against a gold background, the rectangular shape is obvious.

To create a transparent GIF by using the Save for Web method (starting in the RGB mode), I followed these steps:

1. I used the Magic Eraser (🩹) to delete the white background to transparency. If your graphic is already on a transparent layer, you are ready to go.

2. I chose File ➤ Save for Web.

3. In the Save for Web dialog box, I clicked the Transparency check box. This option is available only if your graphic contains transparent areas. If the box is left deselected, your transparent areas will appear in the optimized view as white, or whatever color you choose in the Matte color box next to the word *Transparency*. After you click the Transparency check box, the transparent areas in your graphic will be designated by the familiar gray and white checkerboard pattern.

4. I chose the appropriate palette, dithering, and colors, and optimized the graphic.

5. I used the Save for Web browser preview feature to view the transparent GIF.

At this point, I saw a problem in the browser window. Figure 10.19, which is magnified, shows a halo around the edges.

Figure 10.19: Now I have transparency but I also have a halo.

Before I get into how to fix this problem, it's helpful to explain a basic fact about the GIF transparency. Variable opacity is not an option in the GIF format. It supports only one transparent color, which effectively means a 1-bit mask. Areas are either transparent or not.

To get around the 1-bit mask limitation, you can have Photoshop Elements create a pseudo multi-bit mask. If you know the color of your web page background, all you need to do is choose that color from the Matte pop-up menu in the Save for Web dialog box. Photoshop Elements then adds variations of this color to edges of your graphic. If your web background consists of multiple colors, pick a representative color from your background and use that. Creating this pseudo multi-bit mask adds some file size to your GIF, but not much.

Because I knew my graphic would be placed on a page with a gold background, I chose Other from the Matte pop-up menu, and then in the Color Picker I chose FFCC33, the hexadecimal value for my color. The selected color was displayed in the Matte box. (If you set the Matte to None, no pseudo multi-bit mask is created. Use None if an aliased look is what you want.)

A zoomed-in shot of the edges shown in Figure 10.20 illustrates how Photoshop Elements adds variations of the Matte color to the edges of the graphic. Now when the graphic is placed against the browser background, a nice anti-aliasing effect makes the graphic look much better.

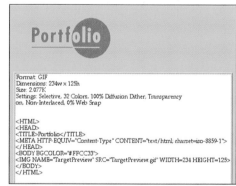

Figure 10.20: When you choose a Matte color, a pseudo multi-bit mask is created (left), which diminishes the jagged look. Now the graphic floats nicely on the page (right).

You can also use the Save As or Image ➤ Mode ➤ Indexed Colors method to designate transparent areas. While in the RGB mode:

1. Use one of the Eraser or Selection tools to delete your background or other areas to transparency. Transparency is signified by a gray and white checkerboard pattern.

2. Choose File ➤ Save As or Image ➤ Mode ➤ Indexed Colors. (If your file contains layers, dialog box will appear asking, "Flatten layers?" To proceed, answer affirmative. If you want to keep your layers intact, work on a copy: File ➤ Duplicate.)

3. Click the Transparency check box in the dialog box. If you know the background color of your web page, and you want to avoid a jagged or halo effect, have Photoshop Elements create a pseudo multi-bit mask. In the Matte pop-up menu, choose from the preset options or enter a color from the Color Picker. Matte will be available only if your image contains transparent areas.

4. Choose the optimal palette, dithering, and color options. When you are finished, click OK. The areas previously signified by a gray and white checkerboard pattern will become transparent.

GIFing a Photograph

Although GIF isn't the ideal format for photographs, if you want true transparency or control over certain colors in an image, there are times when you'll want to GIF a photographic image. If you do this, I recommended that you use the following settings in the Indexed Color dialog box:

Palette Perceptual or Adaptive
Dither option Diffusion
Colors 256
Dither amount 100 percent

Furthermore, there is something else you can do to make certain photographs look better, especially photographs of faces. The method that I'll describe doesn't work with the Save for Web plug-in. You'll need to toggle between Image ➤ Mode ➤ RGB and Image ➤ Mode ➤ Indexed Color.

You have to understand that when Photoshop Elements converts an image from the RGB mode to the Indexed Color mode, it treats all parts of the image equally. It doesn't recognize, for example, that you might be more concerned about the foreground of the image than the background. But you're not stuck with this situation—you can "influence" Photoshop Elements to create a palette that best represents the important parts of your image.

Take the photograph shown in Figure 10.21. I applied the standard GIF settings described in the preceding list, and this is what I got. As you can see by the color table, the Perceptual palette gave a lot of emphasis to the colorful background and not enough to the important skin tones. It's OK, but I can easily do better.

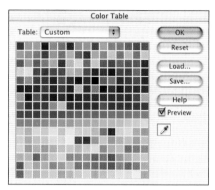

Figure 10.21: Applying the standard GIF settings produced the image shown on the left. The color table (right) shows an equal emphasis on the background colors and the face.

All I need to do is simply use a selection tool to select the area that I want to emphasize. Then when I convert from RGB to Indexed Color mode, Photoshop Elements will automatically weigh the conversion in favor of the selected area.

This is what I've done to get the image shown in Figure 10.22. I made a selection around the child's face with the Elliptical Marquee tool (○), then converted the image to Indexed Color mode. The new palette contains many more of the subtle tonal variations that make the skin tone more realistic. Yeah, the rainbow now has color banding, but the face is the important part.

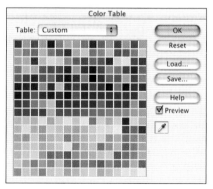

Figure 10.22: By selecting the child's face with the Elliptical Marquee tool and then applying the Indexed Color mode, the conversion is weighed in favor of the selected area (left). The color table (right) now displays more skin tones.

You can also apply selective dithering to make a photographic image look better. When you command Photoshop to dither an image, it applies the dither pattern to the entire image, even to areas that you might not want to dither, such as areas containing flat colors. Wouldn't it be great if you could "tell" Photoshop to selectively dither a small part of an image and yet keep the other parts intact? You can, by following these steps:

1. In RGB mode, select and copy the part of the image to dither (Ctrl/⌘ +C).
2. Index the image (Index ➢ Mode ➢ Indexed Color).
3. Paste the copied portion back from the Clipboard to the indexed but undithered image (Ctrl/⌘ +V). Photoshop automatically dithers the pasted RGB selection, leaving the rest of the image untouched.

By the way, I have CNET's Casey Caston to thank for showing me this very useful method.

Animating GIFs

You can also create simple animations by using the GIF file format and the Save for Web plug-in. Individual animation frames are created from Photoshop Elements layers. You can open an existing GIF animation file and view each frame as a layer in Photoshop Elements. This round-trip GIF animation capability is especially handy if you want to change and edit your animation.

I'll show you how to create an animated GIF by using four frames from a video clip I shot of my daughter riding without training wheels for the first time. I actually created this animation to send to our relatives in Spain and Norway. It was less than 150 KBs, much smaller than a video and almost as effective.

This is what I did:

1. I selected File ➢ Import ➢ Frame from Video from the menu bar. This brought up the dialog box shown in Figure 10.23.
2. I selected Browse, and selected and opened the video of my daughter on the bike. (On the Windows side, Photoshop Elements reads just about anything the Microsoft Media Player supports, that is, AVI, WMV, ASF, MPEG, and MIV. On the Mac side, it supports just about anything QuickTime supports, that is, AVI, MPEG, and MOV3). Using the VCR-like controls I found a frame at the beginning of the sequence. I selected Grab Frame. Then I stepped forward to a frame in the middle of the sequence, paused, and selected Grab Frame. I repeated this two more times at different intervals. When I was finished, I selected Done.
3. Photoshop Elements numbers the frame grabs in sequence. I selected the second frame grab, copied the selection from frame grab 2, and pasted it onto frame grab 1. I selected frame 3, copied, and pasted it on frame grab 1. I selected frame grab 4, copied, and then pasted it on frame grab 1. Now I had one file with four layers, as shown in Figure 10.24. The order of the layers is important because it determines the animated sequence.

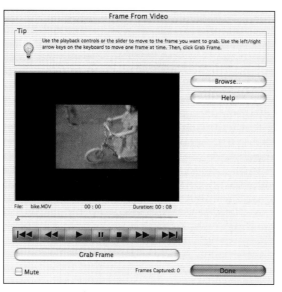

Figure 10.23: The Frame from Video dialog box. From here you can grab as many frames as you wish.

Figure 10.24: My Layers palette showing the four layers that will make up my animated GIF.

4. Next I selected the Save for Web plug-in by choosing File ➤ Save for Web from the menu bar (Figure 10.25). I selected GIF as the file format, chose the Selective palette, chose 256 colors, and selected the Animation check box (Animate on Windows). In the Animation settings, I selected Loop so my animation would play continuously, and experimented with the frame rate settings until I got the look I wanted. You can step frame by frame through an animation by using the Animation controls in the Save for Web dialog box. However, to view the animation in action, you need to click the Preview In check box and view your animation in a selected web browser.

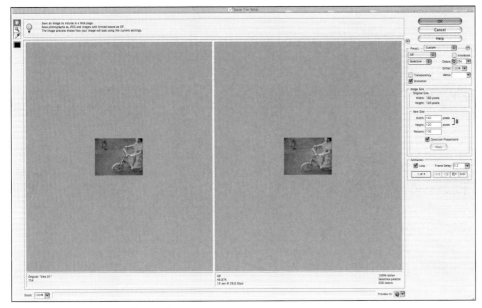

Figure 10.25: My Save for Web settings.

My GIF animation is included on the accompanying CD. The original Photoshop Elements file complete with layers is also there.

Building Web Page Backgrounds

The simplest way to create a web page background is to use HTML-designated colors. However, you can take your web page to another level of professionalism by using Photoshop Elements to create custom backgrounds. This section shows you how to use large images to fill a background and how to create smaller background tiles that automatically fill any size browser window.

The HTML code for adding a graphic to your background page is simple: just add the **BACKGROUND** extension to your **BODY** tag. The tag **<BODY BACKGROUND= "*background*.gif">**, where *background* is the name of your background image, tiles the graphic across and down the browser window. Any text or graphics on your page will be displayed on top of the tiled background.

You can use either GIF or JPEG files for background. Just remember to make your graphic small enough through compression or color indexing so that it appears nearly instantly.

Creating Tiled Patterns

A simple way to create a background image that loads quickly is to create a square tile made in such a way that it tiles seamlessly.

To do this, you can either use one of Photoshop Elements' ready-made patterns or create one of your own.

To use the ready-made pattern:

1. Create a new Photoshop Elements document (File ➤ New ➤ Blank File), 128 × 128 pixels at 72dpi.

2. Choose Edit ➤ Fill Layer. Then choose Use: Pattern and select any of the custom patterns. Play with different opacity settings in the Fill Layer dialog box. Lowering the opacity diminishes the effect of the pattern on the content of your web page. (When you select a pattern, the Pattern window stays open unless you click OK to close the Fill Layer dialog. If you want to play around with the opacity settings, you'll need to click any empty spot in the Fill Layer dialog to close the Pattern window.)

3. Click the OK button.

Now you'll need to convert your pattern into a GIF or JPEG by using the methods described earlier in this chapter. To test your pattern and see what it might look like on a web page, use the method described in the upcoming section "Testing Your Background Tiles." Figure 10.26 shows a tiled background created by using this method and the Water pattern from the Custom Patterns palette.

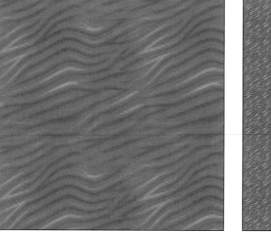

Figure 10.26: This 128 × 128 pixel tile (left) was created using the Water pattern set at 65 percent opacity. On the right is how it will look as a web page background.

To create a tile completely on your own:

1. Create a new Photoshop Elements image (File ➤ New ➤ Blank File), 128 × 128 pixels at 72dpi.

2. Create your own texture by using various filters applied to a background or foreground color. Try any of the filters found under the Texture, Pixelate, or Render categories. If you use the Clouds and Difference Clouds filters found under Filter ➤ Render and use the dimensions suggested in step 1, your tile will automatically tile seamlessly. You'll need to apply these filters to an image with existing texture, not a flat color. If you use these filters on other dimensions or use other filters, your image might not tile seamlessly. In that case, you'll need to use the Offset filter found under Filter ➤ Other.

3. To use the Offset filter shown in Figure 10.27, do the following: In the Horizontal and Vertical boxes, type values equal to half the dimensions of your tile. For example, with a 128 × 128 pixel tile, use the number 64. This moves the image 64 pixels to the right and 64 pixels down. Next, select the Wrap Around option. This inverts the remaining portion of the image and tiles it in the unused areas. Click the OK button.

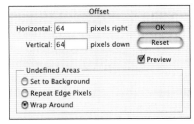

Figure 10.27: The Offset filter helps create tiles that tile seamlessly.

4. Use the Clone Stamp tool (⚓) to remove the seam caused by the outside edges meeting in the center, and smooth out the lines. Convert your tile to the GIF or JPEG file format and test it by using the method described in "Testing Your Background Tiles," later in this chapter. Figure 10.28 shows a background I created by applying the Grain filter (Filter ➤ Texture ➤ Grain) to a 128 × 128 tile, then the Offset filter as described, and touching up the seams with the Clone Stamp tool.

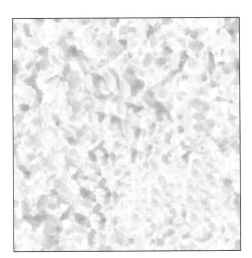

Figure 10.28: I created this 128 × 128 pixel tile (left) by using the Grain filter and the Offset filter. After some touching up with the Clone Stamp tool, the image tiled seamlessly (right).

Creating Tiled Strips

Figure 10.29 shows another type of tile, one that gives you a way to control the placement of color so you can have a bright band of color on one side and a solid band of color on the other.

Figure 10.29: This type of tile (left) gives you a different kind of control. By controlling where the colors go, you can create a horizontal or vertical navigational bar (right).

This is how I created the tile shown:

1. I created a new file (File ➢ New ➢ Blank File), 1200 × 8 pixels. In the New dialog box, I set the Contents option to White.

2. I used the Rectangular Marquee selection tool (⬚) on the left edge of my image to create a selection 150 pixels wide. I opened the Info box from the menu bar (Window ➢ Info) bin so I could see when my selection was exactly 150 pixels. I feathered this selection 10 pixels (Select ➢ Feather).

3. I then filled the selection with red, using the Layer ➢ New Fill Layer ➢ Solid Color command.

4. I saved the tile as a GIF and tested it by using the method described next.

You can fill your selection with any color you want, or you can use a pattern. If you want the color to run horizontally across a web page, just create a vertical tile, 8 × 1200 pixels, and fill the top portion of the tile instead. If you want a band of color on the opposite side, you can do that as well.

Testing Your Background Tiles

To see what your tiles look like tiled, you can test them by designating them as a background in an HTML document and observing how they look on a web browser. Or you can use the following method to test them with Photoshop Elements:

1. Use the Rectangular Marquee selection tool (⬚) to select all of your tiles, or just use the keyboard command Ctrl/⌘ +A.

2. Choose Edit ➢ Define Pattern. Name the pattern and save it.

3. Create a new file 800 × 800 pixels at 72dpi (File ➤ New). Actually, you can make the file any size you want as long as it is large enough to approximate the size of a browser window.

4. Choose Edit ➤ Fill Layer and choose Pattern from the pop-up menu. Find and select your saved defined pattern and click OK. This option will tile your defined pattern to fill the current window in much the same way that a browser would.

Using an Image as a Background

If you use a single image as a background, keep the following suggestions in mind:

- Keep the file size down through heavy JPEG compression or careful color indexing. Unless it is the only graphic on the page, a background image shouldn't be more than 20KB. Some web designers say that a web page should never exceed 50KB total, including the background, all the graphics, and HTML coding. I've compressed JPEG images that were 800 × 800 pixels down to 4KB, using some of the methods described earlier in the chapter (➤ "Optimizing Digital Images for JPEG Compression").

- Make your image at least 640 × 480 pixels and preferably a little larger. Unfortunately, there is no set size to work with, and this is where the drawback to using a single image becomes apparent. Unlike the tiling method described earlier, your image might be too small or too big, depending on the size of the browser window.

- Tone the image down so it doesn't distract from the rest of the page's content. While in the RGB mode, use the Levels or Brightness/Contrast controls to do this. Apply a Gaussian blur filter to diffuse it more.

Creating Navigational Graphics

Navigational aids are an important part of any website or presentation. Photoshop Elements provides several easy ways to make an assortment of appropriate shapes that can be customized in almost an infinite number of ways.

To create all the navigational graphics shown in this section, I started with these two steps:

1. I chose File ➤ New ➤ Blank File and created an image window 160 × 160 pixels at 72dpi.

2. I selected a shape from the toolbox. To access the various shape tools from the toolbox, position the pointer on the tool button, and then click and hold down the mouse button until the tools list appears. You can then select the type of tool you want. You can further specify the tool by using the drop-down lists and fields available on the options bar.

For the graphic shown on the left in Figure 10.30, I did the following:

1. I selected the Custom Shape tool from the toolbox (🗩). On the options bar, I opened the Custom Shape drop-down list and clicked the arrow in the upper-right corner to display the Shape pop-up menu. I selected Arrows from the menu, and then I selected a predefined Arrow 25.

2. In the new image window, I clicked and dragged the shape to size.

3. I opened the Style Picker in the options bar and clicked the arrow in the upper right to open the style pop-up menu. I then chose the Wow Neon category and Wow-Purple Neon. Then from the Glass Buttons category, I chose Teal Glass. Because I used these particular layer styles, it really didn't matter which color was selected in the color box. I left my color black.

Note: After you've selected a style from the Shape Tools options bar, that style will remain selected until you select another style or reset your Shape Tools options by clicking the tool icon at the far left of the options bar and selecting Reset Tool. You can also remove a style by opening the style flyout in the options bar and selecting the arrow on the right. From the pop-up menu select Remove Style. (Using the Undo button in the shortcuts bar or the Undo History palette only removes the style from a shape, it doesn't remove the style from the Style options.) If I had wanted to, I could have adjusted various aspects of the layer styles by double-clicking the *f* in the Layers palette. This would have opened the Style Settings dialog box with its various options.

For the graphic on the right in Figure 10.30, I followed the preceding steps, except I selected the 10 Point Star from the Shapes category. From the Style Picker's Complex category, I chose Color Target.

Figure 10.30: This arrow is a custom shape with Purple Neon and Teal Glass layer styles applied to it (left). This star is a custom shape with the Color Target layer style applied to it (right).

For the triangle shown on the left in Figure 10.31, I followed the same steps, except I selected Sign 4 from the Signs category. I chose red as my color and applied an Inner Ridge layer effect from the Bevels category. I used the Style Settings dialog box to adjust the shape of the bevel and the direction of the light. You can rotate the triangle to any direction by selecting the Shape Selection tool from the options bar (➤) and choosing Image ➤ Rotate and the direction you want to go. You might need to open the Style Settings dialog box and adjust your settings based on the new orientation.

To create the button shown on the right in Figure 10.31, I followed these steps:

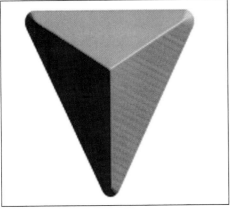 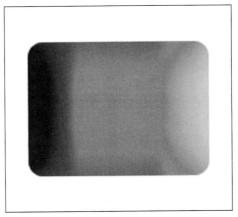

Figure 10.31: This triangle was created by using the Sign 4 custom shape and the Inner Ridge bevel layer effect (left). This button was created using the Rectangle shape tool and a Simple Inner Glows bevel layer style (right).

1. I selected the Rectangle shape tool (□).

2. From the Style Picker's Bevels category, I chose Inner Glows, then Simple. I chose red as a color.

3. I clicked and dragged the rectangle to size. I adjusted the look of the bevel by double-clicking the *f* in the Layers palette. This brought up the Style Settings dialog box, and I played with the various options until I got what I wanted. To create the bullet ball shown in Figure 10.32, I took these steps:

Figure 10.32: This bullet ball was created using the Ellipse shape tool and the Rivet layer style.

1. I selected the Ellipse shape tool (○) from the toolbar. You can also select the various shape tools directly from the options bar.

2. From the Complex category in the Style Picker, I chose Rivet.

3. I held the Shift key and clicked and dragged the ellipse into a centered circle. I then double-clicked the *f* in the Layers palette and adjusted the Style Settings to get the effect I wanted.

Using Camera Raw and Other Advanced Techniques

This chapter includes several examples that require a higher commitment to "getting your hands dirty" and spending a little more time to get an image just right. Ultimately, learning the advanced techniques shown in this chapter will help you take your digital imaging skills to a higher level of expertise.

11

Chapter Contents

Using Adobe's Camera Raw

Many digital cameras offer a choice of file formats. The mostly commonly used file format to save an image in is JPEG. But some of the more advanced digital cameras offer a format that saves the RAW data that comes directly off the sensor. (Check your camera's specs to see whether your camera does. Settings are usually adjusted via the camera's menu.)

Note: When "raw" image data is the product of a digital camera, it's usually called a RAW file to distinguish it from other file formats.

This RAW data is full of potential. It hasn't been touched by on-board camera processing, and is therefore full of information that may be very useful. Think of the RAW data as a negative in traditional photography, and the JPEG or TIFF file as a print. If you save the "negative," you can always make a perfect "prints" later. A print from a print is never as good.

To coax the best image from this data, you need special software that interprets the data. You also need to know what you are doing. Some manufacturers include RAW imaging software with their digital cameras, but because you are using Photoshop Elements 3, no worry: The new version comes with Camera Raw, a powerful plug-in that works with most RAW formats.

Note: RAW data files differ from manufacturer to manufacturer, and even from camera model to camera model. (Here are a few typical file extensions: Nikon **.nef**, Olympus **.orf**, Canon **.crw**, Minolta **.mrw**, and Fuji **.raf**). RAW formats are constantly being changed, so if you find the plug-in doesn't read your RAW file, go to **www.adobe.com** and download the latest version of the plug-in. You can tell which version you are using by selecting the About Plug-In menu and clicking Camera Raw.

Let's start with opening RAW files in Photoshop Elements and then move on to using the powerful Camera Raw plug-in shown in Figure 11.1. I've included a few RAW files on the CD to experiment with if you don't have any of your own.

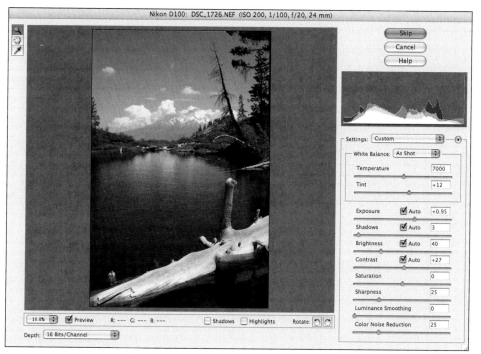

Figure 11.1: The Camera Raw plug-in work area.

Opening RAW Files

There are at least three basic ways to open RAW files into Photoshop Elements (four ways if you are working on the Windows platform). One way opens your RAW file from the File Browser directly into the editing work space of Photoshop Elements. The other methods open your file in the Camera Raw plug-in, where you can work directly on the RAW data before sending the file to Photoshop Elements' editing space for fine-tuning or more extensive editing.

To open a RAW file into the Camera Raw plug-in, do *one* of the following:

- Choose File ➤ Open from the Editor menu bar. Navigate to and open your file. The Camera Raw plug-in will automatically open.
- Choose File ➤ Browse Folders from the Editor menu bar. Navigate to your RAW file and double-click the thumbnail. The Camera Raw plug-in will automatically open. (This is the most efficient way to handle RAW files, because you can see all of them at once.)
- From the Organizer (in Windows only), double-click the image thumbnail or choose Edit ➤ Go to Standard Edit from the Organizer menu bar. Either way will open the Camera Raw plug-in window.

To open a RAW file directly into the editing space of Photoshop Elements and bypass the Camera Raw plug-in window:

1. Open the File Browser from the Editor (File ➤ Browse Folders).
2. Navigate to your RAW files.
3. Select the file you wish to open. (Shift+click to select more than one file at a time.)
4. Hold the Shift key while double-clicking selected files. The images are converted by using the current Camera Raw setting—or, if no settings were specified previously, the Camera Default will be used.

So, double-clicking opens a RAW file into the Camera Raw plug-in, Shift+double-clicking opens it directly into the editing work space. Why open RAW files directly into the editing space? If you are satisfied with using either the previous Camera Raw setting or the Camera Default, this method simply saves time.

Shooting Digital: When to Shoot RAW

Assuming your digital camera supports a RAW format, use RAW when quality is critical and you have the time and means to process the results yourself. Consider this musical analogy: When you listen to a symphony, you want the highest possible fidelity to enjoy the nuances and subtleties. Fidelity is less important as the music itself becomes less complex. When you want to see a symphony, think RAW. Conversely, if space on your memory card is an issue, shoot JPEG, because RAW files are generally much larger.

It's also important to remember that with many digital cameras there is no reason why you can't save one image as a JPEG, a subsequent one as a TIFF, and yet another image as RAW, basing your choice on the content of the shot or your needs. Some professional digital cameras can save a single shot in more than one format simultaneously.

Processing with the Camera Raw Plug-In

As you can see in Figure 11.1, the Camera Raw plug-in offers many options for optimizing your image. Let's go through each component and feature of the plug-in and see how it works. Just keep in mind that in the rapidly evolving world of RAW, the plug-in will be updated—and while the basics of processing a RAW file will remain—you'll likely see additional features in future versions of the plug-in, which can be downloaded for free from the www.adobe.com website.

Image Preview Window and Navigation

To the left of the Camera Raw plug-in window is the image preview. Here you'll find familiar navigation and magnification tools. To magnify an image, use the Zoom tool ($\mathcal{Q}$) from the toolbox. To reduce an image, hold down the Alt (Windows) or Option (Mac) key while using the Zoom tool. You can also choose a percentage from the zoom level menu. Right-clicking (Windows) / Control+clicking (Mac) the image brings up the pop-up menu, where you can also change the magnification level.

You can change the image orientation with the Rotate icons (↺) at the bottom right of the image preview window. Photoshop Elements saves an image's Camera Raw settings so the rotation will still be applied to the dialog box preview when you reopen the camera RAW file.

Move an image around the image preview window by selecting the Hand tool (✋), and clicking and dragging the image window. You can also press and hold the spacebar at any time to move your image around in the image window.

To the far left of the image area, near the bottom of the plug-in window, is the Depth pop-up menu that enables you to choose between 8 Bits/Channel and 16 Bits/Channel. I suggest you set your Depth to 16 Bits/Channel. I'll get into why later in the chapter.

Histogram and Clipping Tools

At the top right of the Camera Raw window is a histogram, which graphically maps the tonal values of the red, green, and blue colors in your image. The histogram changes accordingly as you apply different color and tonal values. An ideally-exposed image will produce a well-distributed histogram, with a range of values spread across the graph. Values clumped to the left or right of the graph indicate the image is too dark or too light, respectively. The histogram also indicates color distribution. Red, Green, and Blue values are graphed separately, and dominance of one of these colors signifies a color shift in that direction.

At the bottom of the image window you'll find other useful indicators for determining proper exposure values. If you select Highlights, any areas containing highlights with no pixels (commonly referred to as *highlight blowout*) will appear red. Select Shadows, and shadow areas of your image containing pure black and no details will appear blue. Figure 11.2 shows an image with both blown-out highlights and blocked shadows. You can confirm this by looking at the histogram in the upper right of the Camera Raw plug-in window. The highlight values are shifted to the right and are *clipped* by the edge of the graph, indicating loss of highlight detail. The tonal values are clumped to the far left of the graph, and are also clipped.

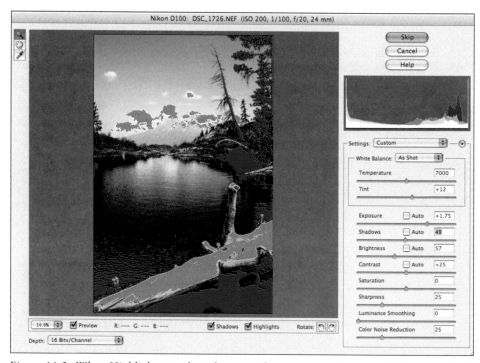

Figure 11.2: When Highlights is selected, areas of your image that contain blown-out high-lights appear red. Note how the values in the histogram (upper right) are clumped to the left, which confirms "highlight clipping." When Shadows is selected, areas of your image that contain pure black appear blue. Note how the values in the histogram are clumped to the right, which confirms "shadow clipping."

Note: *Clipping* refers to the movement of pixel values to either the highest highlight value (255)—which is represented by the far right border of the histogram, or the lowest shadow value (0)—which is represented by the far left border of the histogram. A photo that is *clipped* has areas that are either completely white or completely black and have no image detail. Most people agree that this is not a good thing.

Settings

In the Settings menu of the Camera Raw plug-in, you have the following choices:

Camera Default applies the exposure, white balance. and sharpness settings of your camera to the image. If you select Update or OK, this information is saved and attached to the image file as metadata that is read by the Camera Raw plug-in.

Selected Image is relevant only if you have previously updated an image. The first time you open an image, Camera Default is selected. At that moment, Camera Default and Selected Image are the same. However, if you alter the settings from the Camera Default, the next time you open it the Settings will show Selected Image.

Previous Conversion applies the conversions from a previous RAW file. **Custom** is automatically selected when you change any of the camera RAW plug-in settings. You can save the Custom setting by choosing Set Camera Default from the pop-up menu that appears when you click the arrow to the right of the Settings menu. You can reset the camera default from this menu as well.

White Balance

In the White Balance menu, you have the following choices: As Shot, Auto, Daylight, Cloudy, Shade, Tungsten, Fluorescent, Flash, and Custom.

If you choose As Shot, the Camera Raw plug-in will apply the white balance setting recorded at the time of exposure. If your settings are correct, there is nothing more to do; just leave the setting to As Shot. If you are *not* happy with what you see, you can try the other settings. Start with Auto. The Camera Raw plug-in reads the image data and automatically attempts to adjust the white balance. You can also select the other presets and observe the changes in your image. (The presets are available, in Windows, by placing your cursor over the image area and holding Shift and then right-clicking. If there is a Mac keyboard equivalent, I haven't found it.)

Below the White Balance pop-up menu are two sliders—Temperature and Tint—that can be used to fine-tune the white balance. If you move the Temperature slider to the left, colors will appear bluer (or cooler). Move the slider to the right, and the colors appear more yellow (warmer). If you move the Tint slider to the left (negative values), you'll add green to your image. Move it to the right (positive values) and you'll add magenta.

You can also use the White Balance tool in the image window toolbox (✐). (Alternately, you can hold the Shift key—Windows and Mac—and the cursor becomes the White Balance tool.) Select the tool and click in an area of the image that should be gray, neutral, or white. The White Balance tool then attempts to make the color exactly neutral. The changes are reflected in the Temperature and Tint sliders. You'll also notice a change in the histogram. If you are having trouble finding an area that is white or neutral, note the RGB values at the bottom of the image preview window. These values will change as you move the White Balance tool around. Locate an area that appears white and note the RGB values. If the values for each color are the same, you have a neutral color. If your RGB values are 255 each, you have pure white.

Tonal Controls

You have four ways to make tonal adjustments with the Camera Raw plug-in: Exposure, Shadows, Brightness, and Contrast.

For many images, leaving the Auto check boxes selected for these settings does the job. The Camera Raw plug-in calculates the correct tonal adjustments automatically.

When Auto doesn't work, as illustrated in the left image of Figure 11.3, you can move the sliders manually to get the correct setting. In this particular case, sliding the

Exposure slider to the left to +1.0 and sliding the Shadows slider to the left slightly helped, as shown in the second image in the figure. The histogram confirms the more evenly distributed tonal values.

Figure 11.3: Auto Exposure and Auto Shadows produced an image that was too light (left). Moving the Exposure and Shadows sliders to the left produced a more evenly distributed tonal range, as confirmed by the histogram (right).

In general, sliding the Exposure slider to the right lightens the image and sliding it to the left darkens it. The values are in increments equivalent to f-stops. For example, a +2 is similar to opening the aperture two stops. Sliding the Shadows slider to the right increases the density of the shadow areas without affecting the highlights. Sliding the slider to the left "opens," or lightens, the shadow areas without affecting the highlights.

For this example, I left the Brightness, Contrast, and Saturation settings alone. Brightness is similar to the Exposure slider; however, it redistributes the midtones in only a linear adjustment. Contrast applies an S-curve and leaves the extremes alone. Saturation increases the strength of the colors.

Sharpness

When the Camera Raw plug-in opens a RAW file, it automatically sharpens an image based on camera model, ISO, and exposure compensation. You can increase or decrease sharpening with the Sharpness slider, or leave it alone. A zero value turns sharpening off altogether.

Sharpening, as I explained in Chapter 2, is best saved for last, after you've resized your image to match the needs of your final destination, be it print or screen. With that in mind, I suggest you either leave the default setting or reduce sharpening altogether and do the sharpening later in the editing work space of Photoshop Elements (☞ "Sharpening" in Chapter 2).

Luminance Smoothing and Color Noise Reduction

Use the Luminance Smoothing slider to reduce grayscale image noise that makes an image look grainy. Use the Color Noise Reduction slider to reduce chroma (color) noise, which often occurs when you shoot at a high ISO. Moving the Luminance Smoothing or the Color Noise Reduction sliders to the right reduces noise but also "softens" the appearance of the image. It's best to enlarge your image over 100 percent to see the effects. (You can also bring your image into the Photoshop Elements' editing work space and use the Reduce Noise filter: Filter ➢ Noise ➢ Reduce Noise. This filter, unlike many of the other filters, works in the 16-bit mode.)

And, Finally

When you are finished, click the OK button. The altered image opens in the Photoshop Elements edit work space. Regardless of what you do to the image in the Camera Raw plug-in, the original camera RAW image file remains unaltered for future interpretation.

Note: Hold down the Alt (Windows) or Option (Mac) key to restore all your adjustments to the original settings. The Cancel button will change to a Reset button. While holding down the key, click the Reset button. You can also select Camera Default from the Settings menu to restore your camera's original settings. Deselecting the Preview option at the bottom of the image window will *display* your image unchanged, without the applied image setting adjustments.

Working in 16-Bit Mode

Photoshop Elements 3 supports 16-bit files, which is especially significant if you are working with RAW files and the Camera Raw plug-in. (Remember, as I mentioned earlier in this chapter, the Camera Raw plug-in gives you an option to work with a RAW image in 8 Bits/Channel or 16 Bits/Channel.) Some flatbed and slide scanners generate 16-bit files, and these files are supported by Photoshop Elements as well.

Why work in 16-bit? 8-bit files can contain up to 16.8 million colors, while 16-bit files can contain up to 281 trillion colors; obviously, working in 16-bit is preferred because you'll greatly increase your color gamut. (One way to see the difference is to perform a Levels adjustment with both 8 and 16 bits. With 16-bit, the resulting histogram is much smoother because of the additional data.) Working in 16-bit is also desirable when you are using certain filters or downsampling. When data needs to be thrown out, it's always better for the algorithm to have more data than less to work with.

Unfortunately, saving a 16-bit file doubles your file size, so if memory storage is an issue you might want to convert your images to 8-bit before saving them (I'll show you how to do this shortly). Also, many options and tools available in 8-bit mode, including layering, the Clone Stamp tool, and the Healing Brush tool aren't available in 16-bit mode.

So what should you do? I suggest the following workflow:

1. Bring in a 16-bit image from the Camera Raw plug-in, or if you are scanning, from the scanning software module.
2. Do any necessary work that's available only in 16-bit:
   - Use the histogram (Window ➢ Histogram), for example, to determine whether tonal or color corrections are necessary (☞ Chapter 2).
   - Use Levels, Quick Fix, Enhance, or whatever commands you are comfortable with to fine-tune tones and color.

3. If you need to resize your image, do it now (Image ➤ Resize ➤ Image Size).

4. Save your file in the PSD or TIFF file format (File ➤ Save As). JPEG doesn't support 16-bit files, so don't even try saving your file in that format. As I said earlier, if storage is an issue, you may choose to avoid this step.

5. After you have saved a 16-bit version of the file, change the mode to 8 Bits/Channel (Image ➤ Convert to 8 Bits/Channel).

6. All Photoshop Elements' tools and commands are now available, so finish preparing and editing your image as necessary with techniques that are available only for 8-bit files, such as these:
   Clone Stamp tool (⬚)
   Healing Brush tool (✐)
   Unsharp Mask filter

7. After you are finished, save a copy of your image (File ➤ Save As).

Now you may very well have three versions: the unadulterated RAW file (your negative) or the original 16-bit scanned file, a tonally correct and resized 16-bit file, and a final 8-bit image, ready for print and sharing.

Note: Don't expect good results if you print a 16-bit image with a typical desktop printer. Most desktop printers don't have the capability to print the wider color gamut. In the future this will likely change.

Extending Dynamic Range with Photomerge

Digital cameras notoriously capture a limited dynamic range, certainly when compared with print film. If you look at the left image in Figure 11.4, which was taken with a Nikon D100 digital camera, you'll see what I mean. Although the exposure for the foreground was correct, there was not enough latitude to capture the brighter details. The version on the right shows what happens when the exposure is made for the background. The foreground is now too dark. Professional photographers often use a technique that requires mounting a camera on a tripod and taking a series of images at the same f-stop but different shutter speeds, and then using Photoshop carefully to copy and paste the perfectly aligned images of different exposures into one final image.

Figure 11.4: *The exposure for the foreground is correct, but the exposure for the background is not (left). Here the exposure for the background is correct but not the exposure for the foreground (right).*

You can shoot more casually, avoid using a tripod, and still get good results by using the Photomerge feature in Photoshop Elements. The latest version of Photomerge features a Save As Layers option, which makes the following process—and the results shown in Figure 11.5—possible.

Figure 11.5: *After merging the two images with Photomerge, keeping layers intact, and then erasing unwanted parts of one image, you get this perfectly exposed image.*

Start by taking at least two shots with your digital camera at different exposures. It's best if you can use the same f-stop and vary the shutter speed to produce the different exposures, but not essential. Frame each shot as close to the next as possible. Refer to your camera manual if you don't know how to set your camera to over- or underexpose. Photomerge doesn't support 16-bit files, but you can still shoot in RAW, and the files will be automatically converted to 8-bit by Photomerge.

Then, in Photoshop Elements:

1. Choose File ➤ New ➤ Photomerge. (On the Mac you can also access Photomerge directly from the File Browser Automate menu. Just select the files you wish to merge, hold the Shift key to select multiple files, and apply Photomerge via the Automate menu.)

2. Navigate via the Browse button and select the files containing the different exposures. (If you are using a Mac and the File Browser Automate menu, skip this step.)

3. Click OK. Photomerge automatically attempts to merge the documents. If it fails to do this—and you see a dialog box telling you so—simply drag and drop the images from the photo well on top of each other (☞ Chapter 8 for more on using the Photomerge plug-in).

4. Keep your Photomerge settings at Normal and select Keep as Layers. Keep Snap to Image selected. (Advanced Blending will not be an option if you select Keep as Layers.)

5. Click OK. When Photomerge finishes, you will be left with one image file, and your images perfectly aligned on top of each other in the Layers palette.

6. If it's not already open, open the Layers palette.

7. Erase (✐) unwanted areas of the top layers to reveal corrected versions of those areas underneath. You might want to move layers around to get the "best" version of your image on top, to minimize the amount of erasing needed.

For this example, I moved the image with the correctly exposed background and dark foreground to the top of the Layers palette, as shown in the shot on the left in Figure 11.6. I then selected the top layer and selected the Magic Eraser (✐) from the toolbar. In the Magic Eraser options bar I set the Tolerance to 50 (this number will vary depending on the tonal values of the image you are working on). I left Contiguous selected and Use All Layers deselected. Then I clicked a dark area in the foreground of my image with the Magic Eraser.

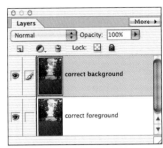 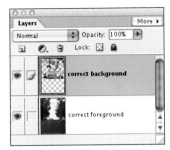

Figure 11.6: I moved the layer containing the correctly exposed background to the top of the Layers palette (left). This is what my palette looks like after applying the Magic Eraser to the dark areas of the image in the top layer (right).

The shot on the right of Figure 11.6 shows my Layers palette after applying the Magic Eraser to the top layer. By removing the dark areas in the top layer, the lighter areas of the bottom layer show through. (I used the Eraser tool to fine-tune the results of the Magic Eraser for the final image.) I slightly cropped the image and flattened my layers, and I was finished.

For this example I used the Magic Eraser and Eraser, but you can use other methods to remove the improperly exposed areas of the image in the top layer. For example, you could use the Selection Brush tool (✐) to create a precise selection, and then delete your selection. I've found the Magic Eraser works quickly and often it works well enough.

> **Note:** I got the idea for this Photomerge procedure while talking with Photomerge's creator, John Peterson.

Using Layer Adjustments with Masks

In Chapter 2, I showed how Photoshop Elements' Smart Fix, Auto Levels, and Levels can be used to correct a poorly exposed image. But these methods don't always work satisfactorily.

Take, for example, the photo of Mt. Shasta in Figure 11.7. When I use the Levels controls to adjust the image, I can either make the foreground trees look good, or the mountain and sky in the background look good. But I can't make both look good at the same time. I need a way to apply a different set of Levels adjustments to each area of the image separately. There are a couple of ways to do this, but I've found a combination of layer adjustments and masks to be the most effective and versatile.

Figure 11.7: The original photo (top). The foreground is okay, but the background is washed out (bottom left). Now the background is okay, but the foreground is too dark (bottom right).

Adjustment layers are layers that apply color and tonal adjustments to an image without permanently modifying the pixels in the image (☞ "All about Layers" in the appendix). A *layer mask* can be added to an adjustment layer to protect sections of an adjustment layer and control the effect that the adjustment layer has on the layer beneath it.

This is what I did to improve the digital photo of Mt. Shasta:

1. I created a new adjustment layer by choosing Layer ➤ New Adjustment Layer ➤ Levels from the menu bar (shown on the left in Figure 11.8). I could have created a new adjustment layer by clicking the Create Adjustment Layer button (◕) at the top of the Layers palette and choosing Levels (shown on the right in Figure 11.8). I named this new layer **Trees**.

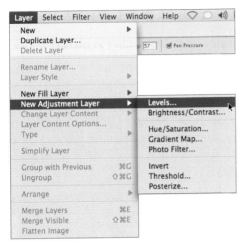
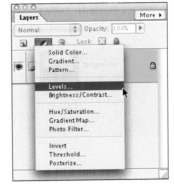

Figure 11.8: Choose an adjustment layer from the Layer menu (left). Or choose an adjustment layer directly from the Layers palette (right).

2. I used the Levels palette to adjust the midtones so my trees looked right. I didn't pay any attention to the sky and the mountain. When I was finished, I turned the layer visibility off by clicking the eye icon in the leftmost column of the Layers palette. I did this so my new adjustment layer wouldn't interfere with the next adjustment in step 3.

3. I created another Levels adjustment layer and called it **Mt./Sky**. I used the Levels controls to adjust the tonal values so Mt. Shasta and the sky looked right, and I didn't worry about my foreground.

4. Next came the tricky part—and if you don't get this part right, this exercise won't work. In the adjustment layer called **Mt./Sky** I created a mask that blocked the effect of the Levels adjustment on the trees. To do this, I clicked the Gradient tool (▭) in the toolbox. In the options bar I selected the following options:

   Gradient: Foreground to Transparent

   Style: Linear Gradient

   Blend mode: Normal

   Opacity: 100 percent

   I made sure that the foreground was set to black: click the Default Colors icon (▪) at the bottom of the toolbox and then click the Switch arrow (↱). This is necessary on an adjustment layer because the default colors are reversed.

5. With the **Mt/Sky** layer selected, I placed my cursor on the image window. While holding the Shift key, I started at the bottom of the image, then clicked and dragged about halfway up the image and let go of the mouse. Holding the Shift key and dragging straight up constrained the Gradient tool to a 90-degree angle.

Note: Because the layer mask is represented in tones of gray, what you paint or fill with black will be hidden, what you paint or fill with white will show, and what you paint or fill with gray shades will show in various levels of transparency. Masks can be edited like a grayscale image with any painting or editing tool. Hold down Alt/Option+Shift and click the adjustment layer thumbnail to view the mask in a rubylith masking color. Hold down Alt/Option+Shift and click the thumbnail again to turn off the rubylith display. Shift+click the adjustment layer thumbnail to turn off the masking effects temporarily; click the thumbnail again to turn on the mask. You can also use the Move tool ( ) to move or resize a mask.

6. I selected the adjustment layer called **Trees** and made another similar mask by using the Gradient tool with the same settings as in step 4. Selecting the **Trees** layer automatically turned on its visibility, which I had turned off in step 2. This time I created a mask by holding the Shift key and dragging straight downward from the top of the image. This blocked the effect of the Levels command on the mountain and sky areas of the image.

7. For the most part, the mask created by the Gradient tool was enough. However, I did go back into the adjustment layer called **Mt./Sky** with the paintbrush and mask in a few other areas, including the tree on the right.

As you can see in Figure 11.9, I've managed to get both the foreground and background right. And as long as I keep my adjustment layers, I can go back and tweak the levels at any time.

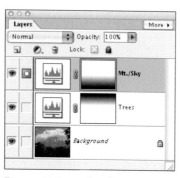

Figure 11.9: Both adjustment layers are selectively masked with gradient fills (left). With just a little work, both the foreground and background look good (right).

Note: You can edit an adjustment layer at any time: double-click the adjustment layer's thumbnail in the Layers palette or choose Layer ➤ Layer Content Options from the menu bar.

Using a Gradient Mask to Combine Multiple Images

In Chapter 8, I showed how you an easy way to use Photoshop Elements' Photomerge feature to combine multiple images into a collage. For more control and precise blending, here is a method that uses layers and gradient masks rather than Photomerge. Obviously, this method isn't as straightforward as using Photomerge, and it's a bit time consuming. But if you master layer adjustments and masking techniques—as you started to do in the previous example—you are on a professional-level track, and a whole new world of options opens up.

As with the previous example, please follow my steps carefully. If you do as I suggest, you'll have no trouble duplicating the effect on images of your own. However, even a slight variation (such as not setting the Gradient tool and the foreground color properly) will produce quite a bit of frustration, and not the results you expect.

Let's begin!

1. Create a new document with the desired dimensions. For this example I created a 10 × 5 inch document at 200dpi (File ➢ New ➢ Blank File).

2. Open two or more images you wish to combine. I'll use the three images shown in Figure 11.10.

Figure 11.10: I'll start with these three images that I wish to combine.

3. Crop and resize the images to match. I did this by selecting the Crop tool (⛶) in the toolbar and setting my width to 3.3 in., height to 5 in., and resolution to 200dpi. I applied the fixed crop separately to each image. When you crop, keep in mind you will eventually overlap the images. (When you are finished doing this, click the Clear button in the Crop tool options bar; otherwise, you may inadvertently apply the fixed dimensions later to another image.)

4. Copy and paste the cropped, resized images to the blank document you created in step 1 (Ctrl/⌘ +A, followed by Ctrl/⌘ +C and, after selecting the blank file, Ctrl/⌘ +V). When you are finished your Layers palette should look like the one in Figure 11.11, with three layers. At this point you can rename the layers if you want.

Figure 11.11: The Layers palette of the blank file after copying and pasting the three images.

5. In the image window, position the images adjacent to each other, with a slight overlap, as shown in Figure 11.12. Do this by selecting the top layer in the Layers palette and the Move tool from the toolbar. In the image window, click and hold while dragging the image to the far left of the image window. Next, select the second layer, and in the image window move the middle image into the middle position, allowing for a slight overlap with the image to the left. Finally, select the bottom layer (but not the background layer), and in the image window move that image to the far right.

Figure 11.12: Position the images adjacent to each other with a slight overlap. Place the image contained in the top layer to the far left, the image contained in the middle layer (if you have one), in the middle, and the image in the bottom layer (but not the background layer) to the far right of the image window.

At this point you've finished the "heavy" lifting. Now it's time to finesse the images so the edges blend into one another. You'll do this by creating a gradient mask that allows only a portion of an image to show through. Because Photoshop Elements doesn't offer gradient "masks" per se, you'll use a clever workaround that will turn an adjustment layer and a clipping path into one.

6. In the Layers palette, starting with the top layer, create a Levels adjustment layer for each layer: click the Create Adjustment Layer button at the top of the palette and select Levels from the pop-up menu, or choose Layer ➤ New

Adjustment Layer ➤ Levels. *Don't* change *anything* in the Levels dialog box that appears. Just click the OK button. Apply an adjustment layer to each image layer until your Layers palette looks like the one in Figure 11.13. (By the way, you could create Brightness/Contrast adjustment layers instead of Levels. It doesn't matter. Just don't touch any setting before clicking OK.)

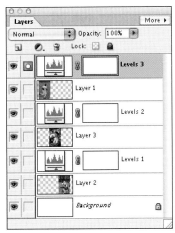

Figure 11.13: After applying a Levels adjustment layer to each layer, your Layers palette will look something like this.

7. Now you need to rearrange the layers in the Layers palette. Move each adjustment layer *below* its image layer by dragging it into the desired position. Your Layers palette should look like the one in Figure 11.14.

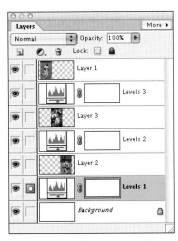

Figure 11.14: Move the adjustment layers below the image layers as shown here.

8. Starting with the top layer, which contains the image located to the far left of the image window, hold the Alt/Option key and (in the Layers palette) click the border between that layer and the adjustment layer located just beneath it. Two intersecting circles, one light and one dark, appear. After you click the top layer, these circles will indent slightly to the right and contain an arrow pointing to the "grouped" layer below. Doing this creates a "clipping" mask, and now the content of the adjustment layer masks the content of the layer above it. You can

also create a clipping mask by selecting the top layer, and in the menu bar selecting Layer ➤ Group with Previous. Now your Layers palette will look something like the one in Figure 11.15. Note that the name of the base layer of the clipping mask is underlined.

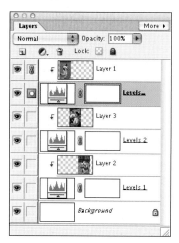

Figure 11.15: After you clip the adjustment layers with the layers containing your images, you'll get something that looks like this.

Now that you have created a "mask" for each image, you need to apply a gradient to the mask that will fade the edges:

9. Select the Gradient tool from the toolbar.

10. In the Gradient options bar, select Foreground to Transparent from the flyout Gradient picker. This is so important I'm going to repeat myself. In the Gradient options bar, select Foreground to Transparent.

11. In the color swatch at the bottom of the toolbar, make sure the foreground color is set to black. Getting the color correct is critical. Again, I repeat: set the foreground color to black!

12. In the Layers palette, select the second layer. This is the layer containing the adjustment layer, which, remember, is clipped to the topmost image.

13. In the image window, place the cursor on the far right of the leftmost image. Hold the Shift key and drag inward, to the left. Go in about 1/2 inch and release the mouse. This applies a gradient to the right edge of the image. You should see the results immediately.

14. Highlight the adjustment layer that is below the layer containing the middle image. You may need to turn off the visibility of the top layer to see the leftmost edge of the middle image; do this by clicking the eye icon next to the top layer.

15. On the left edge of the middle image, Shift+drag inward (to the right) about 1/2 inch and release the mouse. Then Shift+drag from the *right* edge of the middle image about 1/2 inch inward (to the left).

16. Turn off the visibility of the middle image if necessary to see the image on the right. Highlight the adjustment layer that is below the right-image layer.

17. On the left edge of the right image, Shift+drag inward (to the right) about 1/2 inch and release the mouse. Turn on all layer visibility and you will see something like Figure 11.16.

Figure 11.16: With the edges of the three images faded, the images blend together.

To tweak your work, you can move the images in relationship to each other by using the Move tool. However, you must first link the adjustment layer with the layer containing the image. To do this, click on the column immediately to the left of the image layer. A link icon (⅋) will appear in the column. Now when you use the Move tool to move the image, the 'linked' adjustment layer will move also.

Converting a Photo to a Painting

The simplest way to convert a photo into a painting is by using one of the Artistic filters such as Watercolor or Rough Pastels (Filter ➤ Artistic from the main menu bar).

However, if you want to convert a photo into a truly unique-looking "painting," follow this slightly more complex procedure. Start with an original photo containing sharply defined lines and shapes, such as the one shown on the left in Figure 11.17.

Figure 11.17: The original image (left); after applying various filters and blending modes (right).

1. Duplicate the background layer twice (Layer ➢ Duplicate Layer from the menu bar, or drag and drop the layer to be duplicated onto the Create a New Layer icon (🖻) at the top of the Layers palette). Name one of the duplicate layers **Underpainting** and the second **Find Edges**. The Layers palette is shown in Figure 11.18.

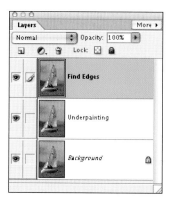

Figure 11.18: The Layers palette so far, with its Background layer and two duplicate layers.

2. Select the layer you named **Underpainting** and apply the Underpainting filter (Filter ➢ Artistic ➢ Underpainting). My settings are shown in Figure 11.19, but you have a lot discretion on your own settings.

*Figure 11.19: My **Underpainting** filter settings. These are just rough guidelines for you to follow.*

3. Select the layer you named **Find Edges** and apply the Find Edges filter to the layer (Filter ➢ Stylize ➢ Find Edges). No options are available for this filter.

4. Make a duplicate of the layer you just applied the Find Edges filter to and call it **Wave**. You can boost the contrast of the duplicate layer, if you want, by using Levels.

5. On the layer you named **Wave**, apply the Wave filter (Filter ➢ Distort ➢ Wave). My settings are shown in Figure 11.20, but again, you can use other settings.

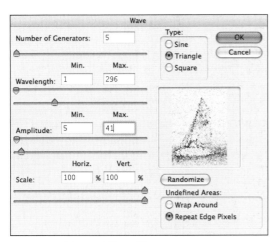

Figure 11.20: My Wave filter settings.

6. Finally, you need to change the blending mode of the **Wave** layer to Soft Light and change the Opacity to 65 percent. Also change the blending mode of the Find Edges layer to Overlay, but keep the mode of the Underpainting layer at Normal. Figure 11.21 shows the final configuration of the Layers palette with the different mode and opacity settings.

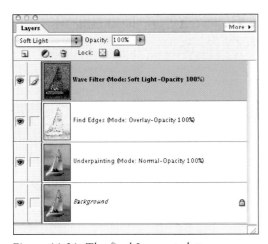

Figure 11.21: The final Layers palette.

My finished Layers palette looked like this, in order from top to bottom:

Wave Filter layer: Soft Light mode, 100 percent% opacity

Find Edges layer: Overlay mode, 68 percent opacity

Underpainting layer: Normal mode, 100 percent opacity

Background layer

Sharing and Auto-Processing Images

What's the good of having all your hard work available in a digital image if you can't easily share it with friends and colleagues? This chapter focuses on ways to use Photoshop Elements to get the most out of your desktop printer or to access an online photo service. It shows you ways to automatically create picture packages of single pages containing various sizes of the same image and to process folders full of several images to the same file format, size, and resolution. It'll also show you how to make web photo galleries, postcards, slide shows, and much more!

12

Chapter Contents

Printing from the Organizer (Windows)

When you choose Print from the Organizer menu—or if you choose File ➢ Print Multiple Photos from the Editor—you'll get the options shown in Figure 12.1.

Figure 12.1: When you print from the Organizer, you have these options.

This is your gateway to some really useful features. If you look under option 2, for example, you'll see you have four choices for printing in the Organizer: Individual Prints, Contact Sheet, Picture Package, and Labels. With these options you'll be able to easily print multiples of the same image on a single page, or a variety of images on a single page.

It's also easy to print individual images on single sheets of paper from the Organizer but I want to caution you: this isn't the best use of the Organizer's print capabilities, which are mostly about convenience and speed. (When you print from the Organizer, for example, you have only limited control over the print.) You can get much better results—with optimal resolution, sharpness, and color fidelity—if you print from the Editor and use its sharpening and resizing controls. I'll get into the details of doing that in a later section, "Printing from the Editor (Windows) or Application (Mac)."

Meanwhile, let's see what your print options are from within the Organizer.

Printing Multiple Images (Windows)

Here's how to print multiple images on a single sheet of paper:

1. Select your images in the Organizer by Ctrl+clicking each one. Do this *before* choosing File ➢ Print. If you have no images selected, you will be asked whether you want to print all the images in your catalog. (You can amend your selections later, but it's quicker to make your selection up front.)

2. Choose File ➢ Print from the Organizer or File ➢ Print Multiple Photos from the Editor.

3. Select the printer from the step 1 drop-down at the top right. (At this point—or at any time in the process before you hit the Print button—you can add more images by clicking the Add button at the bottom-left of the dialog box, or remove images by selecting them and then clicking the trash can icon.)

4. Select Individual Prints in step 2.

5. Select a print size in step 3. (In Figure 12.2, I selected two images, which are displayed on the left of the dialog box. As you can see, I chose 5" × 7" for step 3.)

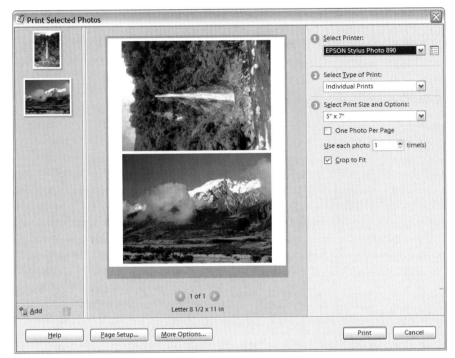

Figure 12.2: For this example I selected two images, set the size to 5" × 7", deselected One Photo Per Page, and selected Crop to Fit. It's easy to preview the results before printing.

6. Deselect the One Photo Per Page check box. If you don't do this, only one image will appear on a page, regardless of size. (If you are printing only one picture per sheet and want optimal quality, I highly recommend you follow the steps I describe later about printing directly from the Editor.)

7. If you want just one copy of each image, leave the Use Each Photo option set to 1. If you want to print two copies of the same image per page, just change Use Each Photo to 2 times.

8. Select Crop to Fit to make your prints exactly the size you chose. Some cropping may occur, because the aspect ratio of digital camera images doesn't always match the aspect ratio of the print.

9. Click the Print button.

Don't be confused by the Page Setup button, which lets you select Portrait or Landscape. The pictures display differently in the preview window, but print the same way in either case.

One point to think about before bringing up the Print dialog box is to enter any information in the Properties dialog box (Window ➤ Properties) that you may want to include with your images. Captions or Dates, which you can include by clicking the More Options button in the Print dialog box, must be entered prior to clicking File ➤ Print. You don't want to set everything up, only to have to start over again.

Printing a Contact Sheet (Windows)

The second option in the Print Selected Photos dialog box, under Select Type of Print, is Contact Sheet. In traditional photography, a *contact sheet* is a sheet of negative-sized photographs made by simply placing the printing paper in direct contact with the negatives during exposure. The results allow a viewer to quickly compare smaller versions of each photo side by side.

Digital photos don't have negatives *per se*, but by using the Contact Sheet option, you can control the size of a series of images and group as many as nine images per column. These images can then be printed and the results used for side-by-side comparison and easy reference, as shown in Figure 12.3.

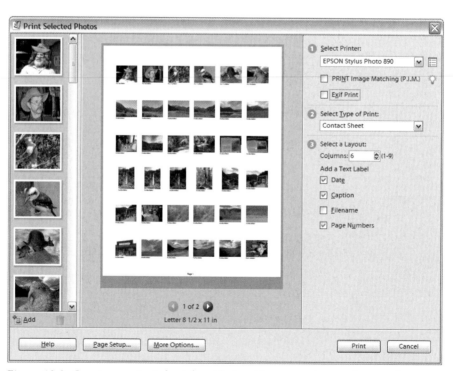

Figure 12.3: Create a contact sheet for side-by-side comparison and easy reference.

To create a Contact Sheet, follow these steps:

1. In the Organizer select the images you want. There is no limit to the number you select, but the most images you'll fit on a single 8.5 × 11 inch sheet of paper is 81 very tiny ones.

2. Choose File ➢ Print (Ctrl+P).
3. Select the printer in step 1.
4. Select Contact Sheet in step 2.
5. Select a Layout in step 3. The smaller the number in the Columns box, the fewer (but larger) the number of thumbnails per page. Choose appropriate text labels, and you are done.
6. Click Print.

Remember, as with the previous example using the Individual Prints option, you can click the Add button at any time to add additional images. Also remember to add any captions prior to bringing up the Contact Sheet dialog box.

Printing a Picture Package (Windows)

The Picture Package option provides a way to automatically create a variety of layouts with your images that otherwise would be extremely time-consuming. Not only can you produce useful layouts—and customize them to boot—you can automatically add a variety of frames to each image as well. Figure 12.4 shows a Picture Package.

Figure 12.4: By using Picture Package you can automatically create a variety of useful layouts and automatically add frames as well.

Here are the steps for creating the Picture Package shown in Figure 12.4:
1. Select an image in the Organizer.
2. Choose File ➢ Print (Ctrl+P).
3. Select the printer in step 1.
4. Select Picture Package in step 2.

5. Select a Layout in step 3. I selected Letter (2) 4×5 (4) 2.5×3.5. I then selected an Antique Oval frame and selected One Photo Per Page. (If I had selected more than one image to begin with, deselecting One Photo Per Page would result in Picture Package arranging different photos together on the same page. Selecting One Photo Per Page would result in multiple picture packages, each containing the same photo on a separate page.)

6. Preview the results and click Print.

It may not be immediately obvious, but you can create custom layouts with Picture Package as well. Simply place your cursor over an image in the preview box— it'll turn into a hand icon—and then click and drag. You can place the image wherever you want on the page, or place it on top of another image and the two images will exchange places. If you aren't satisfied with your new layout, right-click a thumbnail and select Revert to Original. Now that is cool. (What's not so cool is that Picture Packages are all set for 8.5 × 11 inch paper. You also can't add captions or credits.)

Printing Labels (Windows)

This feature is accessed from the Organizer by clicking File ➤ Print and selecting Labels in step 2. The process is similar to Picture Package and fairly straightforward: Select an appropriate layout based on the type of labels you are printing and, if you want, select a frame from the pop-up menu. If you are printing one image, select One Photo Per Page. If you select multiple images, deselect One Photo Per page to print all the images on a single page.

If you want to add text to your labels, you can't do it from the Organizer Label print control. You'll have to use the Editor's text tool to place the text directly on an image and import the edited image into the Organizer for printing.

As anyone who has printed labels knows, printing small labels can be difficult. Even the slightest misalignment of the paper will result in off-registered images. If you are having difficulty printing, try using the Offset Print Area controls to adjust the labels' print position in increments of 0.1mm, up to plus or minus 50mm.

Printing from the Editor (Windows) or Application (Mac)

As I mentioned earlier, if you want to create the best possible print, you'll want to print directly from the Editor and use its resizing and sharpening controls. Everything I write here applies equally as well to Mac users, who don't have the option of printing from the Organizer.

Using Image Size to Set Resolution and Print Dimensions

What if you have a photo taken with a 4-megapixel digital camera? How big of a print can you make without loss of quality?

Let's open such an image in Photoshop Elements and take a closer look at it via the Image Size dialog box shown in Figure 12.5 (Image ➤ Resize ➤ Image Size).

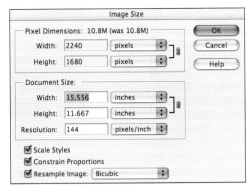

Figure 12.5: The Image Size dialog box for an image taken with a 4-megapixel digital camera.

As you can see near the top of the Image Size dialog box, the pixel dimensions are 2240 for Width, and 1680 for Height. In the Document Size section, you can see the following numbers: 31.111 inches for Width, 23.333 inches for Height, and 72 pixels/inch for Resolution.

If you tried to print this image as is, straight out of Photoshop Elements without changing any parameters, you'd create a print approximately 31 × 23 inches at 72 pixels/inch. (Of course you'd have to have a printer that printed this large.) Most likely the print would appear "grainy" or soft. Technically, there just aren't enough pixels to support this size.

So if 72 pixels/inch isn't enough, how much resolution do you need? Don't be misled by the specifications of your printer. For most desktop inkjet printers, a resolution of 150–250 pixels/inch is plenty, and anything over 250 pixels/inch is a waste. Your print quality won't suffer, nor will it improve with the higher settings. You'll just create a huge file that will take forever to print.

Shooting Digital: Using Metadata to Determine Print Resolution Value

Photoshop Elements uses metadata created by many digital cameras to determine the print resolution value that appears in the Image Size dialog box. You can see this metadata in the bottom-left of the File Browser window (↶ Chapter 1).

Because Photoshop Elements uses the metadata saved with an image, you can open an image taken, say, with a Nikon Coolpix 885, and the numerical value in the Image Size dialog's Resolution field is 300 pixels/inch; you can then open an image taken with an OlympusC- 2500L and find Resolution set to 144 pixels/inch. Both cameras produce images that have similar pixel dimensions (Nikon = 2048 × 1536 pixels; Olympus = 1712 × 1368 pixels), but if you were to print the first image with a resolution of 300 pixels/inch you'd end up with a print size of 6.8 × 5.1 inches. If you printed the second image set at 144 pixels/inch, the print size would be 11.9 × 9.5 inches. If the metadata is absent for some reason, Photoshop Elements defaults to 72 pixels/inch. Remember, you can always change these resolution values by choosing Image ➤ Resize ➤ Image Size and placing a new value in the Resolution box.

So what would be an optimal size for this 4-megapixel image? Look at Figure 12.6 and note an important detail: at the bottom of the Image Size dialog box, I deselected the Resample Image check box. By doing this I prevent Photoshop Elements from adding or deleting pixels. It keeps my original pixel count, and only redistributes the existing pixels. I'll explain exactly what that means shortly.

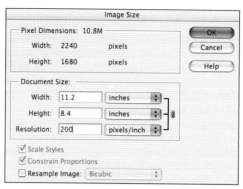

Figure 12.6: By deselecting the Resample Image check box and bumping up the resolution, I arrive at my optimal print size.

Now look at the Resolution input box. I typed in 200 pixels/inch, which is plenty of resolution to produce a high-quality print. Notice the Width and Height numbers have changed. Now, at 200 pixels/inch, I can easily print an 11.2 × 8.4 inch picture.

Again, because I deselected the Resample Image check box, nothing has been added to or taken away from my image. Instead of using the pixels to produce a large print, albeit at low resolution, the pixels are now distributed so that the resolution is higher and the print dimensions lower.

Okay, up to now I haven't done anything to change the pixel count of my image. I've only realigned my pixels for more depth rather than for size. What happens if I don't have enough pixels? What if I wanted to print at, say 18 × 13.5 inches, but with enough resolution?

If I punch in 18 inches in the Width field, the Height is automatically set to 13.5 inches and my Resolution drops to 124 pixels/inch, which isn't enough for a quality print. Figure 12.7 shows what happens when I select the Resample Image check box and punch in 200 pixels/inch in the Resolution field. You can see at the top of the Image Size dialog box that I have increased my Pixel Dimensions from 10.8MB to 27.8MB. Obviously a lot of pixels were added, through a process called interpolation.

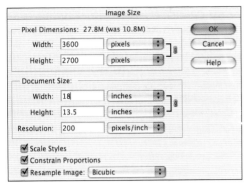

Figure 12.7: Selecting the Resample Image box and typing in 200 pixels/inch at 18 × 13.5 inches increased my pixel count from 10.8 megabytes to 27.8 megabytes.

Remember, for this process to work you must make sure that both the Constrain Proportions and Resample Image: Bicubic options at the bottom of the dialog box are selected, which they should be by default. (Use Bicubic Smoother from the pop-up menu if you are resampling up, or Bicubic Sharper if you are resampling down.)

Note: Allow for at least a 0.25-inch border because many desktop printers aren't capable of printing, or *bleeding,* an image to the edge of the paper.

After you are finished resizing your image, click OK.

Before printing, I suggest you sharpen your image. The Unsharp Mask filter is best suited for this task (Filter ➤ Sharpen ➤ Unsharp Mask). I also highly recommend you try the nik Sharpener plug-in included on the enclosed CD. It's so much easier to use than Unsharp Mask, and the results can be optimized for specific sizes and even specific printers.

When you are finished sharpening, choose File ➤ Print from the menu bar or click the printer icon found in the shortcuts bar. The Print Preview dialog box will appear, which I'll now discuss.

Using Print Preview

In the Print Preview dialog box (Figure 12.8), you can set the image dimensions manually, have Photoshop Elements do it for you based on the size of your paper, or print from the dimensions you established earlier in the Image Size dialog box. (If you are using Windows, you can also click the Print Multiple Images button, which will take you to the Organizer and the options discussed earlier in this chapter. If you are on a Mac you can click the Print Layouts button, which will take you to Picture Package for printing multiple images on the same page.)

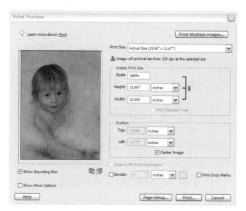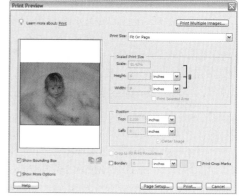

Figure 12.8: The Print Preview dialog box (left). After selecting a smaller size, the warning is gone (right), my image fits in the preview window, and I'm ready to print.

Here, I've used the 4-megapixel image used in the preceding section and kept the default Print Size settings at Actual Size. As you can see, my image is too big for the preview, and I'm being warned that the resolution will be low ("less than 220dpi"). I can easily fix this by choosing a different print size. The second dialog box shows the Print Size changed to Fit on Page; the warning is gone, my image fits in the preview window, and now I'm clear to print.

Note: If you select Custom Size from the Print Size pop-up menu, you can type in your own Height and Width values. If you do this and select the Show Bounding Box check box, you can drag a bounding box handle in the preview area to scale the image. Whatever you do, Photoshop Elements won't override the border settings set by your printer.

Keep in mind that you can set the print size in the Print Preview dialog box, but you can't directly set the resolution of your image. It defaults to the setting in the Image Size dialog box. If your image is enlarged in the Print Preview dialog box, either by using a large print size setting or by you manually, the resolution will be automatically reduced proportionally. If you reduce the size of your image, the resolution will automatically increase proportionally. The bottom line is, if you resize by using the Print Preview dialog box, you don't change the overall number of pixels or affect the original image file in any way.

Other options in the Print Preview dialog box include the following:

Change image orientation with the rotate icons located at the bottom right of the preview area.

Add a colored border. To do this, select the Border check box, type in a border thickness, and click the color box to the right to bring up the Color Picker. You can also drag the bounding box to increase the thickness of the border.

Print any caption text typed in the File Info dialog box in 9 point Helvetica, centered just below the image. You have no control over the size, type, or placement. If a caption doesn't show in the preview, it's because you didn't previously add one in the File Info dialog. Also, if your image fills the page, it's unlikely that the caption or filename will print.

Add corner crop marks to show where a page is to be trimmed by selecting the Print Crop Marks box.

Reposition an image on the paper. In the Position section of the dialog box, either click the Center Image check box to center the image in the printable area, or type values in the Top and Left fields to position the image numerically. You can also select the Show Bounding Box check box and drag the image in the preview area.

Print a selection made with the Rectangular Marquee selection tool (▢), excluding everything else in the image, by selecting the Print Selected Area check box (in the Scaled Print Size section) and clicking the Print button.

Selecting a Paper Size and Orientation

You can select paper size or image orientation through Photoshop Elements' Page Setup dialog box (File ➤ Page Setup, or click the Page Setup button from within the Print Preview dialog box). This dialog will look different depending on the type of printer you are using. However, you can likely access more size/orientation options by using the printer software that comes with your printer.

If the image size you selected in the Image Size dialog box doesn't match the size of the paper set in the Page Setup dialog box (or within your printer software), you'll get a warning message.

Creating and Sharing with the Organizer (Windows)

If you select the Create icon from the Organizer or Editor shortcuts bar, you'll see the window shown in Figure 12.9. There are enough easy-to-use features here to satisfy a variety of creative urges and needs. Most of the features include contextual help and step-by-step procedures. I won't even begin to cover all the details of using these features. Instead, I'll briefly highlight what you can do with them, and point out a few less-than-obvious tips.

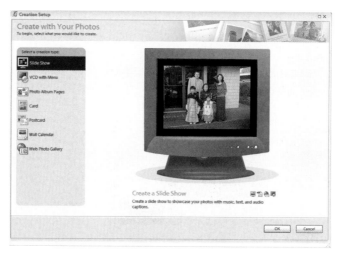

Figure 12.9: The Creation Setup window.

Creating a Slide Show (Windows)

To create a slide show, start by opening the Creation Setup window and clicking Slide Show in the menu panel at the left. You can either create a Custom Slide Show complete with transitions, music, audio annotations, and text, or a Simple Slide Show that will run on any computer platform loaded with Adobe Acrobat Reader. The Custom Slide Show can be saved or burned in the VCD format. (To create a VCD with multiple slide shows and a menu, first create and save your slide shows in the Custom Slide Show window, and then select VCD with Menu from the Creation Setup window.) The slide show work areas are shown in Figure 12.10.

Figure 12.10: The Custom Slide Show work area (left) and Simple Slide Show work area (right).

Creating Specialty Print Layouts: Photo Album Pages, Cards, Postcards, and Calendars (Windows)

You can create printable pages for several specialty purposes by opening the Creation Setup window and clicking a project type in the menu panel at the left. For instance, when you click Photo Album Pages, you'll see the opening window shown in Figure 12.11, with a variety of layouts and styles available. This is step 1 of a five-step procedure. At the end of the process, you can save your creation in a variety of ways. You can save it as PDF, which can be viewed and printed from just about any computer in the world. You can print the pages directly from the Organizer.

Figure 12.11: Creating Photo Album Pages is easy when you follow the five-step procedure. Shown here is step 1 with layout options on the right (a). Also pictured are some of the layout options for cards (b), postcards (c), and calendars (d).

Other special print projects available in the Creation Setup window include Card for a custom fold-over greeting card; Postcard for a single-sided postcard; and Wall Calendar for, well, a calendar. (Figure 12.11 shows some of the layout options for cards, postcards, and calendars.)

Creating a Web Photo Gallery (Windows)

To create a Web Photo Gallery that can be uploaded on the Web, start by selecting the images you want in the gallery *before* clicking the Create icon. Otherwise, the application will assume you want all the images from the catalog included in the gallery.

Next, open the Creation Setup window and select Web Photo Gallery from the menu, to access the window shown in Figure 12.12.

Figure 12.12: The Organizer's Web Photo Gallery option window.

You can choose from over 30 gallery styles, add custom banners and colors, and choose the sizes of your images and thumbnails. The default file extension is **.html** and cannot be changed.

Web Photo Gallery is similar to the feature found in the Mac version, which I explain in more detail later in this chapter. The style options are similar between the two platforms, but there is no Security feature in the Windows version for placing copyrights on the images.

Sharing Images Electronically (Windows)

If you select the Share icon in the Organizer shortcuts bar, a pop-up menu will give you the following choices:

- E-mail
- Share Online
- E-mail to Mobile Phone
- Send to Palm OS Handheld
- Publish to TiVo DVR

The two most useful commands are E-mail and E-mail to Mobile Phone. The other options require you to have other third-party functionality running on your PC.

You can access the Attach to E-mail command via the Share icon in the shortcuts bar, or via the Organizers menu bar: File ➢ Attach to E-mail. For those of you who have used Windows XP's Attach to E-mail feature, you'll be pleasantly surprised by all Photoshop Elements offers.

First, you should open the preferences and select an e-mail client (Edit ➢ Preferences ➢ E-mail). Your choice there will determine your choices later. If, for example, you select Outlook Express as your e-mail client in the Preferences, you'll get the window shown in Figure 12.13 when you select the Share icon in the shortcuts bar and choose Attach to E-mail.

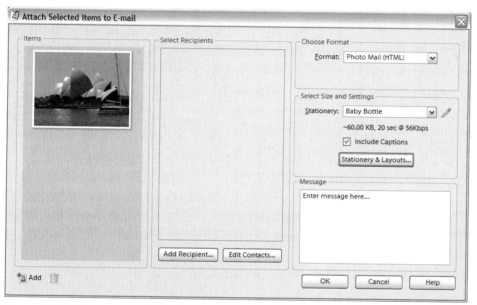

Figure 12.13: If you select Outlook or Outlook Express—or another e-mail client—you'll have the options shown here.

From the Format pop-up menu, you'll have the following options to choose from:

Photo Mail (HTML): Your images are placed directly into your e-mail body and open automatically upon receipt. With this selection you have no choice for the attachment size; the default set in Preferences is used. However, under Select Size and Settings, you can choose from a huge variety of frames or layouts. Simply click the Stationery & Layouts button and follow the prompts.

Individual Attachments: You have three choices of image sizes or you can leave the image as is. If you click the Customize button, visible only when you choose Individual Attachments as an option, you'll have several more size choices, as well as JPEG quality options. (The default can be changed by clicking Edit ➢ Preferences ➢ E-mail.)

Simple Slide Show (PDF): Be sure to keep an eye on your file size. You may find this option unusable because it generates huge files, even when you choose the minimum image dimensions.

Note: If you use Outlook or Outlook Express, you don't need to select a recipient from the Select Recipients box. Just click OK and your e-mail program will launch; you can then add a recipient in that program.

On the other hand, if you select Save to Hard Disk and Attach File(s) Yourself from the E-mail Preferences (Edit ➤ Preferences ➤ E-mail) and then use the Attach to E-mail feature, you will get a slightly different window with fewer options up front. For example, you can no longer select Photo Mail (HTML) as an option in the Format pop-up window, which means you can't add captions or add fancy frames or layout. You'll still be able to change the size for optimal e-mailing. The Save to Hard Disk and Attach File(s) Yourself option is required for Hotmail and Yahoo! users, and might just be preferred by others.

Note: If you click the Share icon in the shortcuts bar and choose E-Mail to Mobile Phone, you see a dialog box very much like Figure 12.13, but the file sizes are optimized for viewing on mobile phone screens.

Warning: If you continually get an error message that reads, "There was a problem with your Internet connection. Please check that you are connected to the Internet and try again," the problem could originate with your e-mail client preference setting. Try a different setting and see if that helps.

Using Online Photography Services

Online photo services can be easier and cheaper to use than making your own print: you simply upload your work to their website and order prints produced with real photographic paper and delivered to your doorstep overnight or in a few days. After you place your images online, anyone you designate, anywhere in the world, can go online, view your digital image, and with a single click of the mouse and a few keystrokes order their own prints in a variety of sizes. Choose File ➤ Order Prints from either the Organizer or the Editor, and follow the prompts.

Processing Multiple Files (Windows and Mac)

If you have a folder of digital images that you want to print at the same size and resolution, or that you want to convert to a similar file format, or resize, or apply a variety of Quick Fix settings to, you can use the Process Multiple Files processing command to automatically do all of the work for you.

To do so, choose File ➤ Process Multiple Files. On a Mac you can also select Process Multiple Files from the File Browser via the Automate menu. You can also select it on Windows from the File Browser but via the main File menu. You can choose from any or all of the possibilities in the Process Multiple Files dialog box (Figure 12.14)—for example, you can rename the output files, change their resolution, and convert them to a different file type simultaneously.

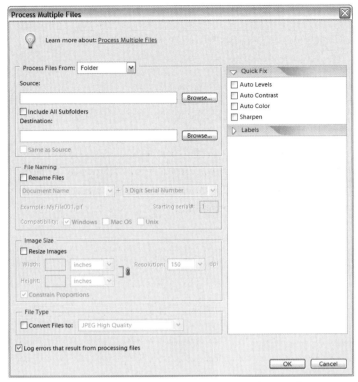

Figure 12.14: The Process Multiple Files dialog box with options.

- Choose a source such as Folder of files, Import, Opened Files, or File Browser. With the Import option, you can import from any source recognized by your computer, including a digital camera or scanner. If you choose Folder, click the Browse button and select the Include All Subfolders check box if you want subfolders included. Next, choose a destination folder and deselect Same as Source, unless you want to overwrite all the originals. If you have selected items in the File Browser, the option to choose the File Browser as the source will become available. It will process only the files selected in the File Browser and will ignore the folders (if any are selected).

- In the File Naming section, you can choose different filenames by selecting the Rename Files check box, and you can add different file extension protocols. You are not limited to the choices in the drop-down box; you can enter any name you wish.

- If you select the Resize Images check box, you can specify a resolution for all the images and specify the width and/or height of the processed images. You are limited to one of the resolution choices presented to you. You also have the option to Constrain Proportions. When this option is enabled, you don't have to place a value in both the Width and Height boxes. You can place a value into just one, and Photoshop Elements will calculate the other value based on the proportions of the image.

- You can also use the features shown on the right either alone or in conjunction with the features on the left. For example, select Auto Contrast and it will be applied to all of the images selected in the source.

Creating and Printing on the Mac OS

The following features are Mac-specific, although the Mac Web Photo Gallery is so similar to the Windows version that much of what is written applies to both platforms.

Creating a Picture Package (Mac)

Picture Package is a way to automatically create a variety of layouts with your images that otherwise would be extremely time-consuming. The Mac version of Picture Package provides three paper-size choices and several labeling options, as well as the option to add more than one image file to a single picture package (see Figure 12.15).

Figure 12.15: The settings in the Picture Package dialog box (top) create the packages shown below.

To create the packages shown in Figure 12.15, I did this:

1. I selected File ➤ Picture Package to open the Picture Package dialog box
2. Under Source I chose Folder instead of File. I navigated to the folder containing three images that I wished to process into three separate packages. I selected the folder and returned to the Picture Package dialog box.
3. Under Document Page Size, I selected 10.0 × 16.0 inches (I've got a large-scale printer...). Under Layout, I chose (1) 5 × 7 (4) 3 × 5. I set my resolution to 200 pixels/inch.

4. Under Label Content, I chose Custom Text, and then in the Custom Text field I typed in Copyright Mikkel Aaland. (If my image files had contained copyright metadata entered via the File Info dialog box—File ➢ File Info—I could have chosen Copyright from the Content drop-down options, and thereby avoided typing in the information.) I set the Font to Helvetica, the Font Size to 12pt, and the Color to Black. I lowered my Opacity to 50 percent to make the type less intrusive. I set the Position to Bottom Right and set Rotate to 90 Degrees to the left, which made the type run up and down along the edge of my images.

5. So far, so good. Now comes the really great part. I placed the cursor over the center thumbnail, the one that represents the 5 × 7 inch image in my package. The words "Click to select a file" appeared. After I clicked, I navigated to an image file and selected Open. After a few moments, the new image appeared in the Picture Package dialog box in place of one of the five images.

6. I selected OK, and Picture Package went to work creating the packages shown in the figure. (You can stop the process at any time by typing ⌘ +period.)

What is a practical application of swapping one image with another? For example, if someone has taken a group picture of a soccer team and also shots of individual players, they may find it very useful to be able to automatically create a picture package that contains one large team picture in addition to images of individual team members. You'd pay a lot of money if you had to custom order picture packages like this.

Attaching to E-mail (Mac)

If you want a quick and easy way to attach an image to an e-mail, and the ultimate file size isn't so critical, consider using Photoshop Elements' Attach to E-mail option.

To do this, with an image open and saved, choose File ➢ Attach to E-mail. You can also click the Attach to E-mail icon found in the shortcuts menu bar (🖼). In two situations, you'll see a prompt:

- If your saved image is larger than 1.3MB (or greater than 1200 pixels in any direction), clicking Auto Convert will automatically create a smaller-size attachment.

- If your image is smaller than 1.3MB (or 1200 pixels) and saved in any file format other than JPEG, clicking Auto Convert will automatically reformat the image for you.

If you're satisfied with the size and format of your image, click Send As Is to have the file attached to an e-mail exactly as it is. Photoshop Elements finds your default messaging software, creates a new e-mail message, and attaches the image file.

If your image is already a JPEG and smaller than the thresholds, and you choose the Attach to E-mail command, no resizing or optimizing is done. The image is automatically attached to a new document within your messaging software.

I suggest you use Attach to E-mail with caution. Check to see what file size it is generating with your images. If you really want to generate a "polite" e-mail attachment, reduce the size of your images for attaching to e-mails, using the Image Size dialog and the JPEG Options in the Save As process.

Preparing a JPEG for E-Mail Transmission

Most of the time it is best to send a JPEG. However, don't just send the JPEG right out of your camera; for a 5-megapixel digital camera, this is huge. There is no optimal size for an e-mail photo–it depends on the recipient's connection speed. I generally recommend that you try to get your digital photo down to between 40KB and 60KB before sending. (Of course, you can settle for a larger byte size if you know your recipient has a DSL connection or a cable modem.) To shrink your JPEG, follow these steps:

1. With your digital photo open, choose File ➢ Save As.
2. Choose JPEG from the file format options.
3. Select a JPEG value from the JPEG Options dialog box. Start with Medium and observe the effect on the actual image. If the quality is acceptable, look at the lower-left corner of the dialog box to see the file size. If it is too high, either choose a lower JPEG value or click Cancel and reduce the actual pixel values of the image by using Photoshop Elements' image resizing features.

To reduce the pixel values, choose Image ➢ Resize ➢ Image Size from the main Photoshop Elements menu. Make sure that the check boxes for Constrained Proportions and Resample Image are selected. Try entering 800 pixels in the Width box under Pixel Dimensions and 72dpi in the Resolution box. When you are finished, click OK. Go back to step 1 and save your image as a JPEG. This time you should be able to get the lower file size that you need.

Creating a PDF Slide Show (Mac)

With Photoshop Elements you can easily create PDF files containing self-running slide shows that can be viewed on just about any computer or Personal Digital Assistant (PDA) using Adobe Reader.

 Note: *PDF*, which stands for *Portable Document Format*, is a universal file format that accurately displays documents and images. A version of Reader is on this book's companion CD.

To create a slide show for viewing on a personal computer monitor or a PDA, you'll need to prepare your images first:

1. Open all of the images that you want to include in your slide show. It doesn't matter how many images you choose; however, if you are targeting a PDA or if you are planning on distributing the slide show via e-mail or the Web, keep in mind that file size is an important consideration, and more images means a larger file size.
2. If needed, crop your images and optimize them for tone and color by using the techniques outlined earlier in the book (☞ "Making Dull Images Shine" in Chapter 2).
3. Choose an optimal image size and then choose Image ➢ Resize ➢ Image Size. If you are creating a slide show for viewing on a 17-inch monitor, I suggest you make your horizontal images 800 pixels and your vertical ones 400 pixels. Larger monitors will require larger pixel values. Type 72 pixels/inch in the Resolution box. To create a slide show for a PDA, you'll need to know the resolution of the destination device. Many Palm Pilots, for example, display only 160 × 160 pixels.

You can also use Photoshop Elements' greatly improved Batch Processing command to quickly resize all your images.

Keep in mind that one of the features of the PDF format is automatic resizing. In other words, Acrobat will fill any size screen with your image, regardless of the inherent pixel dimensions. However, if you prepare an image that is only 300 × 300 pixels and it is viewed on a large monitor, the image will look "grainy" and awful. Conversely, if you prepare an image that is 2000 × 2000 pixels and view it on a smaller monitor, it'll look fine, but you will have created an unnecessarily large file size.

4. After you have finished preparing and resizing all your images, I suggest you rename the images (File ➢ Save As). If you don't, after Photoshop Elements is finished making the slide show, all of your open files are automatically closed and all changes are lost unless you've saved them. The images in the slide show are the optimized ones, of course, but there is no quick and easy way to individually access them. (You can't edit a PDF slide show with Photoshop Elements but you can use File ➢ Import ➢ PDF Image to "extract" individual images from your slide show.)

5. Choose File ➢ Automation Tools ➢ PDF Slideshow. The dialog box shown in Figure 12.16 appears.

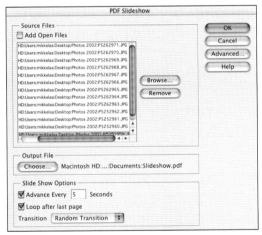
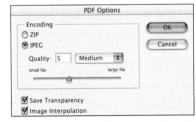

Figure 12.16: The PDF Slideshow dialog box. Advanced options are shown on the right.

6. If you've opened and optimized your images, and they are still on the desktop, select the Add Open Files check box in the Source Files section. Otherwise, just click the Browse button and select the files from your hard disk. You can't select an entire folder, but you can select more than one file at a time from within a folder by holding down the Shift key as you select. Remove unwanted files by selecting them and then clicking the Remove button. Arrange files by clicking and dragging them into the order you wish them to appear.

7. Choose a name and destination for your final file by clicking the Save button. A Save dialog box appears, in which you can name the file and specify where to save it. Under Slide Show Options choose an Advance rate and a type of Transition. You can also choose whether you want your slide show to loop, or repeat itself, when it reaches the end.

After you select Save, Photoshop Elements does the rest. How long it takes will depend on the number of images and the speed of your computer.

Creating a Web Photo Gallery (Mac)

With the Web Photo Gallery command (File ➤ Create Web Photo Gallery), it's easy to convert a folder of images into an interactive online gallery. Photoshop Elements creates both thumbnails and full-size images, and even creates HTML pages and navigable links!

You can choose to display your image files in several distinctly different ways, You can add an active e-mail address link, change the extension from .htm to .html, and customize pages as well. For some gallery styles you can specify a range of options that include the following:

- Banner font and font color (Options: Banner)
- Gallery image information such as size and JPEG quality (Options: Large Images)
- Gallery thumbnail information such as font, font size, and caption information (Options: Thumbnails)
- Custom colors for backgrounds, text, banner, and hyperlinks (Options: Custom Colors)
- Information such as copyrights, titles, or credits included directly on the images (Options: Security)

Some of these options may not apply to a particular gallery style. How do you know which styles have limited options? Just below the visual representation of the style that appears on the right side of the Web Photo Gallery window box, a caution appears to warn you. If this warning occurs, you'll still be able to fill in the option fields, but only some of the information will be used, depending on the style.

Let me walk you through the process of creating the gallery shown in Figure 12.17. This should give you a good idea of how the process works for the other styles as well. Keep in mind that if your images aren't oriented correctly before you begin—as many aren't when they are imported directly from a digital camera—you'll need to rotate (Image ➤ Rotate) and resave them before you start the process of creating a gallery.

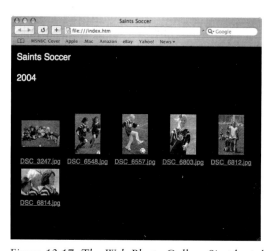

Figure 12.17: The Web Photo Gallery Simple style does it this it way.

Here are the steps for creating the gallery:

1. I placed six photos into a folder and chose File ➤ Create Web Photo Gallery. (I could have also selected six photos in the File Browser and choose Web Photo Gallery from the Automate menu.) The Web Photo Gallery dialog box appeared (shown in Figure 12.18).

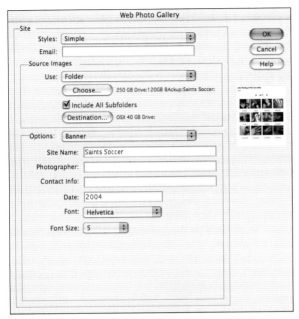

Figure 12.18: The Web Photo Gallery dialog box.

2. I chose the following selections from the Web Photo Gallery dialog box:
   - In Site/Styles I chose Simple. Midway down the dialog box, on the right, a representation of the style appeared.
   - I left the E-mail field blank. However, if you fill it in with your e-mail address, an active link will appear on all the HTML pages.
   - I left the Extension option set to .htm. (Check with your Internet Service Provider to see which protocol, .htm or .html, works for your system.)
   - I navigated to the folder containing my six photos (by clicking the Choose button) and then I chose a destination folder for the HTML files. (If you select Include All Subfolders, then images contained in subfolders will also be included in your gallery.) If you selected your files in the File Browser, select Selected Images from File Browser from the Use pop-up menu.

3. I selected Banner from the Options drop-down list and typed the words *Saints Soccer* as the Site Name, and left the Photographer and Contact Info fields blank. I typed the year 2004 in the Date Field (if you don't put a date in this field, the current date will be automatically generated for you). I set the Font Size to 5 and left the default, Helvetica, as my font.

4. I selected Large Images from the Options drop-down list and then selected the Resize Images check box. I set the size of my images to Large and the JPEG quality setting to Medium. You can also choose a custom size for your images.

However, if you want to display really large images, you'll want to select more JPEG compression to make the image file size smaller. If you want to maintain the original aspect ratio of your image, you can constrain it while resizing by selecting an option from the Constrain drop-down list.

5. I left the Border Size set to 0 pixels and for Titles Use I deselected Filename. I left the other options deselected. (If you use Filename, you may want to rename your files by using descriptive words or phrases before you start the automated Web Photo Gallery process; otherwise, you'll likely get titles consisting of the number sequences generated by your digital camera.)

Note: You can use Photoshop Elements to attach useful file information, such as copyright notices and captions, to your PSD or JPG formatted images. Choose File ➢ File Info from the menu bar and type your information into the provided fields. The information you include will be used, if you choose, by the Web Photo Gallery to generate captions and add other useful data.

6. I selected Thumbnails from the Options drop-down list, and I left all options set to their defaults.

7. I selected Custom Colors from the Options drop-down list, and then changed my background and banner to black and my text to white. Pick your colors carefully. You don't want a black text color and a black background; the type won't be readable. Again, even though this option appears to be functional, not all gallery styles will recognize your color choices.

8. I selected Security from the Options drop-down list, and I left the Content set to None. However, if I had selected Custom Text, I could have typed something like "Photo by Mikkel Aaland" in the Custom Text field, and the words would appear on every image in the font size, color, position, and rotation that I specified. Choosing any of the other Content options would generate type over my image based on File Info information.

9. After I set the options and clicked OK, Photoshop Elements did the rest. It opened each image and created both a thumbnail version and a gallery version and, regardless of the original file format, saved the file as a JPEG. It created an HTML index page and three folders containing the thumbnail images and navigational GIFs, gallery images, and HTML pages.

Elements also generates a separate file called **UserSelections.txt** that stores the settings from the Web Photo Gallery dialog box. This way, if you change, delete, or add only a single new file and don't change any other options, Web Photo Gallery will process only the files it needs to change to make the update.

The amount of time it takes for Photoshop Elements to process the images varies depending on the number of images in the source folder and the speed of the CPU. You can stop the process at any time by pressing Esc/⌘ +period.

If you want to, you can always tweak the HTML later. Just go to the destination folder and you'll find the index and other HTML files that can be opened and edited by using appropriate web-editing software. It's also likely that before you place the gallery on a server, you'll need to edit the links to reflect a proper directory path.

Creating a Contact Sheet (Mac)

Figure 12.19 shows a contact sheet that I created on a Mac.

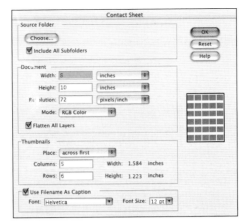

Figure 12.19: A contact sheet (left) helps organize digital images. On the right is the Contact Sheet (Mac) dialog box.

Here's how I made the contact sheet:

1. I chose File ≻ Contact Sheet II. The Contact Sheet dialog box appeared.
2. I clicked the Choose button and selected a folder from my hard disk.
3. Under Document, I kept the default document dimensions. A resolution of 72dpi is adequate for a sheet I'm just using for reference, so I kept that setting too.
4. Under Thumbnails, I kept the default settings for how the thumbnails would be placed on the page. I also selected Use Filename As Caption; this labeled the thumbnails by using the source image filenames.
5. I clicked OK and printed the result.
   Remember to add any captions prior to bringing up the Contact Sheet dialog box.

Appendix

A Reference to the Tools and Features of Photoshop Elements

Up to this point, this book has focused on giving you straightforward solutions to common challenges associated with acquiring, organizing, and processing digital images. This appendix is more reference-oriented, zooming in on the details of some of Photoshop Elements' preferences, tools, and features. This is by no means a definitive guide. For that, it's best to refer to Adobe's excellent online help, where you'll find a massive hyperlinked and searchable document with tons of information not found even in the Adobe Photoshop Elements User Guide.

Chapter Contents

Setting Preferences
Customizing and Organizing the Work Area
Histograms
All about Layers
Effects
Selection Tools
Viewing and Navigation Tools
Brushes
Filters

Setting Preferences

Adobe ships Photoshop Elements with preferences set in a way that may or may not suit your particular needs. Through these settings, you can change how Photoshop Elements handles a whole range of tasks, from color management to memory allocation to saving files. Let's look at some of the more important choices you can make, and see what you can do to customize the program so that it works better for you. (Windows users please note that these preferences refer to the Photoshop Elements Editor workspace, not the Organizer. I've covered many of the Organizer preferences in Chapter 1.)

Resetting Preferences

If at any point you want to reset Photoshop Elements preferences to their original settings, here's how to do so:

Throw away the Photoshop Elements preferences file. Windows users will find the **Photoshop Elements 3.0 Prefs** file here:
> **C:\Windows\Application Data\Adobe\Photoshop\Elements\Photoshop Elements 3.0 Settings**

In Windows 2000/XP, the preferences are located here:
> **C:\Documents and Settings\<username>\Application Data\Adobe\Photoshop\Elements\Photoshop Elements 3.0 Settings**

Mac OS X users will find the preferences file in this folder:
> **/Users/<username>/Library/Preferences/Photoshop Elements 3.0 Settings**

Delete the file, and the next time you launch Photoshop Elements, all your settings will be reset to their defaults. You can also hold down Ctrl+Alt+Shift / ⌘ +Option+Shift while the program launches to trash the preferences file and start up with the default settings.

Color Settings

Every scanner, every computer system, and every printer handles color differently. In order to maintain some control over the way your digital images look in this chaotic world, you need to know how Photoshop Elements handles color.

On the Edit menu at the top of the Photoshop Elements window, you'll see an option for Color Settings. (On the Mac, the Color Settings are found on the Photoshop Elements application menu.) When you choose this, you are faced with three options: No Color Management, Limited Color Management, and Full Color Management (described briefly in the following sections). The default setting is No Color Management, and even if you are tempted otherwise, I suggest you keep it this way. You might be in for some surprises if you select either of the other two options.

No Color Management

If you keep the default setting at No Color Management, you'll work in the RGB color mode, where there is a very slight possibility that some color banding will occur when your work is viewed on some monitors. *Banding* is what happens when you create a graphic in a color space and then view the same graphic on a device that displays a smaller range of colors. (A range of colors is referred to as *gamut*. On a monitor with a narrower gamut, colors are squished, or banded together.) Even though working in RGB mode may result in some banding, I believe that the potential loss of quality on some monitors is worth it, because you don't have to deal with the issues associated with Limited or Full Color Management.

Limited Color Management

If you choose Limited Color Management, you will find yourself working in a color space called sRGB, instead of just plain RGB. The *sRGB* color space is a limited color space that Adobe and others claim is good for Web work and some desktop printers. It has a narrower gamut than the RGB color space and more faithfully represents the color capabilities of most commonly used display systems. However, the difference between the sRGB and RGB color space is slight, and many other applications that you use may not support the sRGB color space. Sure, you'll be able to open your files in those programs, but you may find some maddening color shifts.

Full Color Management

If you choose Full Color Management, you'll work in the Adobe RGB color space, and Photoshop Elements will also assign an ICC color profile to your image file. A *color profile* is a universally accepted point of reference developed by the International Color Consortium (ICC). In theory, this means that when you open the file with another computer and monitor, the image will be displayed exactly as it was on your monitor. Also, in theory, if you have an ICC-compliant printer, you'll get a printout that closely matches the image on your monitor. This is fine in theory, but in reality it doesn't always work. All the devices need to understand your color profile, and if they don't you'll have an even greater mess on your hands.

Preset Manager

When you use a brush, gradient, pattern, or swatch, you are presented with a default set of corresponding brushes, gradients, patterns, or colors. Except for the swatches, these options appear in the options bar at the top of the Photoshop Elements window. The swatches are found in the Color Swatches palette. For most people, the default sets provide enough options, but you can also add or customize sets by using the Preset Manager, which is found on the Edit menu. Select the Preset Type to see the default options. To load a set of *custom libraries,* as the custom sets are called, you can click Load and select a saved library to open, or click the More icon at the top of the Preset Manager dialog box. A pop-up menu will appear with a list of choices, including the choice to reset back to the default set. You can also create your own set by Shift+clicking various brushes and clicking Save Set.

Undo History States

Most of the time, when you work on the pixels of a digital image, Photoshop Elements records each step of the process in the Undo History palette. You can go back to a previous step at any point, but only as long as that step remains in the Undo History palette. Photoshop Elements records 50 steps by default, but if you have enough RAM you can boost that number to as many as 1000. To change the default, choose Edit ➤ Preferences ➤ General (in Mac OS X, Photoshop Elements ➤ Preferences ➤ General) and then simply type in a new number.

Saving Files

When you save a file, Photoshop Elements by default creates an image preview (Windows) or an icon and thumbnail (Mac). Although this makes it easy to identify an image on the desktop or in a dialog box, and the saved thumbnail is used by the File Browser, it adds size to your image. If restricting file size is important to you, consider turning this option off and using only a descriptive name to identify your file. Do this by choosing Edit ➤ Preferences ➤ Saving Files (in Mac OS X, Photoshop Elements ➤ Preferences ➤ Saving Files).

Note: The File Browser (➤ Chapter 1) creates and displays its own temporary thumbnail version of an image, regardless of whether the image file was saved with an image preview or icon/thumbnail. However, if an image preview or icon/thumbnail is saved, the File Browser displays quicker.

If you create a lot of JPEG images for the Web or for e-mail transmission, turn off the image preview options (Windows) or icon and thumbnail options (Mac). This will lessen the chance that your JPEG will become corrupted and unreadable.

In the Saving Files Preferences dialog box, you also have the choice of whether to Always Maximize Compatibility for Photoshop (PSD) Files. To save up to a third of your file size, I suggest you turn this option off. If you leave this option selected, Photoshop Elements creates a second file, one with the layers (if you have any) flattened. You need this option only if you are planning to use Photoshop version 2.5 or earlier, which is unlikely. Keep in mind that turning off backward compatibility affects only PSD files, not GIFs or JPEGs. However, according to Adobe, the File Browser will create thumbnails more quickly if this option is left on. So your decision about whether to enable this option depends on which is more important to you, file size or performance.

You can also choose to turn off Ask Before Saving Layered TIFF Files. If you leave this option selected (which is the default), you'll have the choice of saving layered TIFFs or applying JPEG compression to a TIFF. Unless you are absolutely sure you'll never want to do this, leave this option selected.

By default, the recent file list (found under File ➤ Open Recently Edited File) includes 10 recent files. In the Saving Files Preferences dialog box, you can change this to any value from 0 to 30.

Units and Rulers

Photoshop Elements displays dimensions in inches by default (in the U.S.). You can change that setting to centimeters, millimeters, or pixels in the Units & Rulers dialog box (Edit ➤ Preferences ➤ Units & Rulers) (in Mac OS X, Photoshop Elements ➤ Preferences ➤ Units & Rulers). You can also change these preferences in the Info palette. When I am working on images destined for the Web, I always use pixels; otherwise, I leave my setting at inches. (Picas, points, and percent will be useful for only a select few users.)

Plug-Ins

When Photoshop Elements is launched, it automatically searches for a folder called Plug-Ins in the application folder. *Plug-ins* are mini software programs developed by Adobe or third-party vendors to add various functionalities to Photoshop Elements. You also may be using another program that uses compatible Photoshop plug-ins. You can tell Photoshop Elements where to find, and open those plug-ins as well, by going to Edit ➤ Preferences ➤ Plug-Ins & Scratch Disks (in Mac OS X, Photoshop Elements ➤ Preferences ➤ Plug-Ins & Scratch Disks). You can also hold down Ctrl+Shift / ⌘ +Shift while Photoshop is starting up, and then choose an alternate plug-in directory.

Memory

If you don't have enough RAM, Photoshop automatically creates and uses a portion of your startup hard drive as a scratch disk. It's never as fast or as optimal as having enough RAM, but if you have a large hard disk you'll avoid the dreaded "out-of-memory" warning. If you have more hard drives, you can assign scratch disks to them by choosing Edit ➤ Preferences ➤ Plug-Ins & Scratch Disks (in Mac OS X, Photoshop Elements ➤ Preferences ➤ Plug-Ins & Scratch Disks). Choose the drive that is the fastest and has the most contiguous free space to use as your primary scratch disk. You can create up to 200GB of scratch disk space. To change your scratch disk, hold down Ctrl+Alt / ⌘ +Option while Photoshop Elements is starting up.

The Memory and Image Cache preferences settings allow you to specify how much memory you want to use for Photoshop Elements. The cache levels affect the speed of zooming and drawing, and the Use Cache for Histograms setting affects how quickly histograms display. These settings are best left at the default levels for most projects.

Note: Sometimes cameras and other devices that mount themselves on the desktop as drives will show up as valid options in the Memory Preferences dialog box. It is important that you do not choose them. They are usually small in size and are slow. You should choose only devices that are real hard disks, and not removables.

Customizing and Organizing the Work Area

Look at anyone's desk and you'll see variations in the way people like to work. It's the same with the Photoshop Elements work area. One person might prefer a desktop tiled with palettes, whereas someone else might find this cluttered look distracting. With Photoshop Elements, palettes can be stacked and tiled and moved wherever you want. (Window users: Again, I'm referring here to the Editor. I covered the Organizer in Chapter 1.)

Look at Figure A.1. It shows the entire editing work area of Photoshop Elements. The Windows version is shown at the top. The Mac version is shown below. (As I've said all along, the two editing work areas are very similar. However, as you can see, the Windows version has different icons in the shortcuts bar, three of which take users to the Organizer work space, which is not available on the Mac platform.) This is how your screen should look when you first open the program.

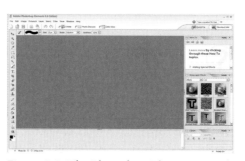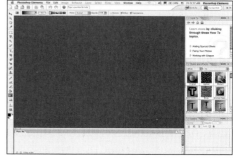

Figure A.1: The Photoshop Elements Windows Editor work area (left). The Macintosh version (right).

At the top is the *menu bar,* which contains drop-down menus for performing tasks. On the Enhance menu, for example, you'll find ways to modify the contrast and color of your digital image. Unlike most of the other components of the work area, the menu bar can't be moved or altered in any way. On Windows, you will find a search field for using keywords to access the help database (this is located on the shortcuts bar on Mac OS X). Additionally, you will find an option to automatically tile open documents (on by default) or view them in a maximized mode (also on the shortcuts bar on Mac OS X).

Below the menu bar is the *shortcuts bar.* You can position the pointer over any icon in the shortcuts bar and its name will appear. Here you'll find buttons for common commands such as Open, Print, Save, and Undo. In Windows you will also find buttons that will jump you to the Organizer (denoted by a sweeping arrow, or *swoosh*). On both the Windows and Mac versions are icons that allow you to switch between the Quick Fix and Standard Edit workspace modes.

Below the shortcuts bar and palette well is the *options bar,* which contains various options for using a selected tool. As you select a tool from the toolbox, different options will appear in the options bar. Some settings are common to several tools, and others are specific to one tool.

To the left of the work area is the *toolbox.* The icons in the toolbox give you access to various tools for creating and editing images. When you position the pointer over an icon in the toolbox, the name of the tool appears. An icon with a small arrow in its lower-right corner indicates a group of tools. When you select one of these icons, the tools it provides appear on the options bar. You can also click and hold the mouse on one of these icons to display a pop-up menu of the tools it provides. By default the toolbox is docked, but it can be torn off into a floating palette by grabbing on to its gripper and dragging.

To the right of the work area is the *palette bin*. Palettes help you modify and monitor images. You open a palette by clicking its "twist down" arrow. A palette will remain open until you click its arrow again. The palette bin can be easily closed by clicking the Close button at the bottom of the bin, or by dragging the bin to the right edge. You can also drag a palette's tab to move the palette from the bin to any place you want on the screen (↷ "Docking, Stacking, and Resizing Tool Palettes," next).

At the bottom of the work area is the *photo bin*. This container displays the currently opened files. For every open image you will see a live thumbnail representation. You can switch between files by clicking the thumbnails. You can also close, minimize, duplicate or rotate images via the photo bin by right/clicking (Windows) or Ctrl/clicking (Mac) on a thumbnail.

Docking, Stacking, and Resizing Tool Palettes

When you open Photoshop Elements for the first time, the How To, Styles and Effects, and Layers palettes are in the palette bin. You can move a palette to and from the palette bin and the work area by dragging the palette's tab in or out of the bin. You can change the order of palettes in the bin by dragging the title bar above or below other palettes found in the bin. You can resize a palette found in the palette bin by grabbing the gripper at the bottom of the palette. You can also dock palettes together on the work area by dragging one palette's tab onto the body of the other palette (see Figure A.2).

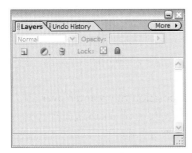

Figure A.2: For easy access, dock palettes together on the work area.

Personally, because I use them so much, I make both the Layers and Undo History palettes visible in the palette bin.

Note: Choosing Window ➢ Reset Palette Locations will place all palettes back in their default locations.

The Welcome Screen

When you open Photoshop Elements, you are greeted with a Welcome screen (Figure A.3). On Windows you have seven options; you can get a brief overview of the product, and you have access to the Organizer's viewing and authoring capabilities, as well as the Editor's editing and Quick Fix workspace modes. On the Mac, you have the ability to open an existing file from your disk, choose to open a recently edited file, or acquire one from your camera or scanner. The Welcome screens on both platforms additionally give you the ability to create a new file or have instant access to Adobe's online tutorials. The Welcome screen disappears when you select an option on it or start to work on an image, but you can get it back at any time by choosing Window ➢ Welcome.

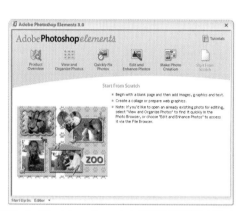
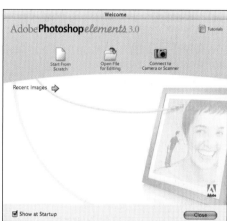

Figure A.3: The Windows Welcome screen (left). The Mac Welcome screen (right).

Histograms

A *histogram* shows the distribution of an image's pixel value in a bar chart representation. The left side (level 0) shows the values of an image's shadow, and the right side (level 255) shows the image's highlight values. For a properly exposed photo you will want the entire spectrum to be covered, with the base high in the center.

You can view the current histogram of your frontmost document by choosing Window ➢ Histogram from the main menu. You can change which channel you view along with the source from the Histogram palette (Figure A.4).

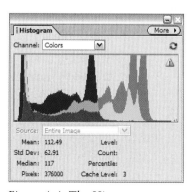

Figure A.4: The Histogram.

From the Channel pop-up menu you can select RGB, Red, Green, Blue, Luminosity, or Colors. RGB displays a composite of individual color channels placed on one another. Red, Green, and Blue display the histogram for the individual color channel. Luminosity displays the luminance (or intensity) values of the composite channel. And Colors displays the RGB composite. The Red, Green, and Blue colors represent those individual channels; Cyan, Magenta, and Yellow colors represent an overlap of channels, and Gray represents an overlap of all three channels.

From the Source pop-up menu you can select Entire Image, Selected Layer, or Adjustment Composite. Entire Image does just that—it looks at the whole image to get its values (including all layers). Selected Layer uses only the selected layer to base the histogram on. And Adjustment Composite displays the histogram of the selected adjustment layer in the Layers palette.

To view information about a range of values, you can click and drag in the histogram to select the range.

All about Layers

Following most of the examples in this book requires an understanding of layers and the Layers palette. Layers are one of the most powerful features in Photoshop Elements, and once you get used to using them, you will never understand how you managed without. Some people use layers as a filing cabinet where they keep various versions of their work, as well as commonly used templates. One such template is a screen shot of a web browser window that is used for previewing web graphics and type. Many users make changes on a duplicate layer while always keeping an original version of their work handy on a separate layer, for comparison.

When you first open a digital image, Photoshop Elements places the image on a layer that is by default called the **Background** layer. Many Elements users may never have a need to go beyond this point. As you saw earlier in the book, you can resize, crop, or apply simple color and tonal corrections to a digital image, without going beyond one layer (☞ Chapter 2). However, even if you never consciously create a new layer, layers will creep into your document. For example, a new layer is added automatically when you cut and paste a selection.

The minute you have more than one layer, the relationship between different layers is controlled by the Mode and Opacity settings in the Layers palette. For example, if the Mode is set to Normal and the Opacity set to 100 percent, pixels in the top layer replace pixels in the layer underneath. This relationship changes when you select another Mode, or you lower the Opacity. Several ways of using different Mode settings for effects have been shown throughout the book.

Figure A.5 shows the Layers palette. Note the various states of the layers. Some have their visibility turned on, as indicated by the eye icon in the leftmost side; others are turned off, as indicated by the absence of the eye. Only a single layer can be *selected* at a time, as indicated by the blue shading. One of the most common mistakes people make is not selecting the layer that they want to work on. The result is that a command, such as a blur filter, doesn't affect the desired image at all, but in fact affects the content of another layer instead.

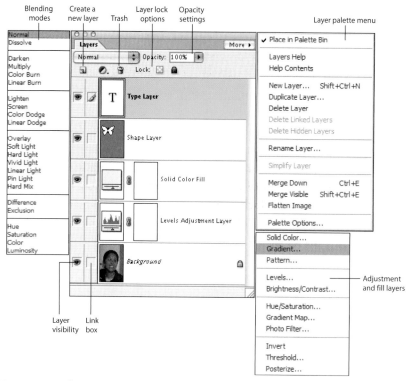

Figure A.5: The Layers palette revealed.

Most of the time, when you add a layer, you increase the file size of your image—how much depends on the contents of the layer. Adjustment and fill layers, which are discussed later, don't add any appreciable file size. Also remember that you'll need to save your work in the PSD or advanced TIFF file formats in order to keep layers intact. The JPEG file format, for example, doesn't allow you to save layers, and if you save your file as an animated GIF, layers are retained, but not in the same state as they were saved.

Here are some of the other things you need to know to create and otherwise work with and manage multiple layers. Photoshop Elements offers many ways to accomplish the same tasks:

Turn the visibility of layers on and off by toggling the eye icon in the leftmost side of the Layers palette.

Select a layer by clicking its thumbnail or name in the Layers palette. Blue highlighting and the paintbrush icon (✐) indicate the layer is active. Selecting the Move tool (▸⊹) from the toolbar and clicking an image in the image window will select the layer containing that image. With the Move tool selected, right-clicking (Windows) or Ctrl+clicking (Mac) will open a pop-up menu listing the names of the various layers and indicating which layer is active. To select a layer, click its name in the pop-up menu.

Link layers by clicking in the link box of an unselected layer. A link icon (⧉) appears, indicating that these layers are treated as one.

Group layers by holding down Alt/Option and positioning the pointer over the line dividing two layers in the Layers palette. Click when the pointer changes to two overlapping circles (⊕). When layers are grouped together, the bottommost layer, called the *base layer*, becomes dominant and defines the subsequent layers.

Imagine a base layer consisting of type grouped with another layer containing texture. The type would define the shape of the texture. You can also choose Layer ➤ Group with Previous (Ctrl+G / ⌘ +G) after selecting a layer. To ungroup layers, choose Layer ➤ Ungroup, or hold down the Alt/Option key, position the pointer over the line dividing the layers, and click.

Lock the properties of a layer by selecting it and clicking the Lock All button (🔒). Note the appearance of a solid black lock icon to the right of the layer name, indicating the layer is protected from any changes.

Lock a layer's transparency by selecting it and clicking the Lock Transparent Pixels button, just to the left of the checked square icon. Note the hollow lock icon in the layer bar, which indicates that changes will be made in this layer only on existing pixels. This is useful for modifying an image while maintaining its exact shape and size.

Move a layer by selecting it and then dragging and dropping it into a new position in the Layers palette. A background layer cannot be moved from its background position without first changing its name. You can also reorder layers by choosing Layer ➤ Arrange.

Add a layer by clicking the More button and choosing New Layer from the palette menu, or by clicking the Create a New Layer icon (🖿) at the top and far left. Some actions, such as cut and paste, automatically create a new layer. You can also choose Layer ➤ New ➤ Layer or press Ctrl+Shift+N / ⌘ +Shift+N.

Duplicate a layer by clicking the More button and choosing Duplicate Layer from the palette menu. Or in the Layers palette, select the layer you wish to duplicate and drag it to the Create a New Layer icon (🖿) at the top of the Layers palette. Or choose Layer ➤ Duplicate Layer.

Delete a layer by dragging a selected layer to the trash icon (🗑) at the top of the Layers palette, or select a layer and click the trash icon. You can also choose Layer ➤ Delete Layer, or choose Delete Layer from the More palette menu.

Rename a layer in the Layers palette by double-clicking the layer name, or clicking the More button and choosing Rename Layer from the palette menu. Or choose Layer ➤ Rename Layer.

Flatten linked layers into one layer by clicking the More button and choosing Merge Linked from the palette menu. Or choose Layer ➤ Merge Linked (Ctrl+E / ⌘ +E).

Flatten visible layers by clicking the More button and choosing Merge Visible from the palette menu. Or choose Layer ➤ Merge Visible, or press Ctrl+Shift+E / ⌘ +Shift+E.

Flatten all layers by clicking the More button and choosing Flatten Image from the palette menu. All layers will become one. All layer information will be lost after the image is flattened. You can also choose Layer ➤ Flatten Image.

Adjustment and Fill Layers

When Adobe first added layers to Photoshop many years ago, I was thrilled. When they came up with adjustment and fill layers, I was amazed. As you've seen throughout the book, adjustment layers enable you to affect a single layer or group of layers while making it possible to remove the effect anytime later without changing the rest of the image or greatly increasing your file size. Adjustment and fill layers retain the same opacity, blending, and grouping properties.

Access adjustment and fill layers by clicking the black-and-white circle at the top of the Layers palette (◑) or by choosing Layer ➢ New Adjustment Layer, or Layer ➢ New Fill Layer.

You can choose from the following kinds of adjustment layers: Levels, Brightness/Contrast, Hue/Saturation, Photo Filter, Gradient Map, Invert, Threshold, and Posterize. In the book, I've mostly referred to the first four types. However, I encourage you to try the others. *Gradient Map*, for example, is a great way to create special color effects by mapping the equivalent grayscale range of your image to a colorful gradient fill. *Invert* makes your image look like a negative. *Threshold* converts images into high-contrast, black-and-white images that look like lithographs. *Posterize* gives you control over the number of tonal levels for each color channel; choosing lower numbers radically changes the look and feel of your image.

Fill layers include fills based on a solid color, a gradient, or a pattern. I've used fill layers throughout the book, especially when manipulating product shots (➤ Chapter 5).

To change an adjustment or fill layer, double-click the thumbnail in the Layers palette or choose Layer ➢ Layer Content Options. To delete an adjustment or fill layer, drag it to the trash icon at the bottom of the Layers palette, or with the adjustment layer selected, choose Layer ➢ Delete Layer.

Layer Styles

Another amazing feature is layer styles. You most likely have no idea how long it used to take to create a simple drop shadow before Photoshop introduced layer styles. Now you can do it with a click of the mouse.

Layer styles provide a way to apply a predetermined look and feel to a layer itself. These are removable and nondestructive, just like adjustment and fill layers. You can choose the way layer styles are displayed—list or thumbnails—via the More button at the top of the Styles and Effects palette. Thumbnails are the most useful in previewing a style's effect. Figure A.6 shows a few layer styles.

Figure A.6: Here are a few of the many layer styles.

To apply a layer style, be sure the Layer Styles option is selected in the first pop-up of the Styles and Effects palette, and then drag and drop a style from the palette onto an image. You can also double-click a style to apply it to the active layer. Be careful: clicking more than one style will apply all your choices additively. This is great if this is what you want, but if not, make liberal use of the Undo History palette or the Undo command.

The Styles and Effects palette offers 14 categories of styles as starting points. However, with the power to customize style settings, the possibilities are endless. You can manipulate layer styles in the following ways:

Customize a layer style by double-clicking the *f* symbol in the Layers palette, which brings up a dialog box where you can specify the exact thickness, angles, and other characteristics of the style you desire. Or choose Layer ➢ Layer Style ➢ Style Settings from the menu.

Repeat a custom layer style on other layers by simply copying and pasting styles from one layer to another. Choose Layer ➢ Layer Style ➢ Copy Layer Style and then choose Layer ➢ Layer Style ➢ Paste Layer Style.

Clear a layer style by choosing Layer ➢ Layer Style ➢ Clear Layer Style or by right-clicking (Windows) / Control+clicking (Mac) the layer in the Layers palette and choosing Clear Layer Style.

Effects

Effects are like automatic cameras. They make you look good even if you don't know what you are doing. Built into most effects are a complex series of filters, layer styles, and/or program functions. Figure A.7 shows all the effects in the Styles and Effects palette window.

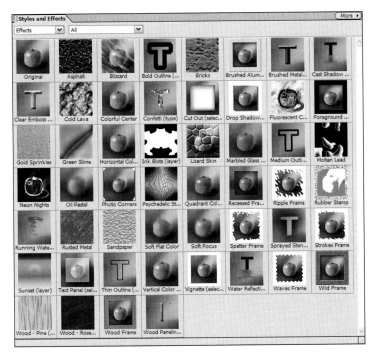

Figure A.7: Thumbnails provide a useful preview of an effect.

To apply an effect, first select Effects from the first pop-up in the Styles and Effects palette. Then you can select an effect and drag it from that palette onto an image, or simply double-click the effect. Remember that you don't have to apply an effect to an entire image. If you make a selection before applying an effect, the effect will apply only to that selection.

It may seem that effects are similar to layer styles, but there are some huge differences: effects are not changeable in the same way that layer styles are, and they often require you to simplify a type layer before you apply an effect to it.

Selection Tools

Much of the power of Photoshop Elements lies in its capability to manipulate both entire images and discrete portions of images. Selection tools enable you to target which pixels to operate upon. As you've seen throughout the book, knowing which selection tool to use when makes a big difference. Some selection tools, such as the Rectangular Marquee, are straightforward to use; others, such as the Magic Wand and the Magnetic Lasso, are more complex and require a little more skill to use. Most users will find that the Selection Brush tool falls somewhere in between. Each selection tool has multiple options for its use, which are accessed via the options bar found below the shortcuts bar.

Marquee Tools

The Marquee tools include the Rectangular ([ ]) and Elliptical (○) selection tools. They share the same spot on the toolbar. When you click the Marquee tool, buttons for both tools appear on the options bar. Switch between the two by clicking one of the buttons, or by clicking and holding the Marquee tool and then selecting Rectangular or Elliptical from the flyout.

Press M at any time (except when you are in text edit mode) to select the Marquee tool. Hold the Shift key while pressing M to toggle back and forth between the Rectangular and Elliptical tools.

These tools are most appropriate for making selections in the general area of what you want. Holding down the Shift key forces a Marquee tool into a circle or square shape. You can also use either Marquee tool as a rectangular cropping tool. Just make your selection and then choose Image ➢ Crop. If you are using the Elliptical Marquee tool, the crop will go to the outermost points of the ellipse but still be rectangular.

Lasso Tools

Lasso tools include the Lasso, Magnetic Lasso, and Polygonal Lasso. All three tools are at the same spot on the toolbar. When you click the Lasso tool, buttons for all three tools appear on the options bar. Switch between the tools by clicking one of the buttons, or by clicking and holding the Lasso tool and then selecting Lasso, Magnetic Lasso, or Polygonal Lasso from the pop-up menu.

Press L at any time (except when you are in text edit mode) to select the Lasso tool. To toggle back and forth between the three Lasso tools, right-click (Windows) or hold the Shift key while pressing L (Mac).

The Lasso tool (○) is great for tracing areas with jagged edges. Hold down the mouse button and freehand trace the desired selection shape. When you release the mouse, Photoshop Elements will close the shape if you haven't already done so. For maximum accuracy, magnify the image to see border details.

The Magnetic Lasso tool (⟨icon⟩) is an enhanced version of the Lasso tool that snaps to pixels of similar colors. Width, edge-contrast, and frequency parameters let you specify the range of pixel similarity to which the lasso is attracted. Double-click to finish making your selection. Again, Photoshop Elements will close the shape if you haven't already done so. I explain the Magnetic Lasso in great detail elsewhere in the book (⟨icon⟩ "Separating a Product from Its Background" and "Adding Motion Blur" in Chapter 5).

The Polygonal Lasso tool (⟨icon⟩) lets you specify the points of a multi-sided shape you wish to select. This is useful for selections with straight edges.

While using either the Magnetic Lasso or Polygonal Lasso selection tools, you can start over by hitting Esc.

Magic Wand

The Magic Wand tool (⟨icon⟩), located in its own spot in the toolbar, magically chooses pixels of the same color within the specified tolerance limits throughout your image. Use this tool for irregularly shaped areas of the same color. I explain the Magic Wand in great detail elsewhere in the book (⟨icon⟩ "Separating a Product from Its Background" in Chapter 5).

Cookie Cutter

The Cookie Cutter tool (⟨icon⟩) crops an image into a shape you can choose. An example of this is shown in Figure A.8. First, choose the shape you would like to constrict your image to by selecting it in the Cookie Cutter's options bar. Then click and drag on your image to see the shape appear. You can move or resize the shape by moving the cursor over the edge of the bounding regions. Once you are happy with the placement, commit the selection by choosing the Commit button in the options bar. There are a few options you can select for your Cookie Cutter tool: the shape's options, the amount to feather the selection, and whether to crop the image.

Figure A.8: The Cookie Cutter tool automatically turns an image into a shape.

Under the shape's options you can choose Unconstrained, Defined Proportions, Defined Size, Fixed Size, and From Center. Choosing Unconstrained enables you to draw the shape to any size you like. Defined Proportions keeps the height and width of the shape in proportion. Use Defined Size to crop the image to the exact size you want, and Fixed Size to enter the exact size you want for the completed shape. Select From Center to draw the shape from the center of your first click.

Selection Brush

The Selection Brush tool (✐), located in its own spot in the toolbar, selects an area by painting over it. To add to a selection, simply paint over the area you wish to add. To subtract from a selection, hold the Alt/Option key, and the areas you paint will be deselected. At any time you can start over by choosing Select ➢ Deselect from the menu bar or by using the keyboard command Ctrl+D / ⌘+D. Holding the Shift key while dragging this tool will approximately constrain it to straight lines or connect two clicked points. In the Selection Brush options bar, you can control the brush size and hardness. Increasing the Hardness setting is much like using the feather command found in the other selection tool options. 0 percent will produce a soft selection edge, while 100 percent makes the edge of the selection more sharply defined. (Keep in mind that this is only a slight feathering. For radical feathering, you need to use Select ➢ Feather and choose higher pixel values.)

In the Selection Brush options bar, you can choose between working in Selection mode or Mask mode. The default, Selection mode, will produce the familiar pulsing, dotted "marching ants" lines that define and protect the area contained within the dots. If you select Mask, the areas you paint over will be colored. The default is a red overlay at a 50 percent opacity, but you can change both the color and the opacity in the options bar.

Keep in mind that Selection and Mask modes are essentially opposite selection methods. When you use Mask mode, areas that are colored by the Selection Brush are "protected" as opposed to being "selected." It's really important to understand the difference. When something is selected, either by using the Selection Brush in Selection mode or one of the other selection tools, you can apply Enhance commands, filters, or effects *only to the selected areas*. But when you use the Selection Brush in Mask mode, the colored areas are the areas that *won't be affected* by such commands. In other words, they are protected (remember this by thinking of the Mask mode as a way to put virtual "masking" tape over parts of an image to protect it). Now this gets really confusing if you go from Mask mode back to Selection mode. The color overlay you created with the Selection Brush will be replaced by the familiar pulsing dotted line; however, don't be fooled. The area within the parameter of the dotted line is still protected, not selected. If you look carefully, you'll see more dotted lines that show the boundaries of the actual selection.

You can selectively deselect masked areas by holding down the Alt/Option key while painting with the Selection Brush in Mask mode.

Selection Tool Options

Generally, options for the selection tools other than the Selection Brush include the following:

Adding, subtracting, or merging selection shapes. You can add to (Shift), subtract from (Alt/Option), or cut multiple selections (Ctrl/⌘) by holding down these additional keys while making selections. You can also click the respective icons in the options bar.

Moving, copying, or pasting selections and layers. After you make a selection shape, you can move the outline of the defined area with the Move tool, or you can more precisely position it with the arrow keys.

Softening edges of a selection. You can blur edges of selections by typing a specific number of pixels in the Feather field, or by choosing Select ➤ Feather (Ctrl+Alt+D for Windows, or ⌘+Option+D for the Mac).

Anti-aliasing a selection. This controls the smoothness of selected shapes' edges by including transition pixels. By default, the anti-aliasing option is selected.

Controlling Selections

There are several ways to control the shape and size of a selection:

- You can specify the exact dimensions or proportions of a Marquee selection in the options bar Style pop-up menu.
- You can reverse any selection and choose nonselected pixels by choosing Select ➤ Inverse or by pressing Ctrl+Shift+I / ⌘+Shift+I.

There are several ways you can modify a selection:

Select ➤ Modify ➤ Border selects a border of pixels the specified number of pixels above and below the current selection.

Select ➤ Modify ➤ Smooth excludes pixels outside the specified range from the current selection. This is especially useful when you use the Magic Wand and get small selections all over the image. The Smooth option unifies the many selections into one.

Select ➤ Modify ➤ Expand makes the current selection larger by the specified number of pixels.

Select ➤ Modify ➤ Contract makes the current selection smaller by the specified number of pixels.

Select ➤ Grow incorporates, into the current selection, pixels that are similar and in a contiguous area.

Select ➤ Similar incorporates, into the current selection, pixels that are similar anywhere within the image.

Select ➤ Save Selection allows you to save a selection and load it for later use.

Except for the options that apply specifically to the Marquee selection tool, all of these commands apply to a selection created by the Selection Brush.

At any time, you can cancel a selection by pressing Ctrl+D / ⌘+D. The trusty Undo command (Ctrl+Z / ⌘+Z) will get it back for you. You can also click the New Selection icon (■) in the floating toolbar. Or, choose Select ➤ Deselect (Ctrl+D / ⌘+D), Select ➤ Reselect (Ctrl+Shift+D / ⌘+Shift+D), or Edit ➤ Undo.

You can turn a selection into a colored outline by using the Stroke command. Make a selection with any of the selection tools and choose Edit ➤ Stroke. In the Stroke dialog box, specify a line width and color, as well as the location of where the pixels fall in relationship to the selection outline: inside, center, or outside. You can also select a blending mode and opacity.

Viewing and Navigation Tools

For precise work, it is essential to be able to zoom in and out of an image, and to navigate around the window if the image is large. Several tools and commands are available to help you.

Zoom Tool

To select the Zoom tool (🔍), click it on the toolbar or press Z. The Zoom In tool (🔍) increases image detail, and the Zoom Out tool (🔍) achieves the opposite effect. You can switch between Zoom In and Zoom Out by clicking their buttons on the toolbar. Hold down the Alt key to temporarily change the currently selected Zoom tool to the opposite tool; when you release the Alt key the tool changes back to its original state. Double-clicking the Zoom tool icon in the toolbox returns the image to 100 percent.

The percent magnification and dimensions (provided this is the option you have chosen) appear in the lower-left corner of the work area. You can type a desired percent magnification in this box. You can also choose View ➤ Zoom In or View ➤ Zoom Out.

With the Zoom In tool selected, you can fill the screen with a particular area of an image by clicking and dragging the mouse to define a bounding box surrounding the area of interest. Let go of the mouse, and zoom!

In the Zoom tool options bar, if Resize Windows to Fit is selected, the Photoshop Elements window is resized as necessary to display the image. When the option is deselected, the window remains the same size regardless of magnification.

If you have more than one image open, you can have the Zoom tool zoom in on all the images at the same time by selecting the Zoom All Windows check box in the options bar. To temporarily set this behavior, you can hold down the Shift key while clicking the Zoom tool. You can also Shift+double-click the Zoom tool to display all open images at 100 percent.

View Commands

Several view commands are found in the main menu bar. These include the following:

View ➤ New Window for ‹File Name› creates multiple views of the same image. Any changes made will apply to all views. You can close any but the last view before you will be prompted to save the file.

View ➤ Fit on Screen fills the entire window with the entire image. This is equivalent to double-clicking the Hand tool.

View ➤ Actual Pixels displays an image at 100 percent while taking into account the height and width of the image, as well as the resolution of the monitor. Two images can have the same height and width and different resolutions, and yet appear the same size on the monitor.

View ➤ Print Size displays an image at 100 percent if the resolution is 72ppi. This view takes into account the resolution of the image, as well as the resolution of the monitor. Two images can have the same height and width in pixels, but if the resolution is different they will appear as different sizes on the monitor.

Navigator Palette

The Navigator palette is hidden by default. (You can find it by choosing Window ➤ Navigator from the main menu bar.) The colored view box in this palette helps orient your current position in the image. This is useful when an image gets too large to display on-screen. The slider at the top of this palette offers yet another option to increase or decrease the percent magnification of the image. Change the color of the view box by selecting Palette Options from the More pop-up menu.

Hand Tool

The Hand tool (🖐), located in the toolbar, is used to move the image around in the work area when the image is magnified outside the boundaries of the work area. The Navigator palette provides a thumbnail view to orient your position relative to the entire image. Use the Hand tool in the Navigator palette to move the view box to target areas within the image. Areas outside the view box remain intact but are simply off-screen.

You can access the Hand tool temporarily at any time by holding down the spacebar, or you can switch to it by pressing H. Double-click the Hand tool to reveal the entire image in the image window. You can optionally select the Scroll All Windows check box in the options bar. This enables you to scroll all windows at the same time, which is useful when you have similar images side by side. To temporarily set this behavior, hold down the Shift key while dragging the Hand tool. You can also Shift+double-click the Hand tool to apply Fit on Screen on all open images.

Scrubbers

Scrubbers are a new addition to Photoshop Elements 3. They originate in Adobe's After Effects and provide a whole new way to control items in numeric entry fields. To use this feature, place your cursor over the numeric field you want to change. Then move your cursor to the left over its textual label. You should see the cursor change to a double-ended arrow, as shown in Figure A.9. If you click and drag to the left, the numeric entry will decrease; to the right, it will increase. A common one you may use can be found in the Layers palette's Opacity field.

Figure A.9: Move your cursor over a label, and it turns into a scrubber, which gives you mouse control over numeric entry fields.

Brushes

Many Photoshop Elements tools use brushes to apply different effects. These brushes can be customized far beyond their size and shape. Version 3 makes it especially easy to customize a brush and control the look and feel of a particular brush stroke.

When you select the Brush (B) tool from the toolbar, options for controlling the brush size, shape, and characteristics appear in the options bar. For the other tools that use brushes—Blur, Sharpen, Sponge, Smudge, Dodge, Burn, Clone Stamp, Pattern Stamp, Pencil (N), Color Replacement Tool (B), Selection Brush (A), Impressionist Brush (B), Spot Healing Brush (J), Healing Brush (J), and eraser tools—you have more limited options.

Available to all tools that use brushes are several brush presets, including the default set shown on the left in Figure A.10. There are several other presets as well, including Calligraphic Brushes, Drop Shadow Brushes, and Web Media Brushes. You can control the size of the preset brushes in the options bar.

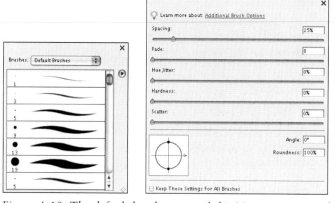

Figure A.10: The default brush presets (left). More presets are found in the drop-down menu. The More Options menu (right) provides additional ways to customize the Brush tool.

When you select the Brush tool, you can use the options on the More Options drop-down menu (shown on the right in Figure A.10) to control the Spacing, Fade, Color Jitter, Hardness, Scatter, and other characteristics of the brush, as well as the precise shape of the tip through Angle and Roundness controls.

If you are feeling really ambitious, you can even create a brush from an image. Make a selection from your image and then choose Edit ➤ Define Brush. Name your brush and select OK. A grayscale brush based on your selection is now available, along with the other preset options.

Impressionist Brush

I don't use the Impressionist Brush in this book. It's a complex tool, and you can spend countless hours just trying to figure out what it does and then realize that you've only scratched the surface. Through different texture and color settings, you can simulate various painting styles—think Van Gogh and Cezanne. Play with different Styles, Fidelity, Area, and Spacing settings. Then when you've figured those out, change the Mode and Opacity settings and see what else you can come up with. The possibilities are limitless. Enjoy!

Healing Brushes

Two new brushes take the pain out of cleaning up and removing unwanted blemishes and artifacts.

If the problem area is small, the Spot Healing Brush (🖊) is ideal at fixing it. In most cases you can choose a brush size that is slightly larger than the area you want to fix, center the brush over the area, and click. You can set two options for the Spot Healing Brush: Proximity Match and Create Texture. The Proximity Match option tries to use the pixels around the edge of the selection as a patch. Create Texture uses all the pixels in the selected area to create a texture to place over the selected area.

If, however, the regions are more complex, you can use the more powerful Healing Brush (🖊). In fact, the Healing Brush not only covers up unwanted areas but also removes objects entirely from view. There are four options available to control the brush: Mode, Source, Aligned, and Use All Layers. The Mode option controls how the source blends with the existing pixels. Source allows you to choose where to get the repairing pixels: Sampled uses pixels from the current image, whereas Pattern uses pixels from a pattern. Aligned will move the sampling point relative to where you are stroking. If you want to always use the original sampling point, deselect this option. Use All Layers samples data from all visible layers. If you want to use only the currently selected layer, deselect this option.

Index

effects
 lighting, **102–104**, *102–103*, **141**, *141*
 removing, 101
 sunlight, 95–96, *95–96*
 for type, **223**, *223*
 working with, **329–330**
electrical outlet shots, 144–145, *144–145*
electronic noise and other artifacts, **45**
 combining tools and techniques, **48–50**, *48–50*
 Reduce Noise filter for, **46**, *46*
 Spot Healing Brush for, **47–48**, *47–48*
Ellipse tool, 265, *265*
Elliptical tool, 330
Elliptical Marquee tool, 256
embossment, **215–217**, *215–217*
enlarging eyes, **71–72**
epic panoramics, **200–201**, *200–201*
Eraser tool
 for clouds, 94
 for dynamic range, 279
 for expanding images, 162
 foreground color with, 126
existing folders, importing images from, **3–5**, *3–4*
Expand option for selections, 333
expanding images, **160–163**, *160–163*
exposure
 for Camera Raw, 273–274, *274*
 for panoramics, 191
exposure lock for Photomerge, 193
exteriors, **171**
 construction sign removal, **177–179**, *177–179*
 keystoning in, **172–175**, *172–175*
 tips for, **187**
 wire removal, **184–187**, *184, 186–187*
Eye-One Display calibrator, 34
Eyedropper tool
 for color cast, 41
 for gradients, 218
 for teeth whitening, 74
eyes
 color, **70–71**, *70–71*
 dog eye, **65–67**, *66–68*
 enlarging, **71–72**
 red eye, **62–65**, *63–65*
 whites, **68–69**, *68–69*

F

facades, slanted looking, **172–175**, *172–175*
faces, **61**
 digital fill flash for, **82**, *82*
 distorted, **83**, *83*
 eyes. *See* eyes
 glasses glare, **89**, *89*
 glow, **79–80**, *79–80*
 grainy look for, **81–82**, *81*
 hair, **84–88**, *84–88*
 lips, **73**, *73*
 noses, **78**, *78*
 order of working on, **62**
 teeth, **73–75**, *74–75*
 wrinkles and blemishes, **75–77**, *77*

Feather Selection dialog box, 165, *165*
feathering
 with Magnetic Lasso, 117
 for perspective, 131
 for seamless pasting, 165, *165*
File association option, 9
File Browser, 2, 9, **21–22**, *21*
 automated tasks in, **24**, *24*
 deleting, moving, and copying files with, **23**
 flags in, **23**
 rotating with, 31
 searching for files in, **24**, *24*
 viewing files with, **22**, *23*
file formats
 advanced, **229**
 in Editor, 9
 GIF. *See* GIF (Graphics Interchange Format) images
 JPEG. *See* JPEG (Joint Photographic Experts Group) images
 Organizer support for, 5
 quality of, 59
 TIFF, 59, **229**, *242, 243*
file size, 54
Fill dialog box, **124–125**, *125*
fill flash
 for faces, **82**, *82*
 for light balancing, 181
 for outside shots, **108–109**, *108–109*
Fill Selection option, 125
fills and fill layers
 for patterns, **124–126**, *125–126*, 260
 for sunset shots, 98–99, *99*
 for tiled strips, 263
 type with images, **222**, *222–223*
 working with, **327–328**
filters
 for backgrounds, 137, *137*, **179–181**, *180*
 for faces, 71–75, *71–73*, 78, *78*
 for interlacing, 55, *55*
 for lighting, **102–104**, *102–103*, **141**, *141*
 for motion, **128–129**, *128–129*
 for noise, **46**, *46*
 for painting, 288–289, *288–289*
 for patterns, 127, *127*, 260–261
 for Photomerge, 193
 for sharpening, 57–59, *58–59*
 for type, **224–225**, *224–225*
Find bar in Organizer, 17, *17*
Find Edges filter, 289
Fit on Screen option, 335
Fixed Center option, 332
fixing
 images, **19**, *19*
 teeth, **74–75**, *75*
flags in File Browser, **23**
flash
 for faces, **82**, *82*
 for light balancing, 181
 for outside shots, **108–109**, *108–109*
 for Photomerge, 193
flat images, 33, *33*
 Auto Levels for, **36–37**, *36–37*, 40
 Levels for, **37–40**, *38–39*
 Smart Fix for, **35**, *35*

Resize Images option, 307
Resize Windows to Fit option, 334
resizing
for composites, 154–156, *154*
for compression, **240–241**, *240–241*
images, **54–56**, *55–57*
multiple files, 307
for slide shows, 311
TIFF images, 242
tool palettes, **323**
resolution
in composites, **152–156**, *153–156*
in cropping, 53, *53*
for printing, **296–299**, *297–299*
for slide shows, 310
Restrictive (Web) color reduction algorithm, 247
Reveal Photos in Stack option, 18
Reveal Photos in Version Set option, 19, *20*
reversing selections, 112
Revert to Saved option, 32
reverting to last saved versions, 32
RGB mode, 51
Robbins, Valerie, 243–244, 252, *253*
Rotate Image tool, 199
Rotate Photo 90 Degrees Counterclockwise option, 31
Rotate transform, 174
rotating
for keystoning, 174
for orientation, **31–33**
for Photomerge, 193
rulers, preferences, **321**
Rutledge, Will, 143, *144*, 150

S

sans serif fonts, 209
Saturation option
for Camera Raw, 274
for Color Variations, 43
Save dialog box for slide shows, 311
Save As dialog box
for GIF images, **248–250**, *249*
for JPEG images, 232, *232*
Save for Web plug-in, 231, **235–237**, *235*
for GIF images, **244–248**, *244–245*
animated, 258, *259*
transparent, 253–254
for JPEG images, **235–237**, *235*
Save Selection option, 333
Save Version Set with Original option, 20
saving
GIF images, **248–250**, *249*
JPEG images, **231–237**, *232*, *235*
preferences for, **320**
TIFF images, 242
Saving Files Preferences dialog box, 320
Scale options bar, 156, *156*
scaling
in composites, 154–156, *156*
in product shots, **130–132**, *130–131*
Scalloped Edge option, 217, *217*
Scanner and Camera Wizard, 5–6, *5*

scanners
flatbed, 205, *205*
importing images from, **7–9**, *8*
scanning
black-and-white photos, 43
services for, **109**
Schwartz, Ed, 150
scratches and other artifacts, **45**
combining tools and techniques, **48–50**, *48–50*
Reduce Noise filter for, **46**, *46*
Spot Healing Brush for, **47–48**, *47–48*
screen captures, **212**
scrubbers, **335**, *336*
seamless pasting, **164–165**, *164–165*
searching
for files in File Browser, **24**, *24*
for tags and properties, **17**, *17–18*
Security option, 314
Selected Image option, 272
Selection Brush tool
for selective focus, 107
working with, **332**
selection marquee, 112
Selection mode, 332
selection tools, **330**
Cookie Cutter, **331–332**, *331*
Lasso, **330–331**
Magic Wand, **331**
Marquee, **330**
options for, **333**
Selection Brush, **332**
selections
controlling, **333–334**
layers, 326
printing, 301
refining, 118, *119*
Selective algorithm, 247, 250
selective blurring, **239**, *239–240*
selective focus, **107–108**, *107*
separating products from background, **112–119**, *113*, *115–116*, *118–119*
sequenced stills, **246**
serifs, 209
Set Date dialog box, 13
Set Vanishing Point tool, 194
Shadow Distance option, 217
shadows
for Camera Raw, 273–274, *274*
drop shadows
for depth, **138–139**, *139–140*
for type, **215–217**, *215–217*
for hair, 86
Levels controls for, 38–39, *38*
Shadows/Highlights dialog box
for digital flash fill, 82, *82*
for light balancing, 181–182, *182*
for outside shots, 108–109, *109*
Shape tool, 212–213, *213*
shapes
for navigational graphics, **263–265**, *264–265*
for type, **219–220**, *220*

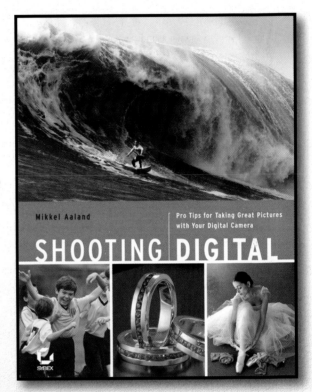

What's on the CD-ROM

The *Photoshop Elements 3 Solutions* CD-ROM contains practice images, plug-ins, utilities, and more, all readily accessible through the graphical CD interface.

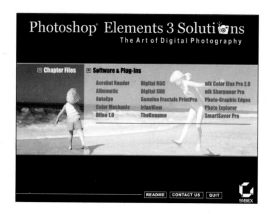

Practice Images

The CD-ROM includes more than 100 of the "before" images used in the book, so you can follow along with the solutions given. The Chapter Files button takes you to the images. Most of the images are in the JPG file format, and others are in the PSD, GIF, or RAW formats.

The images on the CD-ROM are for personal use only. Image copyright is retained by the original copyright holder. Copying or redistribution in any manner for personal or corporate gain is not permitted. Any public or commercial use of these images without prior written permission is a violation of federal copyright law.

Note: A free, downloadable, 30-day trial version of Photoshop Elements 3 is available at www.adobe.com.

Software

The Software & Plug-Ins button takes you to demos of Photoshop Elements–compatible plug-ins and other useful utilities. These include a trial version of Genuine Fractals Print Pro, a resolution-enhancing plug-in from LizardTech; trials of Ulead's Photo Explorer and SmartSaver Pro software; demos of nik Multimedia's Sharpener Pro, Color Efex Pro, and Dfine, plus a fully-functioning sample, tutorial, and special offer from nik; a *fast* image viewer called IrfanView; Digital ROC and Digital SHO, two plug-ins for restoring color and optimizing contrast from Applied Science Fiction; an evaluation of Digital Light & Color's ColorMechanic; a plug-in for 3D text effects; Albumatic, a program from Basepath Software that helps you take your photos to the Web; Acrobat Reader for Palm and Pocket PC versions; and more.

Note: Sybex strives to keep you supplied with the latest tools and information you need. Go to www.sybex.com for additional content and updates that supplement this book and CD.